A SHORT READER OF MEDIEVAL SAINTS

READINGS IN MEDIEVAL CIVILIZATIONS AND CULTURES: XII
series editor: Paul Edward Dutton

A SHORT READER
OF MEDIEVAL SAINTS

edited by

MARY-ANN STOUCK

University of Toronto Press

LIBRARY AND ARCHIVES CANADA CATALOGUING IN PUBLICATION

A short reader of Medieval saints / edited by Mary-Ann Stouck.

(Readings in medieval civilizations and cultures : 12)
Includes bibliographical references and index.
ISBN 978-1-4426-0094-2 (pbk.).–ISBN 978-1-4426-0131-4 (bound)

1. Christian saints – Biography – Early works to 1800.   2. Church history – Primitive and early church, ca. 30–600 – Sources.   3. Church history – Middle Ages, 600–1500 – Sources.   I. Stouck, Mary-Ann, 1941–   II. Series: Readings in medieval civilizations and cultures   12

BX4655.3.S52 2009   270.092'2   C2008-907674-5

We welcome comments and suggestions regarding any aspect of our publications –– please feel free to contact us at news@utphighereducation.com or visit our internet site at www.utphighereducation.com.

North America
5201 Dufferin Street
Toronto, Ontario, Canada, M3H 5T8

2250 Military Road
Tonawanda, New York, USA, 14150

ORDERS PHONE: 1-800-565-9523
ORDERS FAX: 1-800-221-9985
ORDERS EMAIL: utpbooks@utpress.utoronto.ca

UK, Ireland, and continental Europe
NBN International
Estover Road, Plymouth, PL6 7PY, UK
TEL: 44 (0) 1752 202301
FAX ORDER LINE: 44 (0) 1752 202333
enquiries@nbninternational.com

This book is printed on paper containing 100% post-consumer fibre.

The University of Toronto Press acknowledges the financial support for its publishing activities of the Government of Canada through the Book Publishing Industry Development Program (BPIDP).

Book design and composition by George Kirkpatrick.

Printed in Canada

CONTENTS

FOREWORD

This book has been compiled in response to a request from students and instructors for a shorter collection of medieval saints' lives than that found in my earlier volume for this series: *Medieval Saints: A Reader*. That book was put together on the assumption that it would serve as the core primary text for an entire semester's investigation of medieval hagiography. This new book addresses the need for a selection that would serve as the basis for two or three weeks' reading in a larger course on medieval culture and history. Like the earlier book it includes both saints' 'lives' and material related to the cult of the saints – the veneration of relics and the practice of pilgrimage. If virtue naturally rules in the saints' lives, the reader may be assured that there are scoundrels aplenty to be found in these related materials.

The present book also contains some new material. The excerpt from the *Legenda Aurea* now comprises 'lives' of Agnes, Mary of Egypt, and Christopher, as well as the memorable James the Dismembered. Since a short collection such as this must emphasize the standard works of medieval hagiography, I have had to omit accounts of some of the more eccentric and fascinating saints. But the excerpts from the *Legenda Aurea* remind us of the colorful people – martyred virgins, harlots, and giants among them – that figured so prominently in the popular imagination.

Selections from Raymond of Capua's *Life of Catherine of Siena* now conclude the book, along with six of her *Letters*, in recognition of her special importance as a late medieval saint. Her highly individualized voice marks a change from the formulaic materials of the *Legenda Aurea* to the personalized piety of the later Middle Ages. While Raymond of Capua's hagiography describes the rigors of her life, we hear Catherine's unique voice in these letters written to him, to family and friends, and to popes and potentates.

As in the earlier reader, BHL (*Bibliotheca Hagiographica Latina*) numbers are supplied where appropriate, to identify the version of a 'life' that has been used. The introductions to selections have been revised to include material from the section headings in the earlier book, and all selections are now chronologically ordered.

1. THE PASSION OF SS. PERPETUA AND FELICITAS

The persecution of Christians under the Roman Empire during the first three centuries CE constituted for later writers the heroic age of the church and left an indelible imprint on the collective Christian imagination. Nevertheless, there remains considerable argument about the numbers of Christians who were killed. Official suppression of the new faith was sporadic, despite periods of intense persecution under the emperors Decius in 248 and Diocletian in 303-11.

The following account of the martyrdom of a group of Christians in North Africa in 203 CE is exceptional because it is presented mostly in the words of two of the martyrs themselves: a man named Saturus and a young married woman of the Roman upper classes, Vibia Perpetua. Perpetua's words account for the major part of the 'Passion' and take us from the time of her arrest in the town of Thuburbo Minus, a short distance from Carthage, to the point where she is awaiting imminent death in the amphitheater. This document, then, includes one of the few writings by women extant from the early period. However, the account also gives evidence of complex transmission. An unnamed author narrates the opening and closing sections of the narrative and places the martyrdoms in the context of Montanism, an important early Christian movement whose adherents believed in the 'parousia,' that is, the imminence of the second coming of Christ. They also promoted the importance of prophecy and women's special gifts in this domain and took a rigorously ascetic view of earthly life. The 'Passion' is of great intrinsic interest because it includes visions, narrated in detail, received by Perpetua while in prison. The whole account survives in a long version in Latin and Greek known as the 'Passio' (the Latin version is given here), and in a short version in Latin only, known as the 'Acta,' perhaps composed to be read aloud in church on the saints' feast-day.

Source: trans. H.R. Musurillo, *Acts of the Christian Martyrs* (Oxford: Clarendon Press, 1972), pp. 106-31; repr. with permission. BHL 6633.

1. The deeds recounted about the faith in ancient times were a proof of God's favor and achieved the spiritual strengthening of men as well; and they were set forth in writing precisely that honor might be rendered to God and comfort to men by the recollection of the past through the written word. Should not then more recent examples be set down that contribute equally to both ends? For indeed these too will one day become ancient and needful for the ages to come, even though in our own day they may enjoy less prestige because of the prior claim of antiquity.

Let those then who would restrict the power of the one Spirit to times and seasons look to this: the more recent events should be considered the greater, being later than those of old, and this is a consequence of the extraordinary graces promised for the last stage of time. For *in the last days, God declares, I will pour out my Spirit upon all flesh and their sons and daughters shall prophesy and on my manservants and my maidservants I will pour my Spirit, and the young men shall see visions and the old men shall dream dreams.* So too we hold in honor and acknowledge not only new prophecies but new visions as well, according to the promise. And we consider all the other functions of the Holy Spirit as intended for the good of the Church; for the same Spirit has been sent to distribute all his gifts to all, as the Lord apportions to everyone. For this reason we deem it imperative to set them forth and to make them known through the word for the glory of God. Thus no one of weak or despairing faith may think that supernatural grace was present only among men of ancient times, either in the grace of martyrdom or of visions, for God always achieves what he promises, as a witness to the non-believer and a blessing to the faithful.

And so, my brethren and little children, *that which we have heard and have touched with our hands we proclaim also to you, so that* those of you that were witnesses may recall the glory of the Lord and those that now learn of it through hearing *may have fellowship* with the holy martyrs and, through them, *with the Lord Christ Jesus,* to whom belong splendor and honor for all ages. Amen.

2. A number of young catechumens [those receiving instruction in preparation for baptism] were arrested, Revocatus and his fellow slave Felicitas, Saturninus and Secundulus, and with them Vibia Perpetua, a newly married woman of good family and upbringing. Her mother and father were still alive and one of her two brothers was a catechumen like herself. She was about twenty-two years old and had an infant son at the breast. (Now from this point on the entire account of her ordeal is her own, according to her own ideas and in the way that she herself wrote it down.)

3. While we were still under arrest (she said) my father out of love for me was trying to persuade me and shake my resolution. 'Father,' said I, 'do you see this vase here, for example, or water pot or whatever?'

'Yes, I do,' said he.

And I told him: 'Could it be called by any other name than what it is?'

And he said: 'No.'

'Well, so too I cannot be called anything other than what I am, a Christian.'

At this my father was so angered by the word 'Christian' that he moved towards me as though he would pluck my eyes out. But he left it at that and departed, vanquished along with his diabolical arguments. For a few days afterwards I gave thanks to the Lord that I was separated from my father, and I was comforted by his absence. During these few days I was baptized, and

I was inspired by the Spirit not to ask for any other favor after the water but simply the perseverance of the flesh. A few days later we were lodged in the prison; and I was terrified, as I had never before been in such a dark hole. What a difficult time it was! With the crowd the heat was stifling; then there was the extortion of the soldiers; and to crown all, I was tortured with worry for my baby there. Then Tertius and Pomponius, those blessed deacons who tried to take care of us, bribed the soldiers to allow us to go to a better part of the prison to refresh ourselves for a few hours. Everyone then left that dungeon and shifted for himself. I nursed my baby, who was faint from hunger. In my anxiety I spoke to my mother about the child, I tried to comfort my brother, and I gave the child in their charge. I was in pain because I saw them suffering out of pity for me. These were the trials I had to endure for many days. Then I got permission for my baby to stay with me in prison. At once I recovered my health, relieved as I was of my worry and anxiety over the child. My prison had suddenly become a palace, so that I wanted to be there rather than anywhere else.

4. Then my brother said to me: 'Dear sister, you are greatly privileged; surely you might ask for a vision to discover whether you are to be condemned or freed.' Faithfully, I promised that I would, for I knew that I could speak with the Lord, whose great blessings I had come to experience. And so I said: 'I shall tell you tomorrow.' Then I made my request and this was the vision I had:

I saw a ladder of tremendous height made of bronze, reaching all the way to the heavens, but it was so narrow that only one person could climb up at a time. To the sides of the ladder were attached all sorts of metal weapons: there were swords, spears, hooks, daggers, and spikes; so that if anyone tried to climb up carelessly or without paying attention, he would be mangled and his flesh would adhere to the weapons.

At the foot of the ladder lay a dragon of enormous size, and it would attack those who tried to climb up and try to terrify them from doing so. And Saturus was the first to go up, he who was later to give himself up of his own accord. He had been the builder of our strength, although he was not present when we were arrested. And he arrived at the top of the staircase and he looked back and said to me:

'Perpetua, I am waiting for you. But take care; do not let the dragon bite you.'

'He will not harm me,' I said, 'in the name of Christ Jesus.'

Slowly, as though he were afraid of me, the dragon stuck his head out from underneath the ladder. Then, using it as my first step, I trod on his head and went up.

Then I saw an immense garden, and in it a grey-haired man sat in shepherd's garb; tall he was, and milking sheep. And standing around him were many thousands of people clad in white garments. He raised his head, looked at me, and said:

'I am glad you have come, my child.'

He called me over to him and gave me, as it were, a mouthful of the milk he was drawing; and I took it into my cupped hands and consumed it. And all those who stood around said: 'Amen!' At the sound of this word I came to, with the taste of something sweet still in my mouth. I at once told this to my brother, and we realized that we would have to suffer, and that from now on we would no longer have any hope in this life.

5. A few days later there was a rumor that we were going to be given a hearing. My father also arrived from the city, worn with worry, and he came to see me with the idea of persuading me.

'Daughter,' he said, 'have pity on my grey head – have pity on me your father, if I deserve to be called your father, if I have favored you above all your brothers, if I have raised you to reach this prime of your life. Do not abandon me to be the reproach of men. Think of your brothers, think of your mother and your aunt, think of your child, who will not be able to live once you are gone. Give up your pride! You will destroy all of us! None of us will ever be able to speak freely again if anything happens to you.'

This was the way my father spoke out of love for me, kissing my hands and throwing himself down before me. With tears in his eyes he no longer addressed me as his daughter but as a woman. I was sorry for my father's sake, because he alone of all my kin would be unhappy to see me suffer.

I tried to comfort him saying: 'It will all happen in the prisoner's dock as God wills; for you may be sure that we are not left to ourselves but are all in his power.'

And he left me in great sorrow.

6. One day while we were eating breakfast we were suddenly hurried off for a hearing. We arrived at the forum, and straight away the story went about the neighborhood near the forum and a huge crowd gathered. We walked up to the prisoner's dock. All the others, when questioned, admitted their guilt. Then, when it came my turn, my father appeared with my son, dragged me from the step, and said 'Perform the sacrifice – have pity on your baby!'

Hilarianus the governor, who had received his judicial powers as the successor of the late proconsul Minucius Timinianus, said to me: 'Have pity on your father's grey head; have pity on your infant son. Offer the sacrifice for the welfare of the emperors.'

'I will not,' I retorted.

'Are you a Christian?' said Hilarianus.

And I said: 'Yes, I am.'

When my father persisted in trying to dissuade me, Hilarianus ordered him to be thrown to the ground and beaten with a rod. I felt sorry for father, just as if I myself had been beaten. I felt sorry for his pathetic old age.

Then Hilarianus passed sentence on all of us: we were condemned to the beasts, and we returned to prison in high spirits. But my baby had got used to being nursed at the breast and to staying with me in prison. So I sent the deacon Pomponius straight away to my father to ask for the baby. But father refused to give him over. But as God willed, the baby had no further desire for the breast, nor did I suffer any inflammation; and so I was relieved of any anxiety for my child and of any discomfort in my breasts.

7. Some days later when we were all at prayer, suddenly while praying I spoke out and uttered the name Dinocrates. I was surprised; for the name had never entered my mind until that moment. And I was pained when I recalled what had happened to him. At once I realized that I was privileged to pray for him. I began to pray for him and to sigh deeply for him before the Lord. That very night I had the following vision. I saw Dinocrates coming out of a dark hole, where there were many others with him, very hot and thirsty, pale and dirty. On his face was the wound he had when he died.

Now Dinocrates had been my brother according to the flesh; but he had died horribly of cancer of the face when he was seven years old, and his death was a source of loathing to everyone. Thus it was for him that I made my prayer. There was a great abyss between us: neither could approach the other. Where Dinocrates stood there was a pool full of water; and its rim was higher than the child's height, so that Dinocrates had to stretch himself up to drink. I was sorry that, though the pool had water in it, Dinocrates could not drink because of the height of the rim. Then I woke up, realizing that my brother was suffering. But I was confident that I could help him in his trouble; and I prayed for him every day until we were transferred to the military prison. For we were supposed to fight with the beasts at the military games to be held on the occasion of the emperor Geta's birthday. And I prayed for my brother day and night with tears and sighs that this favor might be granted me.

8. On the day we were kept in chains, I had this vision shown to me. I saw the same spot that I had seen before, but there was Dinocrates all clean, well dressed, and refreshed. I saw a scar where the wound had been; and the pool that I had seen before now had its rim lowered to the level of the child's waist. And Dinocrates kept drinking water from it, and there above the rim was a golden bowl full of water. And Dinocrates drew close and began to

drink from it, and yet the bowl remained full. And when he had drunk enough of the water, he began to play as children do. Then I awoke, and I realized that he had been delivered from his suffering.

9. Some days later, an adjutant named Pudens, who was in charge of the prison, began to show us great honor, realizing that we possessed some great power within us. And he began to allow many visitors to see us for our mutual comfort.

Now the day of the contest was approaching, and my father came to see me overwhelmed with sorrow. He started tearing the hairs from his beard and threw them on the ground; he then threw himself on the ground and began to curse his old age and to say such words as would move all creation. I felt sorry for his unhappy old age.

10. The day before we were to fight with the beasts I saw the following vision. Pomponius the deacon came to the prison gates and began to knock violently. I went out and opened the gate for him. He was dressed in an un-belted white tunic, wearing elaborate sandals. And he said to me: 'Perpetua, come; we are waiting for you.'

Then he took my hand and we began to walk through rough and broken country. At last we came to the amphitheater out of breath, and he led me into the center of the arena.

Then he told me: 'Do not be afraid. I am here, struggling with you.' Then he left.

I looked at the enormous crowd who watched in astonishment. I was sur-prised that no beasts were let loose on me; for I knew that I was condemned to die by the beasts. Then out came an Egyptian against me, of vicious ap-pearance, together with his seconds, to fight with me. There also came up to me some handsome young men to be my seconds and assistants. My clothes were stripped off, and suddenly I was a man. My seconds began to rub me down with oil (as they are wont to do before a contest). Then I saw the Egyptian on the other side rolling in the dust. Next there came forth a man of marvelous stature, such that he rose above the top of the amphitheater. He was clad in a beltless purple tunic with two stripes (one on either side) run-ning down the middle of his chest. He wore sandals that were wondrously made of gold and silver, and he carried a wand like an athletic trainer and a green branch on which there were golden apples.

And he asked for silence and said: 'If this Egyptian defeats her he will slay her with the sword. But if she defeats him, she will receive this branch.' Then he withdrew.

We drew close to one another and began to let our fists fly. My opponent tried to get hold of my feet, but I kept striking him in the face with the heels of my feet. Then I was raised up into the air and I began to pummel him without as it were touching the ground. Then when I noticed there was a lull, I put my two hands together linking the fingers of one hand with those of the other and thus I got hold of his head. He fell flat on his face and I stepped on his head.

The crowd began to shout and my assistants started to sing psalms. Then I walked up to the trainer and took the branch. He kissed me and said to me: 'Peace be with you, my daughter!' I began to walk in triumph towards the Gate of Life [the *Porta Sanavivaria* by which victorious gladiators or those spared by the people could leave]. Then I awoke. I realized that it was not with wild animals that I would fight but with the Devil, but I knew that I would win the victory. So much for what I did up until the eve of the contest. About what happened at the contest itself, let him write of it who will.

11. But the blessed Saturus has also made known his own vision and he has written it out with his own hand. We had died, he said, and had put off the flesh, and we began to be carried towards the east by four angels who did not touch us with their hands. But we moved along not on our backs facing upwards but as though we were climbing up a gentle hill. And when we were free of the world, we first saw an intense light. And I said to Perpetua (for she was at my side): 'This is what the Lord promised us. We have received his promise.'

While we were being carried by these four angels, a great open space appeared, which seemed to be a garden, with rose bushes and all manner of flowers. The trees were as tall as cypresses, and their leaves were constantly falling. In the garden there were four other angels more splendid than the others. When they saw us they paid us homage and said to the other angels in admiration: 'Why, they are here! They are here!'

Then the four angels that were carrying us grew fearful and set us down. Then we walked across to an open area by way of a broad road, and there we met Jucundus, Saturninus, and Artaxius, who were burnt alive in the same persecution, together with Quintus who had actually died as a martyr in prison. We asked them where they had been. And the other angels said to us: 'First come and enter and greet the Lord.'

12. Then we came to a place whose walls seemed to be constructed of light. And in front of the gate stood four angels, who entered in and put on white robes. We also entered and we heard the sound of voices in unison chanting endlessly: 'Holy, holy, holy!' In the same place we seemed to see an aged man with white hair and a youthful face, though we did not see his feet. On his right and left were four elders, and behind them stood other aged men. Surprised, we entered and stood before a throne: four angels lifted us up and we kissed the aged man and he touched our faces with his hand. And the elders said to us: 'Let us rise.' And we rose and gave the kiss of peace.

Then the elders said to us: 'Go and play.'

To Perpetua I said: 'Your wish is granted.'

She said to me: 'Thanks be to God that I am happier here now than I was in the flesh.'

13. Then we went out and before the gates we saw the bishop Optatus on the right and Aspasius the presbyter and teacher on the left, each of them far apart and in sorrow. They threw themselves at our feet and said: 'Make peace between us. For you have gone away and left us thus.'

And we said to them: 'Are you not our bishop, and are you not our presbyter? How can you fall at our feet?'

We were very moved and embraced them. Perpetua then began to speak with them in Greek, and we drew them apart into the garden under a rose arbor.

While we were talking with them, the angels said to them: 'Allow them to rest. Settle whatever quarrels you have among yourselves.' And they were put to confusion. Then they said to Optatus: 'You must scold your flock. They approach you as though they had come from the games, quarreling about the different teams.'

And it seemed as though they wanted to close the gates. And there we began to recognize many of our brethren, martyrs among them. All of us were sustained by a most delicious odor that seemed to satisfy us. And then I woke up happy.

14. Such were the remarkable visions of these martyrs, Saturus and Perpetua, written by themselves. As for Secundulus, God called him from this world earlier than the others while he was still in prison, by a special grace that he might not have to face the animals. Yet his flesh, if not his spirit, knew the sword.

15. As for Felicitas, she too enjoyed the Lord's favor in this wise. She had been pregnant when she was arrested, and was now in her eighth month. As the day of the spectacle drew near she was very distressed that her martyrdom would be postponed because of her pregnancy; for it is against the law for women with child to be executed. Thus she might have to shed her holy, innocent blood afterwards along with others who were common criminals. Her comrades in martyrdom were also saddened; for they were afraid that they would have to leave behind so fine a companion to travel alone on the same road to hope. And so, two days before the contest, they poured forth a prayer to the Lord in one torrent of common grief. And immediately after their prayer the birth pains came upon her. She suffered a good deal in her labor because of the natural difficulty of an eight months' delivery.

Hence one of the assistants of the prison guards said to her: 'You suffer so much now – what will you do when you are tossed to the beasts? Little did you think of them when you refused to sacrifice.'

'What I am suffering now,' she replied, 'I suffer by myself. But then another will be inside me who will suffer for me, just as I shall be suffering for him.'

And she gave birth to a girl; and one of the sisters brought her up as her own daughter.

16. Therefore, since the Holy Spirit has permitted the story of this contest to be written down and by so permitting has willed it, we shall carry out the command or, indeed, the commission of the most saintly Perpetua, however unworthy I might be to add any thing to this glorious story. At the same time I shall add one example of her perseverance and nobility of soul.

The military tribune had treated them with extraordinary severity because on the information of certain very foolish people he became afraid that they would be spirited out of the prison by magical spells.

Perpetua spoke to him directly. 'Why can you not even allow us to refresh ourselves properly? For we are the most distinguished of the condemned prisoners, seeing that we belong to the emperor; we are to fight on his very birthday. Would it not be to your credit if we were brought forth on the day in a healthier condition?'

The officer became disturbed and grew red. So it was that he gave the order that they were to be more humanely treated; and he allowed her brothers and other persons to visit, so that the prisoners could dine in their company. By this time the adjutant who was head of the jail was himself a Christian.

17. On the day before, when they had their last meal, which is called the free banquet [the public feast given to the condemned], they celebrated not a banquet but rather a love feast. They spoke to the mob with the same steadfastness, warned them of God's judgment, stressing the joy they would have in their suffering, and ridiculing the curiosity of those that came to see them. Saturus said: 'Will not tomorrow be enough for you? Why are you so eager to see something that you dislike? Our friends today will be our enemies on the morrow. But take careful note of what we look like so that you will recognize us on the day.' Thus everyone would depart from the prison in amazement, and many of them began to believe.

18. The day of their victory dawned, and they marched from the prison to the amphitheater joyfully as though they were going to heaven, with calm faces, trembling, if at all, with joy rather than fear. Perpetua went along with shining countenance and calm step, as the beloved of God, as a wife of Christ, putting down everyone's stare by her own intense gaze. With them also was Felicitas, glad that she had safely given birth so that now she could fight the beasts, going from one blood bath to another, from the midwife to the gladiator, ready to wash after childbirth in a second baptism. They

were then led up to the gates and the men were forced to put on the robes of priests of Saturn, the women the dress of the priestesses of Ceres. But the noble Perpetua strenuously resisted this to the end. 'We came to this of our own free will that our freedom should not be violated. We agreed to pledge our lives provided that we would do no such thing. You agreed with us to do this.' Even injustice recognized justice. The military tribune agreed. They were to be brought into the arena just as they were. Perpetua then began to sing a psalm: she was already treading on the head of the Egyptian. Revocatus, Saturninus, and Saturus began to warn the onlooking mob. Then when they came within sight of Hilarianus, they suggested by their motions and gestures: 'You have condemned us, but God will condemn you' was what they were saying.

At this the crowds became enraged and demanded that they be scourged before a line of gladiators. And they rejoiced at this that they had obtained a share in the Lord's sufferings.

19. But he who said, 'Ask and you shall receive,' answered their prayer by giving each one the death he had asked for. For when ever they would discuss among themselves their desire for martyrdom, Saturninus indeed insisted that he wanted to be exposed to all the different beasts, that his crown might be all the more glorious. And so at the outset of the contest he and Revocatus were matched with a leopard, and then while in the stocks they were attacked by a bear. As for Saturus, he dreaded nothing more than a bear, and he counted on being killed by one bite of a leopard. Then he was matched with a wild boar; but the gladiator who had tied him to the animal was gored by the boar and died a few days after the contest, whereas Saturus was only dragged along. Then when he was bound in the stocks awaiting the bear, the animal refused to come out of the cages, so that Saturus was called back once more unhurt.

20. For the young women, however, the Devil had prepared a mad heifer. This was an unusual animal, but it was chosen that their sex might be matched with that of the beast. So they were stripped naked, placed in nets and thus brought out into the arena. Even the crowd was horrified when they saw that one was a delicate young girl and the other was a woman fresh from child birth with the milk still dripping from her breasts. And so they were brought back again and dressed in unbelted tunics.

First the heifer tossed Perpetua and she fell on her back. Then sitting up she pulled down the tunic that was ripped along the side so that it covered her thighs, thinking more of her modesty than of her pain. Next she asked for a pin to fasten her untidy hair: for it was not right that a martyr should die with her hair in disorder, lest she might seem to be mourning in her hour of triumph.

Then she got up. And seeing that Felicitas had been crushed to the ground, she went over to her, gave her hand, and lifted her up. Then the two stood side by side. But the cruelty of the mob was by now appeased, and so they were called back through the Gate of Life.

There Perpetua was held up by a man named Rusticus who was at the time a catechumen and kept close to her. She awoke from a kind of sleep (so absorbed had she been in ecstasy in the Spirit) and she began to look about her. Then to the amazement of all she said: 'When are we going to be thrown to that heifer or whatever it is?'

When told that this had already happened, she refused to believe it until she noticed the marks of her rough experience on her person and her dress. Then she called for her brother and spoke to him together with the catechumens and said: 'You must all *stand fast in the faith* and love one another, and do not be weakened by what we have gone through.'

21. At another gate Saturus was earnestly addressing the soldier Pudens. 'It is exactly,' he said, 'as I foretold and predicted. So far not one animal has touched me. So now you may believe me with all your heart: I am going in there and I shall be finished off with one bite of the leopard.' And immediately as the contest was coming to a close a leopard was let loose, and after one bite Saturus was so drenched with blood that as he came away the mob roared in witness to his second baptism: 'Well washed! Well washed [an ironic use of the greeting to bathers in the public baths]!' For well washed indeed was one who had been bathed in this manner.

Then he said to the soldier Pudens: 'Good-bye. Remember me, and remember the faith. These things should not disturb you but rather strengthen you.'

And with this he asked Pudens for a ring from his finger, and dipping it into his wound he gave it back to him again as a pledge and as a record of his bloodshed.

Shortly after he was thrown unconscious with the rest in the usual spot to have his throat cut. But the mob asked that their bodies be brought out into the open that their eyes might be the guilty witnesses of the sword that pierced their flesh. And so the martyrs got up and went to the spot of their own accord as the people wanted them to, and kissing one another they sealed their martyrdom with the ritual kiss of peace. The others took the sword in silence and without moving, especially Saturus, who, being the first to climb the stairway, was the first to die. For once again he was waiting for Perpetua. Perpetua, however, had yet to taste more pain. She screamed as she was struck on the bone; then she took the trembling hand of the young gladiator and guided it to her throat. It was as though so great a woman, feared as she was by the unclean spirit, could not be dispatched unless she herself were willing.

Ah, most valiant and blessed martyrs! Truly are you called and chosen for the glory of Christ Jesus our Lord! And any man who exalts, honors, and worships his glory should read for the consolation of the Church these new deeds of heroism which are no less significant than the tales of old. For these new manifestations of virtue will bear witness to one and the same Spirit who still operates, and to God the Father almighty, to his Son Jesus Christ our Lord, to whom is splendor and immeasurable power for all the ages. Amen.

2. CHRISTIANITY IN THE DESERT:
ST. ANTONY THE GREAT

With the conversion of the emperor Constantine in 312, the immediate threat of perse-
cution was removed. The standard for acknowledging a saint continued to be martyrdom
but now extended to include extreme self-deprivation, heroic resistance to temptation,
and extraordinary virtue manifested especially in miracles. Many Christians in Syria
and Egypt found it impossible to live the life exemplified by Christ and his disciples
within their communities, so they fled to the desert to confront privation and tempta-
tion as Christ had done before them. The chief among them became the subjects of
hagiographies that were an important influence on the genre.

The most famous of the desert fathers was Antony (c. 250-356), whose 'life' was
written in Greek by Athanasius, bishop of Alexandria (293-373), shortly after Antony's
death. Translated into Latin by Evagrius, it was widely read in both the East and the
West: Augustine tells us that his own conversion was initiated by hearing about Ant-
ony's life and his influence on others ('Confessions,' 8, 6-12). A short prologue included
in Evagrius's version suggests that the 'life' may have been written at the request of
western monks who wished to emulate desert asceticism, and it was instrumental in
introducing monasticism to the West. More than any other single work, 'The Life of
St. Antony' also influenced the form and content of later hagiographies. Originally an
adaptation of classical biography to Christian purposes, it became the primary model for
later writers of saints' lives, and Antony was the outstanding example for those seeking
perfection in the monastic life.

Source: trans. from Migne, *Patrologia Graeca*, 26 (1887), pp. 835-976, by Dom J.B. McLaughlin,
St. Antony the Hermit, by St. Athanasius (London: Burns Oates and Washbourne, 1924), pp.
1-122, abridged.

Book 1
Antony's conversion to the ascetic life, his early temptations, and his solitary withdrawal into the desert.

1. Antony was of Egyptian race, his parents of good birth and good means;
Christians too, so that he also was brought up [as a Christian]. As a child he
lived with his parents, knowing nothing but them and his home; and when
he grew to be a boy and was advancing in age, he refused to learn letters,
desiring to be away from the company of children; all his wish was, as is
written of Jacob, to dwell unspoiled at home.

With his parents he frequented the church, not with a child's inattention,
nor with the contempt [of a youth], but obeying his parents, and listening to
the lessons that were read, and carefully keeping the fruits of them in his own
life. Nor again, though he found himself in a fairly rich home, did he worry

his parents for rich and varied food, nor care for the enjoyment of it; he was satisfied with what was there, and asked no more.

After his parents' death he was left alone with one very young sister. He was eighteen or twenty years old, and had charge of the home and of his sister. Less than six months after the death of his parents he was going out to church as usual, and collecting his thoughts he pondered as he went how the apostles, leaving all things, followed the Savior; and the people in the [Book of] Acts who sold their possessions and brought the price and laid it at the feet of the apostles for distribution among the needy – what good and great hope was laid up in heaven for these. With these thoughts in his mind he entered the church; and it so fell that the Gospel was being read then, and he heard the Lord saying to the rich man: "If thou wilt be perfect, go sell all that thou hast and give to the poor, and come follow me and thou shalt have treasure in heaven." Then, as though it was from God that his thoughts of the saints had come, and this reading had been for his sake, as soon as he went out of the church he gave to the villagers the property he had from his parents (it was 300 acres of land, fertile and very beautiful) [so] that they might not interfere with him and his sister. And all else that they had, in personal property, he sold, and raised a fair sum of money, which he gave to the poor, keeping a little because of his sister.

But when, again entering the church, he heard the Lord saying in the Gospel, "Be not solicitous for the morrow," he could not bear to wait longer, but went out and distributed this also to the poor. His sister he commended to known and trusty virgins, and put her with a sisterhood to be brought up; and then he gave himself for the future to the religious life, minding himself and living a life of hardship, in front of his own house. For as yet monasteries were not so universal in Egypt, and no monk yet knew the great desert; but each who wished to attend to his soul exercised himself alone not far from his own village. Now there was at the time in the neighboring village an old man who had practised the solitary life from youth. Antony, seeing him, was eager to imitate him, so he too at first began to stay in the places near the village. From there, if he heard anywhere of an earnest soul, he went forth like a wise bee and sought him out; nor would he return to his own place till he had seen him and got from him what would help him on his way to virtue; then he went back. There, then, he made his first steps, steadying his mind not to turn back to his inheritance nor to think of his kindred, but to give all its desire and all its energy to keeping up the religious life. He worked with his hands, having heard "He that will not work neither let him eat," spending the money partly on bread, partly on the poor. He prayed constantly, having learned that in private we must pray without ceasing. For he so listened to the reading that nothing of what is written escaped him, but he retained everything, and for the future his memory served him instead of books.

Living this manner of life, Antony was beloved by all. He made himself really subject to the devout men whom he visited, and learned for himself the special religious virtues of each of them: the graciousness of one, the continual prayer of another; he observed the meekness of one, the charity of another; studied one in his long watchings, another in his love of reading; admired one for his steadfastness, another for his fasting and sleeping on the ground; watched one's mildness, another's patience; while in all alike he remarked the same reverence for Christ and the same love for each other. Having thus gathered his fill, he returned to his own place of discipline, and thereafter pondered with himself what he had learned from each, and strove to show in himself the virtues of all. He had no contentions with those of his own age, save only that he would not be found second to them in the better things; and this he did in such manner that none was grieved, but they too were glad on his account. Seeing him such, then, all the village people and the devout with whom he had intercourse called him a man of God, and loved him as a son or as a brother.

2. But the devil, the hater and envier of good, could not bear to see such resolution in a young man, but attempted to use against him the means in which he is skilled. First he tried to draw him back from the religious life by reminding him of his property, of the care of his sister, his intimacy with his kindred, the love of money, the love of fame, the many pleasures of the table, and the other relaxations of life; and lastly the hardness of virtue, and how great is the labor of it: suggesting that the body is weak, and time is long. So he raised in his mind a great dust-cloud of arguments, to drive him aside from his straight purpose. But when the enemy saw himself powerless in face of Antony's resolution, and that rather he [the devil] was himself overthrown by his firmness and routed by his great faith and beaten by Antony's constant prayer, then, placing his trust in "the weapons that hang at his waist" and glorying in these (for these are his first snare against the young), he advances against the young man, disturbing him by night, and so besetting him by day that even onlookers could see the struggle that was going on between the two. He suggested evil thoughts; and the other turned them away by his prayers. He roused feelings; and Antony, ashamed, defended himself by faith and prayers and fastings. The wretched fiend even stooped to masquerade as a woman by night, simply to deceive Antony; and he quenched the fire of that temptation by thinking of Christ and of the nobility we have through him, and of the dignity of the soul. Again the enemy suggested the delight of pleasure; but he, angered and grieved, thought over the threat of the fire and the torment of the worm: these he opposed to his temptations, and so

came through them unhurt. So all these things turned to the confusion of the adversary; for he who thought to be like to God was now mocked by a youth; and he who gloried over flesh and blood was now defeated by a man clad in the flesh. For with him wrought the Lord who for us took flesh and gave to the body the victory over the devil; so that those who truly strive can each say, "Not I, but the grace of God with me."

As the serpent could not conquer Antony by this means either, but saw himself thrust out of his heart, at length, gnashing his teeth, as it is written, like one in a frenzy, he showed himself in appearance as he is in mind, coming to Antony in the shape of a black boy, and as it were flattering him. He no longer assailed him with thoughts, for the deceiver had been cast out, but now using a human voice he said, "Many have I deceived, and very many have I overthrown; yet now, when I attacked you and your works as I have attacked others, I was not strong enough." Antony asked, "Who are you that say such things to me?" Then at once he answered in piteous tones, "I am the lover of uncleanness, I take charge of the ensnaring and the tempting of the young; and I am called the spirit of fornication. How many have I deceived who meant to be careful! How many that were chaste have I drawn away with temptations! I am he through whom the prophet reproaches the fallen, saying, 'You were deceived by a spirit of fornication'; for it was through me that they were tripped up. I am he that so often beset you and as often was defeated by you." Then Antony thanked God, and taking courage against him said to him, "Then you are much to be despised; for your mind is black, and your strength as a child's. I have not one anxiety left on your account, 'the Lord is my helper, and I will despise my enemies.'" Hearing this the black spirit instantly fled, cowering at his words and fearing even to approach the man.

This was Antony's first victory over the devil; or rather, this was the triumph in Antony of the Savior, "who condemned sin in the flesh that the justice of the law may be fulfilled in us who walk not according to the flesh but according to the spirit."

But thereafter Antony did not grow careless and neglect himself as though the devil were beaten; neither did the enemy cease his wiles, as having failed. For he wandered round again like a lion seeking some chance against him. And Antony, having learned from the scriptures that the craftiness of the enemy are many, gave himself earnestly to the religious life, deeming that though the foe had not been able to beguile his heart with bodily pleasures he would surely try to ensnare him by other means; for the devil is a lover of sin. More and more, therefore, did he repress the body and bring it into subjection, lest after winning at one point he should be dragged down at another. He decided, therefore, to accustom himself to harder ways. And many wondered, but he easily bore the hardship; for the eagerness of the spirit, long abiding with him, [created] in him a good habit, so that a small occasion given by others led him to a great exercise of zeal. For such was his watching that often he passed the whole night unsleeping; and this not once, but it was seen with wonder that he did it most frequently. He ate once in the day, after sunset; and at times he broke his fast only after two days, and often even after four days. His food was bread and salt, his drink only water. Of meat and wine it is needless to speak, for nothing of this sort was to be found among the other monks either. For sleep a rush mat sufficed him; as a rule he simply lay on the ground. The oiling of the skin he refused, saying that it would be better for young men to prefer exercise and not seek for things that make the body soft, [but] rather to accustom it to hardships, mindful of the apostle's word, "When I am weak then am I strong." For he said that when the enjoyments of the body are weak, then is the power of the soul strong.

He had also this strange-seeming principle: he held that not by length of time is the way of virtue measured, and our progress in it; but by desire, and by strong resolve. Accordingly he himself gave no thought to previous time; but each day, as though then beginning his religious life, he made greater effort to advance, constantly repeating to himself St. Paul's saying, "Forgetting the things that are behind, and reaching out to the things that are before," keeping in mind, too, the voice of Elijah the prophet saying, "The Lord liveth, before whose sight I stand this day." For he observed that, in saying "this day," he did not count the time gone by; but as though always making a beginning, he was earnest each day to present himself such as one ought to appear before God – clean of heart, and ready to obey his will and none other. And he used to say within himself that from the way of life of the great Elijah a religious man must always study his own way of life, as in a mirror.

3. Having thus mastered himself, Antony departed to the tombs that lay far from the village, having asked one of his acquaintances to bring him bread from time to time. He entered one of the tombs, his friend closed the door of it on him, and he remained alone within. This the enemy would not endure, for he feared lest by degrees Antony should fill the desert too with monks; and coming one night with a throng of demons, he so scourged him that he lay on the ground speechless from the pain. For, he declared, the pain was so severe that blows from men could not have caused such agony. By God's providence (for the Lord does not overlook those who hope in him) his friend came the next day bringing him bread, and when he opened the door and saw him lying on the ground, as [if] dead, he lifted him and took him to the village church and laid him on the ground. Many of his kin and the village people watched beside Antony as if he were dead. But towards midnight Antony came to himself and woke, and seeing all asleep and only

his friend waking, he signed to him to come near, and asked him to lift him again and carry him back to the tombs without waking anyone. So he was carried back by the man, and the door was closed as before, and he was again alone within. He could not stand because of the blows, but he prayed lying down. And after his prayer he shouted out, "Here am I, Antony; I do not run away from your blows. For though you should give me yet more, nothing shall separate me from the love of Christ." Then he sang the psalm: "If camps shall stand against me, my heart shall not fear."

The monk, then, thought and spoke in this way. But the enemy of all good, marveling that even after the blows he had courage to go back, called together his hounds [other demons] and burst out in fury, "Do you see that we have not stopped this man either by the spirit of fornication or by blows, but he challenges us; let us attack him another way." For plans of ill are easy to the devil.

Thereupon in the night they made such a crashing that it seemed the whole place was shaken by an earthquake; and, as if they had broken through the four walls of the building, the demons seemed to rush in through them in the guise of beasts and creeping things, and the place was at once filled with the forms of lions, bears, leopards, bulls, serpents, asps, scorpions, wolves. And each moved according to its own likeness. The lion roared, ready to spring, the bull seemed thrusting with its horns, the serpent crept yet reached him not, the wolf held itself in act to strike. And the noise of all the visions was terrible, and their fury cruel. Antony, beaten and goaded by them, felt keener bodily pain. Nevertheless he lay fearless and more alert in spirit. He groaned with the soreness of his body, but in mind he was cool, and said jokingly, "If you had any power in you, it would have been enough that just one of you should come; but the Lord has taken your strength away, and that is why you try to frighten me if possible by your numbers. It is a sign of your helplessness that you have taken the shapes of brutes." Again he said cheerily, "If you can, and if you have received power over me, do not wait, but lay on. But if you cannot, why are you [upsetting] yourselves for nothing? For our trust in the Lord is like a seal to us, and like a wall of safety."

So after making many attempts they gnashed their teeth at him because they were [making fools of] themselves and not of him.

And the Lord in this also forgot not Antony's wrestling, but came to his defence. For looking up he saw as it were the roof opening and a beam of light coming down to him. And the demons suddenly disappeared, and the soreness of his body ceased at once, and the building was again sound.

Antony, seeing that help had come, breathed more freely, being eased of his pains. And he asked the vision, "Where wert thou? Why didst thou not show thyself from the beginning, to end my suffering?" And a voice came to him: "I was here, Antony, but I waited to see thy resistance. Therefore since thou hast endured and not yielded, I will always be thy helper, and I will make thee renowned everywhere." Hearing this he arose and prayed, and he was so strengthened that he perceived that he had more power in his body than formerly. He was at this time about thirty-five years old.

4. The next day, going out with still greater zeal for the service of God, he met the old man before mentioned, and asked him to live in the desert with him. He refused, because of his age and because this was not as yet usual; but Antony at once set out for the mountain [at Pispir, east of the Nile, about 50 miles south of Memphis]. Yet once more the enemy, seeing his zeal and wishing to check it, threw in his way the [illusory shape] of a large disc of silver. Antony, understanding the deceit of the evil one, stood and looked at the disc, and confuted the demon in it, saying, "Whence [comes] a disc in the desert? This is not a trodden road, and there is no track of any faring this way. And it could not have fallen unnoticed, being of huge size. And even if it had been lost, the loser would certainly have found it had he turned back to look, because the place is desert. This is a trick of the devil. You will not hinder my purpose by this, Satan; let this thing perish with thee." And as Antony said this, it disappeared like smoke before the face of the fire.

Now as he went on he again saw, not this time a phantom, but real gold lying in the way. Whether it was the enemy that pointed it out or whether it was a higher power training the disciple and proving to the devil that he cared nothing even for real riches, he himself did not say, and we do not know; only that it was gold that he saw. Antony marveled at the quantity, but avoided it like fire and passed on without looking back, running swiftly on till he lost sight of the place and knew not where it was.

So with firmer and firmer resolution he went to the mountain, and finding beyond the river a fort long deserted and now full of reptiles, he betook himself there and dwelt in it. The reptiles fled at once as though chased by someone; and he, closing up the entrance and laying in bread for six months (the Thebans do this, and often it keeps unspoiled for a whole year), and having water in the fort, went down into the inner rooms and lived there alone, not going out himself, and not seeing any who came to visit him. For a long time he continued this life of asceticism, only receiving his loaves twice in the year from the house above.

His acquaintance who came to see him often spent days and nights outside, since he would not let them enter. They seemed to hear a tumultuous crowd inside, making noises, uttering piteous cries, shrieking, "Stand off from our domain. What have you to do with the desert? You cannot stand against our contrivings." At first those outside thought there were men fighting with him who had got in to him by a ladder, but when they bent down through a hole and saw no one, then they thought it was demons, and feared for themselves and called to Antony. He listened to them, though he gave no thought to the demons, and going near to the door he urged the people to go home and fear not, saying that the demons made these displays against the timid. "Do you therefore sign yourselves and go away bravely, and leave them to make fools of themselves." So they went away, protecting themselves with the sign of the cross, and he remained and was [not at all] hurt by them. Nor did he weary of the struggle. For the aid of the visions that came to him from on high, and the weakness of his enemies, brought him much ease from his labors, and prepared him for greater earnestness. His friends used to come constantly, expecting to find him dead; but they heard him singing, "Let God arise and his enemies be scattered, and those who hate him flee from his face. As smoke fades away so may they fade away. As wax melts before the face of the fire so may sinners perish before the face of God." And again: "All the nations surrounded me, and by the name of the Lord I drove them off."

He spent nearly twenty years in this solitary religious life, neither going out, nor being seen regularly by any. After that, many longed and sought to copy his holy life, and some of his friends came and forcibly broke down the door and removed it; and Antony came forth as from a holy of holies, filled with heavenly secrets and possessed by the spirit of God. This was the first time he showed himself from the fort to those who came to him. When they saw him they marveled to see that his body kept its former state, being neither grown heavy for want of exercise, nor shrunken with fastings and strivings against demons. For he was such as they had known him before his retirement. The light of his soul, too, was absolutely pure. It was not shrunk with grieving nor dissipated by pleasure; it had no touch of levity nor of gloom. He was not bashful at seeing the crowd, nor elated at being welcomed by such numbers; but was unvaryingly tranquil, a man ruled by reason, whose whole character had grown firm-set in the way that nature had meant it to grow.

Through him the Lord healed many of those present who were suffering from bodily ills and freed others from evil spirits. And the Lord gave Antony grace in speech so that he comforted many in sorrow; others who were at strife he made friends; charging all not to prefer anything in the world to the love of Christ. And when he spoke and exhorted them to be mindful of the good things to come and of the love of God for us, who "spared not his own son but delivered him up for us all," he induced many to take up the solitary life. And so from that time there were monasteries in the mountains, and the desert was peopled with monks, who went forth from their own [people] and became citizens of the kingdom of heaven.

Book 2, omitted here, records Anthony's discourse on the nature of demons, the problem of distinguishing good visions from bad ones, and the ultimate powerlessness of Satan.

Book 3
The persecution under Maximinus (c.305-11) and Antony's life in the inner mountain, between the Nile and the Red Sea.

11. As Antony made this discourse, all rejoiced. It increased the love of virtue in some, in some it cast out carelessness, and in others it ended self-conceit. All were persuaded to despise the plottings of the devil, admiring the grace which God had given to Antony for the discerning of spirits.

The monasteries in the hills were like tents filled with heavenly choirs, singing, studying, fasting, praying, rejoicing for the hope of the life to come, laboring in order to give alms, having love and harmony among themselves. And in truth it was like a land of religion and justice to see, a land apart. For neither wronger nor wronged was there, nor complaint of tax-gathering; but a multitude of ascetics, all with one aim of virtue; so that, looking back on the monasteries and on so fair an array of monks, one cried aloud saying, "How lovely are thy dwellings, O Jacob, thy tents, O Israel; like shady groves, and like a garden by a river, and like tents that the Lord hath pitched, and like cedars beside the waters."

Antony himself retired as usual to his own monastery by himself, and went on with his holy life, groaning daily at the thought of the mansions of heaven, longing for them, and seeing the shortness of man's life. For when going to food, and sleep, and the other needs of the body, shame came on him thinking of the spirituality of the soul. Often when he was to eat with many other monks the thought of the spirit's food came back on him, and he excused himself and went a long way from them, thinking it a shame that he should be seen eating by others. Yet he ate alone, for the needs of the body; and often too with the brethren, ashamed on their account, but emboldened by the words of help he gave them. He used to say that we should give all our time to the soul rather than to the body. A little time indeed we must of necessity allow to the body; but in the main we must devote ourselves to the soul and seek its profit, that it may not be dragged down by the pleasures of the body, but rather that the body be made subject to the soul, this being what the Savior spoke of: "Be not solicitous for your life what you shall eat, nor for your body what you shall put on. And seek not what you may eat or what you may drink, and be not lifted up; for all these things do the nations of the world seek. But your Father knoweth that you have need of all these things. But seek ye first his kingdom, and all these things shall be added to you."

After this, the persecution which then befell under Maximinus overtook the Church. When the holy martyrs were taken to Alexandria, Antony also quitted his monastery and followed, saying, "Let us too go that we may suffer if we are called, or else may look on the sufferers." He had a longing to be martyred; but not wishing to give himself up, he ministered to the confessors in the mines and in the prisons. In the hall of judgment he was full of zeal for those who were called, stirring them to generosity in their struggles, and in their martyrdom receiving them and escorting them to the end. Then the judge, seeing the fearlessness of Antony and his companions, and their zeal in this work, gave orders that none of the monks should appear in the judgment hall, nor stay in the city at all. All the others thought best to be hidden that day, but Antony cared so much for it that he washed his tunic all the more, and on the next day stood on a high place in front and showed himself plainly to the prefect. While all wondered at this, and the prefect saw as he went through with his escort, Antony himself stood fearless, showing the eagerness that belongs to us Christians; for he was praying that he too might be martyred, as I have said. He himself mourned because he was not martyred; but God was keeping him to help us and others, that to many he might be a teacher of the strict life that he had himself learned from the scriptures. For simply at seeing his behavior many were eager to become followers of his way of life. Again, therefore, he ministered as before to the confessors; and as though sharing their bonds, he wearied himself in serving them. When later the persecution ceased, and the bishop Peter of blessed memory had died a martyr [Peter, bishop of Alexandria, executed in 311], Antony departed and went back to his monastery and abode there, a daily martyr to conscience, fighting the fights of the faith. He practised a high and more intense asceticism; he fasted constantly; his clothing was hair within and skin without, and this he kept till his death. He never bathed his body in water for cleanliness, nor even washed his feet; nor would he consent to put them in water at all without necessity. Neither was he ever seen undressed; nor till he died and was buried did any ever see the body of Antony uncovered.

12. When he retired and purposed to pass a season neither going forth himself nor admitting any, a certain captain of soldiers, Martinianus, came and disturbed him, for he had a daughter beset by a demon. As he stayed long, beating the door and asking him to come and pray to God for the child, Antony would not open, but leaned down from above and said, "Man, why do you cry to me? I am a man like yourself. But if you trust in Christ whom I serve, go, and as you trust so pray to God, and it shall be done." And he at once believing and calling on Christ, went away with his daughter made clean from the demon. Many other things did the Lord through Antony for he says, "Ask and it shall be given to you." For though he opened not the

door very many sufferers simply slept outside the monastery, and trusted and prayed sincerely, and were cleansed.

As he saw that many thronged to him, and that he was not suffered to retire in his own way as he wished, and being anxious lest from what the Lord did through him, either he himself should be lifted up, or another should think about him above the truth, he looked around him and set out to go to the upper Thebaid, where he was not known. He had got loaves from the brethren, and was sitting by the banks of the river watching if a boat should pass, that he might embark and go up with them. While he was thus minded, a voice came to him from above: "Antony, where are you going, and why?" He was not alarmed, being used to be often thus called, but listened and answered, "Since the crowds will not let me be alone, therefore I want to go to the upper Thebaid because of the many annoyances here, and especially because they ask me things beyond my power."And the voice said to him, "Though you should go up to the Thebaid, or, as you are considering, down to the pastures, you will have greater and twice as great a burden to bear. But if you wish to be really alone, go up now to the inner desert." Antony said, "And who will show me the way? For I know it not." And at once he was shown some Saracens [desert tribespeople] setting out that way. Advancing and drawing near, Antony asked to go with them into the desert, and they welcomed him as though by the command of Providence. He traveled with them three days and three nights and came to a very high hill. There was water under the hill, perfectly clear, sweet and very cold; beyond was flat land, and a few wild date palms.

Antony as though moved by God, fell in love with the place; for this was the place indicated by the voice that spoke to him at the river-bank. At the beginning he got bread from his fellow-travelers and abode alone on the hill, none other being with him; for he kept the place from then on as one who has found again his own home. The Saracens themselves, who had seen Antony's earnestness, used to travel by that way on purpose and were glad to bring him bread; he had besides a small and frugal refreshment from the date-palms. Afterwards, when the brethren learned the place, they were careful to send to him, as children mindful of their father. But Antony, seeing that by occasion of the bread some were footsore and endured fatigue, and wishing to spare the monks in this matter also, took counsel with himself, and asked some of those who visited him to bring him a pronged hoe, an axe, and some corn. When they were brought he went over the ground about the hill, and finding a very small patch that was suitable, he tilled it and sowed it, having water in abundance from the spring. This he did every year, and had bread from it; being glad that he should trouble no one on this account, but in all things kept himself from being a burden. But later, seeing that people were coming to him again, he grew a few vegetables also, that the visitor might have some little refreshment after the weariness of that hard road. At first the beasts in the desert used often to damage his crops and his garden when they came for water; but he catching one of the beasts said graciously to all, "Why do you harm me when I do not harm you? Begone, and in the name of the Lord do not come near these things again." And thereafter, as though fearing his command, they did not approach the place.

He then was alone in the inner hills, devoting himself to prayer and spiritual exercise. But the brethren who ministered to him asked that they might bring him each month olives and pulse and oil; for he was now an old man.

How many wrestlings he endured while he dwelt there we have learned from those who visited him, not against flesh and blood, as it is written, but against opposing demons. For there also they heard tumults and many voices and clashing as of weapons; and at night they saw the hill full of wild beasts; and they saw him fighting as with visible foes, and praying against them. He comforted his visitors; but he himself fought, bending his knees and entreating the Lord. And it was indeed a thing to admire, that being alone in such a wilderness, he was neither dismayed by the attacks of devils, nor with so many four-footed and creeping things there did he fear their savageness; but according to the scripture he trusted the Lord truly like Mount Zion, with a mind tranquil and untossed; so that rather the devils fled, and the wild beasts kept peace with him, as it is written.

Thus the devil watched Antony and gnashed his teeth against him, as David says in the psalm, while Antony had consolations from the Savior, and abode unharmed by his wickedness and his many arts. He [the devil] set wild beasts on him when watching at night. Almost all the hyaenas in that desert, coming out from their dens, surrounded him. He was in their midst, and each with open mouth threatened to bite him. But knowing the enemy's craft, he said to them all, "If you have received power over me I am ready to be eaten by you, but if you are sent by devils, delay not, but go; for I am Christ's servant." On this they fled, his words chasing them like a whip.

A few days after, while he was working (for he was careful to work), someone stood at the door and pulled the string of his work; for he was weaving baskets, which he gave to his visitors in exchange for what they brought. He rose and saw a beast, resembling a man as far as the thighs, but with legs and feet like a donkey. Antony simply crossed himself and said, "I am Christ's servant; if you are sent against me, here I am," and the monster with its demons fled so fast that for very speed it fell and died. And the death of the beast was the demons' fall; for they were hasting to do everything to drive him back from the desert, and they could not....

14. This was his instruction to those who visited him. To sufferers he gave

compassion, and prayed with them, and often the Lord heard him in many ways. He neither boasted when he was heard, nor murmured when not; but always gave thanks to God, and urged the sufferers to be patient and to know that healing belonged not to him nor to any man, but to God who acts when he will and to whom he will. The sufferers took the old man's words in place of healing, since they had learned to suffer with patience and not with shrinking; and the cured learned not to thank Antony, but God alone.

A man named Fronton from Palatium had a terrible disease; for he was biting his tongue, and his eyes were in danger. He came to the hill and begged Antony to pray for him. When he had prayed he said to Fronton, "Depart and you shall be healed." Fronton objected, and for days stayed in the house, while Antony continued saying, "You cannot be healed while you stay here. Go, and when you reach Egypt you shall see the sign that is wrought on you." The man believed and went; and as soon as he came in sight of Egypt he was freed from his sickness and made well, according to the word of Antony which he had learned from the Savior in prayer.

A girl from Busiris in Tripoli had a dreadful and distressing sickness, a discharge from eyes, nose and ears which turned to worms when it fell to the ground; and her body was paralyzed and her eyes unnatural. Her parents hearing of monks who were going to Antony, and having faith in the Lord who healed the woman troubled with an issue of blood, asked to accompany them with their daughter, and they consented. The parents and their child remained below the hill with Paphnutius, the confessor and monk. The others went up, but when they wished to tell about the girl, Antony interrupted them and described the child's sufferings and how they had traveled with them. On their asking that these also might come to him, he would not allow it, but said, "Go, and you will find her cured if she is not dead. For this is not my work, that she should come to a wretched man like me; but healing is the Savior's, who doeth his mercy in all places to them that call on him. To this child also the Lord hath granted her prayer, and his love has made known to me that he will heal her sickness while she is there." So the marvel came to pass; and going out they found the parents rejoicing and the girl in sound health.

Two of the brethren were traveling to him, when the water failed, and one died and the other was dying; he had no longer strength to go, and lay on the ground awaiting death. But Antony sitting on the hill called two monks who happened to be there, and urged them saying, "Take a jar of water and run down the road towards Egypt; for two were coming, and one has just died, and the other will if you do not hasten. This has just been shown me in prayer." The monks therefore went and found the one lying a corpse, and buried him; the other they revived with water, and brought him to the old man; for the distance was a day's journey. If anyone asks why he did not speak before the other died, he asks amiss in so speaking. For the sentence of death was not from Antony, but from God, who so decreed about the one and revealed concerning the other. In Antony this only is wonderful, that while he sat on the hill and watched in heart, the Lord revealed to him things far off.

For another time also, as he was sitting there and looking up, he saw in the air someone borne along, and great rejoicing in all that met him. Wondering at such a choir, and thinking of their blessedness, he prayed to learn what this might be. And at once a voice came to him that this was the soul of the monk Amun in Nitria [a famous monk, Amun had been a wealthy Alexandrian, who founded a series of monastic retreats in the desert of Nitria]. He had lived as an ascetic till old age. Now the distance from Nitria to the hill where Antony was is thirteen days' journey. Those who were with Antony, seeing the old man in admiration, asked to know, and heard from him that Amun had just died. He was well known, because he often visited there, and because through him also many miracles had come to pass, of which this is one. Once, when he had need to cross the river called the Lycus, the waters being in flood, he asked his companion Theodore to keep far from him that they might not see each other naked in swimming the river. Theodore went; but he was again ashamed to see himself naked. While, therefore, he was ashamed, and pondering, he was suddenly carried to the other side. Theodore, himself a devout man, came up; and seeing that Amun was first and unwetted by the water, asked to know how he had crossed. And seeing that he did not wish to speak, he seized his feet, declaring that he would not let him go till he had heard. Amun, seeing Theodore's obstinacy, especially from his speech, asked him in turn not to tell anyone till his death, and then told him that he had been carried across and set down on the other side; that he had not walked on the water, and that this was a thing not possible to men, but only to the Lord and those to whom he granted it, as he did to the great apostle Peter. And Theodore told this after Amun's death. Now the monks to whom Antony spoke of Amun's death noted the day; and when, thirty days later, the brethren came from Nitria they enquired and found that Amun had fallen asleep at the day and hour when the old man saw his soul carried up. And both these and the others were all amazed how pure was the soul of Antony, that he should learn at once what happened thirteen days away, and should see the soul in its flight.

Again, Archelaus the Count once met him in the outer hills and asked him only to pray for Polycratia, the renowned and Christ-like virgin of Laodicea; for she was suffering much in her stomach and side, through her great mortifications, and was weak throughout her body. Antony therefore prayed, and the Count made a note of the day when the prayer was made and departing to Laodicea he found the virgin well. Asking when and on what day she was freed from her sickness, he brought out the paper on which he had written the time of the prayer; and when he heard he immediately showed the writing on the paper, and all recognized with wonder that the Lord had freed her from her pains at the moment when Antony was praying and invoking the goodness of the Savior on her behalf.

Often he spoke days beforehand of those who were coming to him, and sometimes a month before; and of the cause for which they came. For some came simply to see him, some through sickness, some suffering from devils. And all thought the toil of the journey no trouble or loss; for each returned feeling helped. Antony, while he said and saw such things, begged that none should admire him in this regard, but rather should admire the Lord, who grants to us men to know him in our own measure. Another time when he had gone down to the outer monasteries and was asked to enter a ship and pray with the monks, he alone perceived a horrible, pungent smell. The crew said that there was fish and pickled meat in the boat, and that the smell was from them, but he said it was different; and even as he spoke came a sudden shriek from a young man having a devil, who had come on board earlier and was hiding in the vessel. Being charged in the name of our Lord Jesus Christ, the devil went out and the man was made whole and all knew that the foul smell was from the evil spirit.

Another came to him, one of the nobles, having a devil. This demon was so dreadful that the possessed man did not know he was going to Antony; also he used to eat the filth of his own body. Those who brought him begged Antony to pray for him; and Antony, pitying the youth, prayed and watched the whole night with him. Towards dawn the youth suddenly sprang on Antony, pushing him. His friends were indignant, but Antony said, "Do not be angry with the youth; it is not he, but the demon in him, for being rebuked and commanded to depart into waterless places, he became furious, and has done this. Therefore glorify God; for his attacking me in this way is a sign to you of the demon's going." And when Antony had said this the youth was at once made whole; and then, in his right mind, recognized where he was and embraced the old man, thanking God.

The omitted chapters of Book 3 record how Antony taught the monks and the visions he received from God.

Book 4
Antony as the champion of orthodoxy against heresies; his last years and death.

18. The renown of Antony reached even to kings. For on hearing of these things, Constantine Augustus and his sons, Constantius Augustus and Constans Augustus, wrote to him as to a father and begged to receive answers from him. He, however, did not value these writings nor rejoice over the letters, but was just what he had been before the kings wrote to him. When the letters were brought to him he called the monks and said, "Do not admire if a king writes to us, for he is a man; but admire rather that God has written the law for men, and has spoken to us by his own Son." He wished not to receive the letters, saying that he knew not what to answer to such. But being urged by the monks because the kings were Christians, and they might be scandalized as though he made them outcasts, he allowed them to be read. And he wrote back, welcoming them because they worshiped Christ; and advised them, for their salvation, not to think much of things present, but rather to remember the coming judgment; and to know that the only true and eternal king is Christ. He begged them also to be lovers of men, to care for justice, and to care for the poor. And they were glad to get his letter. So was he beloved by all, and so did all wish to hold him as a father.

With this character, and thus answering those who sought him, he returned again to the mount in the interior, and continued his usual life. Often when sitting or walking with visitors he would become dumb, as it is written in Daniel. After a time he would resume his former discourse with the brethren but they perceived that he was seeing some vision. For often in the mountain he saw things happening in Egypt, and described them to the bishop Serapion [bishop of Thmuis, in lower Egypt, a personal friend of Antony also involved in the Arian controversy], who was within and saw Antony occupied with the vision. Once as he sat working he became as in ecstasy, and in the vision he groaned constantly. Then after a time he turned to his companions groaning; and trembling he prayed, bending his knees and abiding a long time, and when he arose the old man was weeping. Then the others trembled and were much afraid and begged him to tell; and they urged him for a long time till he was compelled to speak. Then with a great groan he said, "Ah, my children, better is it to die than that there happen what I have seen in this vision." And when they asked again he said with tears, "Wrath shall overtake the Church, and she shall be delivered up to men who are like to senseless beasts. For I saw the table of the Lord, and around it mules standing on all sides in a ring and kicking what was within, as might be the kicking of beasts in a wild frolic. You heard surely," he said, "how I was groaning; for I heard a voice saying, 'My altar shall be made an abomination.'" So the old man said; and two years after [356, when the imperial government handed over the church buildings of Alexandria to the Arians] came this present onset of the Arians, and the plundering of the churches; wherein, seizing by force the vessels, they had them carried away by pagans; when, too, they forced the pagans from the workshops to their meetings, and in their presence did what they would on the sacred table. Then we all understood that the kicking of the mules had foreshown to Antony what the Arians are now doing, brutishly as beasts. When he saw this vision, he comforted his companions, saying, "Do not lose heart, children; for as the Lord has been angry, so later will he bring healing. And the Church shall quickly regain her own beauty, and shine as before. And you shall see the persecuted restored, and impiety retiring to its own hiding places, and the true faith in all places speaking openly with all freedom. Only, defile not yourselves with the Arians. For this teaching is not of the apostles, but of the demons and their father the devil; and indeed from no source, from no sense, from a mind not right it comes; like the senselessness of mules."...

20. The manner of the end of his life I ought also to tell, and you to hear eagerly; for this also is a pattern to imitate. He was visiting as usual the monks in the outer hills; and learning of his end from Providence, he spoke to the brethren saying, "This is the last visiting of you that I shall make; and I wonder if we shall see each other again in this life. It is time now for me to be dissolved; for I am near a hundred and five years." Hearing this they wept, clasping and embracing the old man. But he talked joyously, as one leaving a foreign town to go to his own; and bade them "not to fail in their labors nor lose heart in their strict life, but live as dying daily; and, as I have said before, to be earnest to guard the heart from unclean thoughts; to vie with the holy; not to go near the Meletian schismatics, for you know their wicked and profane heresy; nor to have any fellowship with the Arians, for the impiety of these is plain to all. Be not troubled if you see judges protecting them, for their triumph will end, it is mortal and short-lived. Therefore do ye keep yourselves clean from these, and guard the tradition of the Fathers, and above all the loving faith in our Lord Jesus Christ, which you have learned from the Scriptures and have often been put in mind of by me."

When the brethren pressed him to stay with them and die there, he would not for many reasons, as he implied without saying; but on this account chiefly. To the bodies of religious men, especially of the holy martyrs, the Egyptians like to give funeral honors and wrap them in fine linens, but not to bury them in the earth, but to place them on couches and keep them at home with them; thinking by this to honor the departed. Antony often asked the bishops to tell the people about this; and likewise shamed laymen and reproved women, saying it was not right nor even reverent; for that the bodies of the patriarchs and prophets are preserved even till now in tombs; and the very body of our Lord was put in a sepulcher, and a stone set against it hid it till he rose the third day. He said this to show that he does wrong who after death does not bury the bodies of the dead, holy though they be. For what is greater or holier than the Lord's body? Many therefore, hearing him, buried [the dead] thenceforward in the ground, and thanked God that they had the right teaching.

Now knowing this, and fearing lest they might so treat his body also, Antony hastened and took leave of the monks in the outer hills; and returning to the inner hills where he was used to dwell, he fell sick after a few months. He called those who were there (there were two who lived in the house, who had been fifteen years in the religious life, and ministered to him because of his great age) and said to them: "I am going the way of my fathers, as the Scripture says; for I see myself called by the Lord. Be you wary, and undo not your long service of God, but be earnest to keep your strong purpose as though you were but now beginning. You know the demons who plot against you, you know how savage they are, and how powerless; therefore fear them not. Let Christ be as the breath you breathe; in him put your trust. Live as dying daily, heeding yourselves and remembering the counsel you have heard from me. And let there be no communion between you and the schismatics, nor the heretical Arians. For you know how I also have avoided them for their false and anti-Christian heresy. So do you also be earnest always to be in union first with the Lord and then with the saints; that after death they also may receive you into everlasting tabernacles as known friends. Ponder these things, and mean them. And if you have any care for me, and remember me as your father, do not allow anyone to take my body to Egypt lest they should deposit it in houses; for that is the reason why I entered the mountains and came here. And you know how I have always reproached those who do this, and bade them stop the practice. Therefore care for my body yourselves, and bury it in the earth; and let my words be so observed by you, that no one shall know the place but yourselves only. For in the resurrection of the dead I shall receive it back from the Savior incorruptible. Distribute my garments; the one sheepskin give to Athanasius the bishop, and the cloak I used to lie on, which he gave me new, but has worn out with me; and the other sheepskin give to Serapion the bishop; and do you have the hair-cloth garment. And now God save you, children; for Antony departs and is with you no more." Having said this and been embraced by them, he drew up his feet; then gazing as it seemed on friends who came for him, and filled by them with joy, for his countenance glowed as he lay, he died and was taken to his fathers. Then they, as he had given them orders, cared for his body and wrapped it up and buried it there in the earth; and no man yet knows where it is laid save only those two. And they who received the sheepskins of the blessed Antony and the cloak that he wore out, each guard them as some great treasure. For to look on them is like looking on Antony; and to wear them is like joyously taking on us his teachings.

This is the end of Antony's life in the body, as that was the beginning of his religious life. And if this is but little to tell of such virtue as his, yet from this little do you judge what manner of man was Antony the man of God, who from youth to such great age held unchanged his keen quest of a better life; who never for old age yielded to the desire of varied meats; nor for failing strength of body changed his form of dress nor even bathed his feet with water. And yet in all respects he was to the end untouched by decay. He saw well, his eyes being sound and undimmed; and of his teeth he had not lost one; only they were worn near the gums, through the old man's great age. In feet and hands, too, he was quite healthy; and altogether he seemed brighter and more active than all those who use rich diet and baths and many clothes.

That he was everywhere spoken of, and by all admired, and sought even by those who had not seen him — these things are proof of his virtue and of a soul dear to God. For Antony was known not for his writings, nor for worldly wisdom, nor for any art, but simply for his service of God. That this is God's gift none could deny. For how was he heard of even to Spain, and to Gaul, to Rome and to Africa, he sitting hidden in the hills, unless it were God who everywhere makes known his own people, who also had in the beginning announced this to Antony? For though they themselves act in secret, and wish to be unnoticed, yet the Lord shows them as lanterns to all; that even from this the hearers may know that the commandments are able to be fulfilled, and so may take courage on the path of virtue.

Now, therefore, read this to the other brethren that they may learn what should be the life of monks, and may believe that our Lord and Savior Jesus Christ glorifies them that glorify him, and not only brings to the kingdom of heaven those who serve him to the end, but even here (though they hide themselves and seek retirement) he makes them everywhere known and spoken of for their own goodness and for the helping of others. And if need arise, read it also to the pagans, that perhaps thus they may learn not only that our Lord Jesus Christ is God and the Son of God, but also that through him the Christians, who serve him sincerely and who piously trust in him, not only prove that the demons whom the Greeks think gods are no gods, but trample on them and drive them out as deceivers and corrupters of men, through Christ Jesus our Lord, to whom is glory for ages of ages. Amen.

3. THE LIFE AND MIRACLES OF ST. BENEDICT

With the spread of monasticism from the Mediterranean world into Gaul and the eventual Christianization of northern Europe, the predominant model of sanctity continued to be that of the confessor who exemplified a life of heroic virtue. The majority of the saints in this period came from the ranks of the Church, especially from among bishops, abbots, and abbesses. One reason for this was that positions of power offered more opportunity for heroic virtue and also made that virtue more visible to the community, whose veneration might decide whether or not a successful cult developed. The continuing influence of stories of the desert fathers and mothers meant that, ideally, the qualities of the wise administrator were linked with a commitment to solitary asceticism, and we often find saints struggling with the tension between these two modes of spirituality.

The earliest 'life' that we have for St. Benedict of Nursia (c. 480-547) was written by Gregory the Great (c. 540-604) during a chaotic time in Italy: the wars between the emperor Justinian and the invading Goths had devastated the country; the Lombards continued their sporadic attacks; and the last decade of the century was marked by floods, plague, and a series of famines. In these difficult times Gregory, who became pope in 590, wrote a work titled 'The Dialogues' (594) that was intended to encourage people by showing them that saints existed in Italy just as they had in the Egyptian desert and elsewhere, and that through their miraculous powers God continued to protect his people. Book 2 of 'The Dialogues' consists of the 'life' of St. Benedict; Books 1 and 3 describe a number of other Italian saints, and Book 4 concludes the work with a treatise on the 'Immortality of the Soul,' for the continuing presence and power of the saints after their deaths was understood to give certain evidence of the resurrection.

Before he became pope, Gregory had experienced an ascetic conversion: he resigned as prefect of Rome, founded monasteries on his family estates in Sicily, and turned his own home in Rome into the monastery of St. Andrew. He lived there as an ordinary monk under the Benedictine Rule (whose compilation is the major achievement ascribed to St. Benedict) until recalled to public service, but he continued to regret the loss of a life withdrawn from the world. He therefore felt a close relationship to Benedict, who also withdrew from the world for a time before becoming a busy abbot overseeing several monasteries and receiving visits from the temporal powers of the day. Gregory tells us that he got his information about Benedict from other people, but clearly he was well-read in hagiography too, for like other saints, Benedict is to be admired not primarily for his unique personality (though he does emerge as a memorable individual) but because he conforms to the virtuous ideal represented by the desert fathers and their followers.

Source: trans. Odo John Zimmerman, *St. Gregory the Great: Dialogues* (New York: Fathers of the Church, Inc., 1959), pp. 3-6 and 55-110; repr. with permission. BHL 1102.

Prologue to Book 1

Some men of the world had left me feeling quite depressed one day with all their noisy wrangling. In their business dealings they try, as a rule, to make us pay what we obviously do not owe them. In my grief I retired to a quiet spot congenial to my mood, where I could consider every unpleasant detail of my daily work and review all the causes of my sorrow as they crowded unhindered before my eyes. I sat there for a long time in silence and was still deeply dejected when my dear son, the deacon Peter, came in. He had been a very dear friend to me from his early youth and was my companion in the study of sacred Scripture. Seeing me so sick at heart he asked, 'Have you met with some new misfortune? You seem unusually sad.'

'Peter,' I replied, 'this daily sadness of mine is always old and always new: old by its constant presence, new by its continual increase. With my unhappy soul languishing under a burden of distractions, I recall those earlier days in the monastery where all the fleeting things of time were in a world below me, and I could rise far above the vanities of life. Heavenly thoughts would fill my mind, and while still held within the body I passed beyond its narrow confines in contemplation. Even death, which nearly everyone regards as evil, I cherished as the entrance into life and the reward for labor.

'But now all the beauty of that spiritual repose is gone, and the contact with worldly men and their affairs, which is a necessary part of my duties as bishop, has left my soul defiled with earthly activities. I am so distracted with external occupations in my concern for the people that even when my spirit resumes its striving after the interior life it always does so with less vigor. Then, as I compare what I have lost with what I must now endure, the contrast only makes my present lot more burdensome. I am tossed about on the waves of a heavy sea, and my soul is like a helpless ship buffeted by raging winds. When I recall my former way of life, it is as though I were once more looking back toward land and sighing as I beheld the shore. It only saddens me the more to find that, while flung about by the mighty waves that carry me along, I can hardly catch sight any longer of the harbor I have left.

'Such, in fact, is generally the way our mind declines. First we lose a prized possession but remain aware of the loss; then as we go along even the remembrance of it fades, and so at the end we are unable any longer to recall what was once actually in our possession. That is why, as I have said, when we sail too far from shore, we can no longer see the peaceful harbor we have left. At times I find myself reflecting with even greater regret on the life that others lead who have totally abandoned the present world. Seeing the heights these men have reached only makes me realize the lowly state of my own soul. It was by spending their days in seclusion that most of them pleased their Creator. And to keep them from dulling their spiritual fervor with human activities, God chose to leave them free from worldly occupations.'

And now I think it will be best if I present the conversation that took place between us by simply putting our names before the questions and the answers we exchanged.

Peter: I do not know of any persons in Italy whose lives give evidence of extraordinary spiritual powers, and therefore I cannot imagine with whom you are comparing yourself so regretfully. This land of ours has undoubtedly produced its virtuous men, but to my knowledge no signs or miracles have been performed by any of them; or, if they have been, they were till now kept in such secrecy that we cannot even tell if they occurred.

Gregory: On the contrary, Peter, the day would not be long enough for me to tell you about those saints whose holiness has been well established and whose lives are known to me either from my own observations or from the reports of good, reliable witnesses.

Peter: Would you do me the favor, then, of saying at least something about them? Interrupting the study and explanation of the Scriptures for such a purpose should not cause grave concern, for the amount of edification to be gained from a description of miracles is just as great. An explanation of holy Scripture teaches us how to attain virtue and persevere in it, whereas a description of miracles shows us how this acquired virtue reveals itself in those who persevere in it. Then, too, the lives of the saints are often more effective than mere instruction for inspiring us to love heaven as our home. Hearing about their example will generally be helpful in two ways. In the first place, as we compare ourselves with those who have gone before, we are filled with a longing for the future life; secondly, if we have too high an opinion of our own worth, it makes us humble to find that others have done better.

Gregory: I shall not hesitate to narrate what I have learned from worthy men. In this I am only following the consecrated practice of the Scriptures, where it is perfectly clear that Mark and Luke composed their Gospels, not as eyewitnesses, but on the word of others. Nevertheless, to remove any grounds for doubt on the part of my readers, I am going to indicate on whose authority each account is based. You should bear in mind, however, that in some instances I retain only the substance of the original narrative; in others, the words as well. For if I had always kept to the exact wording, the crude language used by some would have been ill suited to my style of writing....

Book 2:
Life and Miracles of St. Benedict, Founder and Abbot of the Monastery Which Is Known as the Citadel of Campania [Monte Cassino].

There was a man of saintly life; blessed Benedict was his name, and he was blessed also with God's grace. Even in boyhood he showed mature understanding, for he kept his heart detached from every pleasure with a strength of character far beyond his years. While still living in the world, free to enjoy its earthly advantages, he saw how barren it was with its attractions and turned from it without regret.

He was born in the district of Norcia [a little town about 112 km/70 miles northeast of Rome] of distinguished parents, who sent him to Rome for a liberal education. But when he saw many of his fellow students falling headlong into vice, he stepped back from the threshold of the world in which he had just set foot. For he was afraid that if he acquired any of its learning he, too, would later plunge, body and soul, into the dread abyss. In his desire to please God alone, he turned his back on further studies, gave up home and inheritance and resolved to embrace the religious life. He took this step, well aware of his ignorance, yet wise, uneducated though he was.

I was unable to learn about all his miraculous deeds. But the few that I am going to relate I know from the lips of four of his own disciples: Constantine, the holy man who succeeded him as abbot; Valentinian, for many years superior of the monastery at the Lateran [in Rome]; Simplicius, Benedict's second successor; and Honoratus, who is still abbot of the monastery where the man of God first lived [Subiaco].

1. When Benedict abandoned his studies to go into solitude, he was accompanied only by his nurse, who loved him dearly. As they were passing through Affile, a number of devout men invited them to stay there and provided them with lodging near the church of St. Peter. One day, after asking her neighbors to lend her a tray for cleaning wheat, the nurse happened to leave it on the edge of the table and when she came back found it had slipped off and broken in two. The poor woman burst into tears; she had only borrowed this tray and now it was ruined. Benedict, who had always been a devout and thoughtful boy, felt sorry for his nurse when he saw her weeping. Quietly picking up both the pieces, he knelt down by himself and prayed earnestly to God, even to the point of tears. No sooner had he finished his prayer than he noticed that the two pieces were joined together again, without even a mark to show where the tray had been broken. Hurrying back at once, he cheerfully reassured his nurse and handed her the tray in perfect condition. News of the miracle spread to all the country around Affile and

stirred up so much admiration among the people that they hung the tray at the entrance of their church. Ever since then it has been a reminder to all of the great holiness Benedict had acquired at the very outset of his monastic life. The tray remained there many years for everyone to see, and it is still hanging over the doorway of the church in these days of Lombard rule [Italy was ruled by the Lombards, a Germanic people from the upper Danube, from 568 until 774]. Benedict, however, preferred to suffer ill-treatment from the world rather than enjoy its praises. He wanted to spend himself laboring for God, not to be honored by the applause of men. So he stole away secretly from his nurse and fled to a lonely wilderness about thirty-five miles from Rome called Subiaco [8 km/5 miles north of Affile, on the Anio River]. A stream of cold, clear water running through the region broadens out at this point to form a lake, then flows off and continues on its course. On his way there Benedict met a monk named Romanus, who asked him where he was going. After discovering the young man's purpose, Romanus kept it secret and even helped him carry it out by clothing him with the monastic habit and supplying his needs as well as he could.

At Subiaco, Benedict made his home in a narrow cave and for three years remained concealed there, unknown to anyone except the monk Romanus, who lived in a monastery close by under the rule of Abbot Deodatus. With fatherly concern this monk regularly set aside as much bread as he could from his own portion; then from time to time, unnoticed by his abbot, he left the monastery long enough to take the bread to Benedict. There was no path leading from the monastery down to his cave because of a cliff that rose directly over it. To reach him Romanus had to tie the bread to the end of a long rope and lower it over the cliff. A little bell attached to the rope let Benedict know when the bread was there, and he would come out to get it. The ancient enemy of mankind grew envious of the kindness shown by the older monk in supplying Benedict with food, and one day, as the bread was being lowered, he threw a stone at the bell and broke it. In spite of this, Romanus kept on with his faithful service.

At length the time came when almighty God wished to grant him rest from his toil and reveal Benedict's virtuous life to others. Like a shining lamp his example was to be set on a lampstand to give light to everyone in God's house. The Lord therefore appeared in a vision to a priest some distance away, who had just prepared his Easter dinner. 'How can you prepare these delicacies for yourself,' he asked, 'while my servant is out there in the wilds suffering from hunger?'

Rising at once, the priest wrapped up the food and set out to find the man of God that very day. He searched for him along the rough mountainsides, in the valleys, and through the caverns, until he found him hidden in the cave.

They said a prayer of thanksgiving together and then sat down to talk about the spiritual life. After a while the priest suggested that they take their meal. 'Today is the great feast of Easter,' he added.

'It must be a great feast to have brought me this kind visit,' the man of God replied, not realizing after his long separation from men that it was Easter Sunday.

'Today is really Easter,' the priest insisted, 'the feast of our Lord's resurrection. On such a solemn occasion you should not be fasting. Besides, I was sent here by almighty God so that both of us could share in his gifts.'

After that they said grace and began their meal. When it was over they conversed some more and then the priest went back to his church.

At about the same time some shepherds also discovered Benedict's hiding place. When they first looked through the thickets and caught sight of him clothed in rough skins, they mistook him for some wild animal. Soon, however, they recognized in him a servant of God, and many of them gave up their sinful ways for a life of holiness. As a result, his name became known to all the people in that locality and great numbers visited his cave, supplying him with the food he needed and receiving from his lips in return spiritual food for their souls.

2. One day, while the saint was alone, the tempter came in the form of a little blackbird, which began to flutter in front of his face. It kept so close that he could easily have caught it in his hand. Instead, he made the sign of the cross and the bird flew away. The moment it left, he was seized with an unusually violent temptation. The evil spirit recalled to his mind a woman he had once seen and before he realized it his emotions were carrying him away. Almost overcome in the struggle, he was on the point of abandoning the lonely wilderness, when suddenly with the help of God's grace he came to himself.

He then noticed a thick patch of nettles and briers next to him. Throwing his garment aside he flung himself into the sharp thorns and stinging nettles. There he rolled and tossed until his whole body was in pain and covered with blood. Yet, once he had conquered pleasure through suffering, his torn and bleeding skin served to drain the poison of temptation from his body. Before long, the pain that was burning his whole body had put out the fires of evil in his heart. It was by exchanging these two fires that he gained the victory over sin. So complete was his triumph that from then on, as he later told his disciples, he never experienced another temptation of this kind. Soon after, many forsook the world to place themselves under his guidance, for now that he was free from these temptations he was ready to instruct others in the practice of virtue. That is why Moses commanded the Levites to begin their service when they were twenty-five years old or more and to become guardians of the sacred vessels only at the age of fifty.

Peter: The meaning of the passage you quote is becoming a little clearer to me now. Still, I wish you would explain it more fully.

Gregory: It is a well-known fact, Peter, that temptations of the flesh are violent during youth, whereas after the age of fifty concupiscence dies down. Now, the sacred vessels are the souls of the faithful. God's chosen servants must therefore obey and serve and tire themselves out with strenuous work as long as they are still subject to temptations. Only when full maturity has left them undisturbed by evil thoughts are they put in charge of the sacred vessels, for then they become teachers of souls.

Peter: I like the way you interpreted that passage. Now that you have explained what it means, I hope you will continue with your account of the holy man's life.

3. Gregory: With the passing of this temptation, Benedict's soul, like a field cleared of briers, soon yielded a rich harvest of virtues. As word spread of his saintly life, the renown of his name increased. One day the entire community from a nearby monastery came to see him. Their abbot had recently died, and they wanted the man of God to be their new superior. For some time he tried to discourage them by refusing their request, warning them that his way of life would never harmonize with theirs. But they kept insisting, until in the end he gave his consent.

At the monastery he watched carefully over the religious spirit of his monks and would not tolerate any of their previous disobedience. No one was allowed to turn from the straight path of monastic discipline either to the right or to the left. Their waywardness, however, clashed with the standards he upheld, and in their resentment they started to reproach themselves for choosing him as abbot. It only made them the more sullen to find him curbing every fault and evil habit. They could not see why they should have to force their settled minds into new ways of thinking.

At length, proving once again that the very life of the just is a burden to the wicked, they tried to find a means of doing away with him and decided to poison his wine. A glass pitcher containing this poisoned drink was presented to the man of God during his meal for the customary blessing. As he made the sign of the cross over it with his hand, the pitcher was shattered, even though it was well beyond his reach at the time. It broke at his blessing as if he had struck it with stone.

Then he realized it had contained a deadly drink which could not bear the sign of life. Still calm and undisturbed, he rose at once and, after gathering the community together, addressed them. 'May almighty God have mercy on you,' he said. 'Why did you conspire to do this? Did I not tell you at the outset that my way of life would never harmonize with yours? Go and find yourselves an abbot to your liking. It is impossible for me to stay here any longer.' Then he went back to the wilderness he loved, to live alone with himself in the presence of his heavenly Father.

Peter: I am not quite sure I understand what you mean by saying 'to live with himself.'

Gregory: These monks had an outlook on religious life entirely unlike his own and were all conspiring against him. Now, if he had tried to force them to remain under his rule, he might have forfeited his own fervor and peace of soul and even turned his eyes from the light of contemplation. Their persistent daily faults would have left him almost too weary to look to his own needs, and he would perhaps have forsaken himself without finding them. For, whenever anxieties carry us out of ourselves unduly, we are no longer with ourselves even though we still remain what we are. We are too distracted with other matters to give any attention whatever to ourselves.

Surely we cannot describe as 'with himself' the young man who traveled to a distant country where he wasted his inheritance and then, after hiring himself out to one of its citizens to feed swine, had to watch them eat their fill of pods while he went hungry. Do we not read in scripture that, as he was considering all he had lost, he came to himself and said, 'how many hired servants there are in my father's house who have more bread than they can eat'? If he was already 'with himself,' how could he have come 'to himself'?

Blessed Benedict, on the contrary, can be said to have lived 'with himself' because at all times he kept such close watch over his life and actions. By searching continually into his own soul he always beheld himself in the presence of his creator. And this kept his mind from straying off to the world outside.

Peter: But what of Peter the apostle when he was led out of prison by an angel? According to the scriptures, he, too, 'came to himself.' 'Now I can tell for certain,' he said, 'that the Lord has sent his angel, to deliver me out of Herod's hands, and from all that the people of the Jews hoped to see.'

Gregory: There are two ways in which we can be carried out of ourselves, Peter. Either we fall below ourselves through sins of thought or we are lifted above ourselves by the grace of contemplation. The young man who fed the swine sank below himself as a result of his shiftless ways and his unclean life. The apostle Peter was also out of himself when the angel set him free and raised him to a state of ecstasy, but he was above himself. In coming to themselves again, the former had to break with his sinful past before he could find his true and better self, whereas the latter merely returned from the heights of contemplation to his ordinary state of mind.

Now, the saintly Benedict really lived 'with himself' out in that lonely wilderness by always keeping his thoughts recollected. Yet he must have left his own self far below each time he was drawn heavenward in fervent contemplation.

Peter: I am very grateful to you for that explanation. Do you think it was right, though, for him to forsake this community, once he had taken it under his care?

Gregory: In my opinion, Peter, a superior ought to bear patiently with a community of evil men as long as it has some devout members who can benefit from his presence. When none of the members is devout enough to give any promise of good results, his efforts to help such a community will prove to be a serious mistake, especially if there are opportunities nearby to work more fruitfully for God. Was there anyone the holy man could have hoped to protect by staying where he was, after he saw that they were all united against him?

In this matter we cannot afford to overlook the attitude of the saints. When they find their work producing no results in one place, they move on to another where it can do some good. This explains the action of the blessed apostle Paul. In order to escape from Damascus, where he was being persecuted, he secured a basket and a rope and had himself secretly lowered over the wall. Yet this outstanding preacher of the Gospel longed to depart and be with Christ, since for him life meant Christ, and death was a prize to be won. Besides being eager for the trials of persecution himself, he even inspired others to endure them. Can we say that Paul feared death, when he expressly declared that he longed to die for the love of Christ? Surely not. But, when he saw how little he was accomplishing at Damascus in spite of all his toil, he saved himself for more fruitful labors elsewhere. God's fearless warrior refused to be held back inside the walls and sought the open field of battle. And if you do not mind continuing to listen, Peter, you will soon discover that after blessed Benedict left that obstinate community he restored to life many another soul that was spiritually dead.

Peter: I am sure your conclusion is correct, after the simple proof you gave and that striking example from sacred Scripture. Would you be good enough to return now to the story of this great abbot's life?

Gregory: As Benedict's influence spread over the surrounding countryside because of his signs and wonders, a great number of men gathered round him to devote themselves to God's service. Christ blessed his work and before long he had established twelve monasteries there, with an abbot and twelve monks in each of them. There were a few other monks whom he kept with him, since he felt that they still needed his personal guidance.

It was about this time that pious noblemen from Rome first came to visit the saint and left their sons with him to be schooled in the service of God.

Thus, Euthicius brought his son Maurus; and Senator Tertullus, Placid – both very promising boys. Maurus, in fact, who was a little older, had already acquired solid virtue and was soon very helpful to his saintly master. But Placid was still only a child.

4. In one of the monasteries Benedict had founded in that locality, there was a monk who would never remain with the rest of the community for silent prayer. Instead, he left the chapel as soon as they knelt down to pray, and passed the time aimlessly at whatever happened to interest him. His abbot corrected him repeatedly and at length sent him to the man of God. This time the monk received a stern rebuke for his folly and after his return took the correction to heart for a day or two, only to fall back the third day into his old habit of wandering off during the time of prayer. On learning of this from the abbot, the man of God sent word that he was coming over himself to see that the monk mended his ways. Upon his arrival at the monastery, Benedict joined the community in the chapel at the regular hour. After they had finished chanting the psalms and had begun their silent prayer, he noticed that the restless monk was drawn outside by a little black boy who was pulling at the edge of his habit. 'Do you see who is leading that monk out of the chapel?' he whispered to Abbot Pompeianus and Maurus. 'No,' they replied. 'Let us pray, then,' he said, 'that you may see what is happening to him.' They prayed for two days, and after that Maurus also saw what was taking place, but Abbot Pompeianus still could not. The next day, when prayers were over, Benedict found the offender loitering outside and struck him with his staff for being so obstinate of heart. From then on the monk remained quietly at prayer like the rest, without being bothered again by the tempter. It was as if that ancient enemy had been struck by the blow himself and was afraid to domineer over the monk's thoughts any longer.

5. Three of the monasteries the saint had built close by stood on the bare rocky heights. It was a real hardship for these monks always to go down to the lake to get water for their daily needs. Besides, the slope was steep and they found the descent very dangerous. The members of the three communities therefore came in a body to see the servant of God. After explaining how difficult it was for them to climb down the mountainside every day for their water supply, they assured him that the only solution was to have the monasteries moved somewhere else. Benedict answered them with fatherly words of encouragement and sent them back. That same night, in company with the little boy Placid, he climbed to the rocky heights and prayed there for a long time. On finishing his prayer, he placed three stones together to indicate the spot where he had knelt and then went back to his monastery, unnoticed by anyone.

The following day, when the monks came again with their request, he told them to go to the summit of the mountain. 'You will find three stones there,' he said, 'one on top of the other. If you dig down a little, you will see that almighty God has the power to bring forth water even from that rocky summit and in his goodness relieve you of the hardship of such a long climb.'

Going back to the place he had described, they noticed that the surface was already moist. As soon as they had dug the ground away, water filled the hollow and welled up in such abundance that today a full stream is still flowing from the top of the mountain into the ravine below.

6. At another time a simple, sincere Goth came to Subiaco to become a monk, and blessed Benedict was very happy to admit him. One day he had him take a brush hook and clear away the briers from a place at the edge of the lake where a garden was to be planted. While the Goth was hard at work cutting down the thick brush, the iron blade slipped off the handle and flew into a very deep part of the lake, where there was no hope of recovering it.

At this the poor man ran trembling to Maurus and, after describing the accident, told him how sorry he was for his carelessness. Maurus in turn informed the servant of God, who on hearing what had happened went down to the lake, took the handle from the Goth and thrust it in the water. Immediately the iron blade rose from the bottom of the lake and slipped back onto the handle. Then he handed the tool back to the Goth and told him, 'Continue with your work now. There is no need to be upset.'

7. Once while blessed Benedict was in his room, one of his monks, the boy Placid, went down to the lake to draw water. In letting the bucket fill too rapidly, he lost his balance and was pulled into the lake, where the current quickly seized him and carried him about a stone's throw from the shore. Though inside the monastery at the time, the man of God was instantly aware of what had happened and called out to Maurus: 'Hurry, Brother Maurus! The boy who just went down for water has fallen into the lake, and the current is carrying him away.'

What followed was remarkable indeed, and unheard of since the time of Peter the apostle! Maurus asked for the blessing and on receiving it hurried out to fulfil his abbot's command. He kept on running even over the water till he reached the place where Placid was drifting along helplessly. Pulling him up by the hair, Maurus rushed back to shore, still under the impression that he was on dry land. It was only when he set foot on the ground that he came to himself and looking back realized that he had been running on the surface of the water. Overcome with fear and amazement at a deed he would never have thought possible, he returned to his abbot and told him what had taken place. The holy man would not take any personal credit for the deed, but attributed it to the obedience of his disciple. Maurus on the contrary, claimed that it was due entirely to his abbot's command. He could not have been responsible for the miracle himself, he said, since he had not even known he was performing it. While they were carrying on this friendly contest of humility, the question was settled by the boy who had been rescued. 'When I was being drawn out of the water,' he told them, 'I saw the abbot's cloak over my head; he is the one I thought was bringing me to shore.'

Peter: What marvelous deeds these are! They are sure to prove inspiring to all who hear of them. Indeed, the more you tell me about this great man, the more eager I am to keep on listening.

8. Gregory: By this time the people of that whole region for miles around had grown fervent in their love for Christ, and many of them had forsaken the world in order to bring their hearts under the light yoke of the Savior. Now, in a neighboring church there was a priest named Florentius, the grandfather of our subdeacon Florentius. Urged on by the bitter enemy of mankind, this priest set out to undermine the saint's work. And envious as the wicked always are of the holiness in others which they are not striving to acquire themselves, he denounced Benedict's way of life and kept everyone he could from visiting him.

The progress of the saint's work, however, could not be stopped. His reputation for holiness kept on growing, and with it the number of vocations to a more perfect state of life. This infuriated Florentius all the more. He still longed to enjoy the praise the saint was receiving, yet he was unwilling to lead a praiseworthy life himself. At length, his soul became so blind with jealousy that he decided to poison a loaf of bread and send it to the servant of God as though it was a sign of Christian fellowship. Though aware at once of the deadly poison it contained, Benedict thanked him for the gift.

At mealtime a raven used to come out of the nearby woods to receive food from the saint's hands. On this occasion he set the poisoned loaf in front of it and said, 'In the name of our Lord Jesus Christ, take this bread and carry it to a place where no one will be able to find it.' The raven started to caw and circled round the loaf of bread with open beak and flapping wings as if to indicate that it was willing to obey, but found it impossible to do so. Several times the saint repeated the command. 'Take the bread,' he said, 'and do not be afraid! Take it away from here and leave it where no one will find it.' After hesitating for a long while, the raven finally took the loaf in its beak and flew away. About three hours later, when it had disposed of the bread, it returned and received its usual meal from the hands of the man of God.

The saintly abbot now realized how deep the resentment of his enemy was, and he felt grieved not so much for his own sake as for the priest's. But Florentius, after his failure to do away with the master, determined instead to destroy the souls of the disciples and for this purpose sent seven depraved women into the garden of Benedict's monastery. There they joined hands and danced together for some time within sight of his followers, in an attempt to lead them into sin.

When the saint noticed this from his window, he began to fear that some of his younger monks might go astray. Convinced that the priest's hatred for him was the real cause of this attack, he let envy have its way and, taking only a few monks with him, set out to find a new home. Before he left, he reorganized all the monasteries he had founded, appointing priors to assist in governing them, and adding some new members to the communities.

Hardly had the man of God made his humble escape from all this bitterness when almighty God struck the priest down with terrible vengeance. As he was standing on the balcony of his house congratulating himself on Benedict's departure, the structure suddenly collapsed, crushing him to death, though the rest of the building remained undamaged. This accident occurred before the saint was even ten miles away. His disciple Maurus immediately decided to send a messenger with the news and ask him to return, now that the priest who had caused him so much trouble was dead. Benedict was overcome with sorrow and regret on hearing this, for not only had his enemy been killed, but one of his own disciples had rejoiced over his death. And for showing pleasure in sending such a message he gave Maurus a penance to perform.

Peter: This whole account is really amazing. The water streaming from the rock reminds me of Moses, and the iron blade that rose from the bottom of the lake, of Eliseus. The walking on the water recalls St. Peter, the obedience of the raven, Elias, and the grief at the death of an enemy, David. This man must have been filled with the spirit of all the just.

Gregory: Actually, Peter, blessed Benedict possessed the Spirit of only one person, the Savior who fills the hearts of all the faithful by granting them the fruits of his redemption. For St. John says of him, 'There is one who enlightens every soul born into the world; he was the true light.' And again, 'We have all received something out of his abundance.' Holy men never were able to hand on to others the miraculous powers which they received from God. Our Savior was the only one to give his followers the power to work signs and wonders, just as he alone could assure his enemies that he would give them the sign of the prophet Jonas. Seeing this sign fulfilled in his death, the proud looked on with scorn. The humble, who saw its complete fulfilment in his rising from the dead, turned to him with reverence and love. In this mystery, then, the proud beheld him dying in disgrace, whereas the humble witnessed his triumph over death.

Peter: Now that you have finished explaining this, please tell me where the holy man settled after his departure. Do you know whether he performed any more miracles?

Gregory: Although he moved to a different place, Peter, his enemy remained the same. In fact, the assaults he had to endure after this were all the more violent, because the very master of evil was fighting against him in open battle.

The fortified town of Cassino lies at the foot of a towering mountain that shelters it within its slope and stretches upward over a distance of nearly three miles. On its summit stood a very old temple, in which the ignorant country people still worshiped Apollo as their pagan ancestors had done, and went on offering superstitious and idolatrous sacrifices in groves dedicated to various demons.

When the man of God arrived at this spot, he destroyed the idol, overturned the altar and cut down the trees in the sacred groves. Then he turned the temple of Apollo into a chapel dedicated to St. Martin [of Tours, who had also destroyed pagan temples], and where Apollo's altar had stood, he built a chapel in honor of St. John the Baptist. Gradually, the people of the countryside were won over to the true faith by his zealous preaching.

Such losses the ancient enemy could not bear in silence. This time he did not appear to the saint in a dream or under a disguise, but met him face to face and objected fiercely to the outrages he had to endure. His shouts were so loud that the brethren heard him, too, although they were unable to see him. According to the saint's own description, the devil had an appearance utterly revolting to human eyes. He was enveloped in fire and, when he raged against the man of God, flames darted from his eyes and mouth. Everyone could hear what he was saying. First he called Benedict by name. Then, finding that the saint would not answer, he broke out in abusive language. 'Benedict, Benedict, blessed Benedict!' he would begin, and then add, 'You cursed Benedict! Cursed, not blessed! What do you want with me? Why are you tormenting me like this?'

From now on, Peter, as you can well imagine, the devil fought against the man of God with renewed violence. But, contrary to his plans, all these attacks only supplied the saint with further opportunities for victory.

9. One day while the monks were constructing a section of the abbey, they noticed a rock lying close at hand and decided to use it in the building. When two or three did not succeed in lifting it, others joined in to help. Yet it remained fixed in its place as though it was rooted to the ground. Then they were sure that the devil himself was sitting on this stone and preventing them from moving it in spite of all their efforts.

Faced with this difficulty, they asked Abbot Benedict to come and use his prayers to drive away the devil who was holding down the rock. The saint began to pray as soon as he got there, and after he had finished and made the sign of the cross, the monks picked up the rock with such ease that it seemed to have lost all its previous weight.

10. The abbot then directed them to spade up the earth where the stone had been. When they had dug a little way into the ground they came upon a bronze idol, which they threw into the kitchen for the time being. Suddenly the kitchen appeared to be on fire and everyone felt that the entire building was going up in flames. The noise and commotion they made in their attempt to put out the blaze by pouring on buckets of water brought Benedict to the scene. Unable to see the fire which appeared so real to his monks, he quietly bowed his head in prayer and soon had opened their eyes to the foolish mistake they were making. Now, instead of the flames the evil spirit had devised, they once more saw the kitchen standing intact.

11. On another occasion they were working on one of the walls that had to be built a little higher. The man of God was in his room at the time, praying, when the devil appeared to him and remarked sarcastically that he was on his way to visit the brethren at their work. Benedict quickly sent them word to be on their guard against the evil spirit who would soon be with them. Just as they received his warning, the devil overturned the wall, crushing under its ruins the body of a very young monk who was the son of a tax collector.

Unconcerned about the damaged wall in their grief and dismay over the loss of their brother, the monks hurried to Abbot Benedict to let him know of the dreadful accident. He told them to bring the mangled body to his room. It had to be carried in on a blanket, for the wall had not only broken the boy's arms and legs but had crushed all the bones in his body. The saint had the remains placed on the reed matting where he used to pray and after that told them all to leave. Then he closed the door and knelt down to offer his most earnest prayers to God. That very hour, to the astonishment of all, he sent the boy back to his work as sound and healthy as he had been before. Thus, in spite of the devil's attempt to mock the man of God by causing this tragic death, the young monk was able to rejoin his brethren and help them finish the wall.

Meanwhile, Benedict began to manifest the spirit of prophecy by foretelling future events and by describing to those who were with him what they had done in his absence.

12. It was a custom of the house, strictly observed as a matter of regular discipline, that monks away on business did not take food or drink outside the monastery. One day, a few of them went out on an assignment which kept them occupied till rather late. They stopped for a meal at the house of a devout woman they knew in the neighborhood. On their return, when they

presented themselves to the abbot for the usual blessing, he asked them where they had taken their meal.

'Nowhere,' they answered.

'Why are you lying to me?' he said. 'Did you not enter the house of this particular woman and eat these various foods and have so many cups to drink?'

On hearing him mention the woman's hospitality and exactly what she had given them to eat and drink, they clearly recalled the wrong they had done, fell trembling at his feet, and confessed their guilt. The man of God did not hesitate to pardon them, confident that they would do no further wrong in his absence, since they now realized he was always present with them in spirit.

13. The monk Valentinian, mentioned earlier in our narrative, had a brother who was a very devout layman. Every year he visited the abbey in order to get Benedict's blessing and see his brother. On the way he always used to fast. Now, one time as he was making this journey he was joined by another traveler who had brought some food along. 'Come,' said the stranger after some time had passed, 'let us have something to eat before we become too fatigued.' 'I am sorry,' the devout layman replied. 'I always fast on my way to visit Abbot Benedict.' After that the traveler was quiet for a while. But when they had walked along some distance together, he repeated his suggestion. Still mindful of his good resolve, Valentinian's brother again refused. His companion did not insist and once more agreed to accompany him a little further without eating.

Then, after they had covered a great distance together and were very tired from the long hours of walking they came upon a meadow and a spring. The whole setting seemed ideal for a much needed rest. 'Look,' said the stranger, 'water and a meadow! What a delightful spot for us to have some refreshments! A little rest will give us strength to finish our journey without any discomfort.'

It was such an attractive sight and this third invitation sounded so appealing that the devout layman was completely won over and stopped there to eat with his companion. Toward evening he arrived at the monastery and was presented to the abbot. As soon as he asked for the blessing, however, the holy man reproved him for his conduct on the journey. 'How is it,' he said, 'that the evil spirit who spoke with you in the person of your traveling companion could not persuade you to do his will the first and second time he tried, but succeeded in his third attempt?' At this Valentinian's brother fell at Benedict's feet and admitted the weakness of his will. The thought that even from such a distance the saint had witnessed the wrong he had done filled him with shame and remorse.

Peter: This proves that the servant of God possessed the spirit of Eliseus. He, too, was present with one of his followers who was far away.

Gregory: If you will listen a little longer, Peter, I have an incident to tell you that is even more astonishing.

14. Once while the Goths [the Ostrogoths, a people from eastern Europe who had established a kingdom in Italy under Theodoric in 493] were still in power, Totila their king [541-52] happened to be marching in the direction of Benedict's monastery. When still some distance away, he halted with his troops and sent a messenger ahead to announce his coming, for he had heard that the man of God possessed the gift of prophecy. As soon as he received word that he would be welcomed, the crafty king decided to put the saint's prophetic powers to a test. He had Riggo, his sword-bearer, fitted out with royal robes and riding boots and directed him to go in this disguise to the man of God. Vul, Ruderic, and Blidin, three men from his own bodyguard, were to march at his side as if he really were king of the Goths. To supplement these marks of kingship, Totila also provided him with a swordbearer and other attendants. As Riggo entered the monastery grounds in his kingly robes and with all his attendants, Benedict caught sight of him and as soon as the company came within hearing called out from where he sat. 'Son, lay aside the robes you are wearing,' he said. 'Lay them aside. They do not belong to you.' Aghast at seeing what a great man he had tried to mock, Riggo sank to the ground, and with him all the members of his company. Even after they had risen to their feet they did not dare approach the saint, but hurried back in alarm to tell their king how quickly they had been detected.

15. King Totila then went to the monastery in person. The moment he noticed the man of God sitting at a distance, he was afraid to come any closer and fell down prostrate where he was. Two or three times Benedict asked him to rise. When Totila still hesitated to do so in his presence, the servant of Christ walked over to him and with his own hands helped him from the ground. Then he rebuked the king for his crimes and briefly foretold everything that was going to happen to him. 'You are the cause of many evils,' he said. 'You have caused many in the past. Put an end now to your wickedness. You will enter Rome and cross the sea. You have nine more years to rule, and in the tenth year you will die.'

Terrified at these words, the king asked for a blessing and went away. From that time on he was less cruel. Not long after, he went to Rome and then crossed over to Sicily. In the tenth year of his reign he lost his kingdom and his life as almighty God had decreed.

There is also a story about the bishop of Canossa, who made regular visits to the abbey and stood high in Benedict's esteem because of his saintly life. Once while they were discussing Totila's invasion and the downfall of Rome, the bishop said, 'The city will be destroyed by this king and left without a single inhabitant.' Benedict assured him, 'Rome will not be destroyed by the barbarians. It will be shaken by tempests and lightnings, hurricanes and earthquakes, until finally it lies buried in its own ruins.' [Totila captured Rome in 546 but stopped short of destroying the entire city.]

The meaning of this prophecy is perfectly clear to us now. We have watched the walls of Rome crumble and have seen its homes in ruins, its churches destroyed by violent storms, and its dilapidated buildings surrounded by their own debris.

Benedict's disciple Honoratus, who told me about the prophecy, admits he did not hear it personally, but he assures me that some of his own brethren gave him this account of it.

16. At about the same time there was a cleric from the church at Aquino [8 km/5 miles from Monte Cassino] who was being tormented by an evil spirit. Constantius, his saintly bishop, had already sent him to the shrines of various martyrs in the hope that he would be cured. But the holy martyrs did not grant him this favor, preferring instead to reveal the wonderful gifts of the servant of God.

As soon as the cleric was brought to him, Benedict drove out the evil spirit with fervent prayers to Christ. Before sending him back to Aquino, however, he told him to abstain from meat thereafter and never to advance to sacred orders. 'If you ignore this warning,' he added, 'and present yourself for ordination, you will find yourself once more in the power of Satan.'

The cleric left completely cured, and as long as his previous torments were still fresh in his mind he did exactly as the man of God had ordered. Then with the passing of years, all his seniors in the clerical state died, and he had to watch newly ordained young men moving ahead of him in rank. Finally, he pretended to have forgotten about the saint's warning and, disregarding it, presented himself for ordination. Instantly he was seized by the devil and tormented mercilessly until he died.

Peter: The servant of God must even have been aware of the hidden designs of Providence, to have realized that this cleric had been handed over to Satan to keep him from aspiring to holy orders.

Gregory: Is there any reason why a person who has observed the commandments of God should not also know of God's secret designs? 'The man who unites himself to the Lord becomes one spirit with him,' we read in sacred Scripture.

Peter: If everyone who unites himself to the Lord becomes one spirit with him, what does the renowned apostle mean when he asks, 'Who has ever understood the Lord's thoughts, or been his counselor?' It hardly seems possible to be one spirit with a person without knowing his thoughts.

Gregory: Holy men do know the Lord's thoughts, Peter, in so far as they are one with him. This is clear from the apostle's words, 'Who else can know a man's thoughts, except the man's own spirit that is within him? So no one else can know God's thoughts but the spirit of God.' To show that he actually knew God's thoughts, St. Paul added: 'And what we have received is no spirit of worldly wisdom; it is the Spirit that comes from God.' And again: 'No eye has seen, no ear has heard, no human heart conceived, the welcome God has prepared for those who love him. To us, then, God has made a revelation of it through his spirit.'

Peter: If it is true that God's thoughts were revealed to the apostle by the Holy Spirit, how could he introduce his statement with the words, 'How deep is the mine of God's wisdom, of his knowledge; how inscrutable are his judgments, how undiscoverable his ways!' Another difficulty just occurred to me now as I was speaking. In addressing the Lord, David the Prophet declares, 'With my lips I have pronounced all the judgments of thy mouth.' Surely it is a greater achievement to express one's knowledge than merely to possess it. How is it, then, that St. Paul calls the judgments of God inscrutable, whereas David says he knows them all and has even pronounced them with his lips?

Gregory: I already gave a brief reply to both of these objections when I told you that holy men know God's thoughts in so far as they are one with him. For all who follow the Lord wholeheartedly are living in spiritual union with him. As long as they are still weighed down with a perishable body, however, they are not actually united to him. It is only to the extent that they are one with God that they know his hidden judgments. In so far as they are not yet one with him, they do not know them. Since even holy men cannot fully grasp the secret designs of God during this present life, they call his judgments inscrutable. At the same time, they understand his judgments and can even pronounce them with their lips; for they keep their hearts united to God by dwelling continually on the words of holy scripture and on such private revelations as they may receive, until they grasp his meaning. In other words, they do not know the judgments which God conceals but only those which he reveals. That is why, after declaring, 'With my lips I have pronounced all the judgments,' the Prophet immediately adds the phrase, 'of thy mouth,' as if to say, 'I can know and pronounce only the judgments you have spoken to me. Those you leave unspoken must remain hidden from our minds.' So the prophet and the apostle are in full agreement. God's decisions are truly unfathomable. But, once his mouth has made them known, they can also be proclaimed by human lips. What God has spoken man can know. Of the thoughts he has kept secret man can know nothing.

Peter: That is certainly a reasonable solution to the difficulties that I raised. If you know any other miraculous events in this man's life, would you continue with them now?

17. Gregory: Under the direction of Abbot Benedict a nobleman named Theoprobus had embraced monastic life. Because of his exemplary life he enjoyed the saint's personal friendship and confidence. One day, on entering Benedict's room, he found him weeping bitterly. After he had waited for some time and there was still no end to the abbot's tears, he asked what was causing him such sorrow, for he was not weeping as he usually did at prayer, but with deep sighs and lamentation. 'Almighty God has decreed that this entire monastery and everything I have provided for the community shall fall into the hands of the barbarians,' the saint replied. 'It was only with the greatest difficulty that I could prevail upon him to spare the lives of its members.'

This was the prophecy he made to Theoprobus, and we have seen its fulfilment in the recent destruction of his abbey by the Lombards [in 589; it was rebuilt in 720]. They came at night while the community was asleep and plundered the entire monastery, without capturing a single monk. In this way God fulfilled his promise to Benedict, his faithful servant. He allowed the barbarians to destroy the monastery, but safeguarded the lives of the religious. Here you can see how the man of God resembled St. Paul, who had the consolation of seeing everyone with him escape alive from the storm, while the ship and all its cargo were lost.

18. Exhilaratus, a fellow Roman who, as you know, later became a monk was once sent by his master to Abbot Benedict with two wooden flasks of wine. He delivered only one of them, however; the other he hid along the way. Benedict, who could observe even what was done in his absence, thanked him for the flask, but warned him as he turned to go: 'Son, be sure not to drink from the flask you have hidden away. Tilt it carefully and you will see what is inside.' Exhilaratus left in shame and confusion and went back to the spot, still wishing to verify the saint's words. As he tilted the flask a serpent crawled out, and at the sight of it he was filled with horror for his misdeed.

19. Not far from the monastery was a village largely inhabited by people the saintly Benedict had converted from the worship of idols and instructed in the true faith. There were nuns living there too, and he used to send one of his monks down to give them spiritual conferences.

After one of these instructions they presented the monk with a few handkerchiefs, which he accepted and hid away in his habit. As soon as he got back to the abbey he received a stern reproof. 'How is it,' the abbot asked him, 'that evil has found its way into your heart?' Taken completely by surprise, the monk did not understand why he was being rebuked, for he had entirely forgotten about the handkerchiefs. 'Was I not present,' the saint continued, 'when you accepted those handkerchiefs from the handmaids of God and hid them away in your habit?' The offender instantly fell at Benedict's feet, confessed his fault, and gave up the present he had received.

20. Once when the saintly abbot was taking his evening meal, a young monk whose father was a highranking official happened to be holding the lamp for him. As he stood at the abbot's table the spirit of pride began to stir in his heart. 'Who is this,' he thought to himself, 'that I should have to stand here holding the lamp for him while he is eating? Who am I to be serving him?' Turning to him at once, Benedict gave the monk a sharp reprimand. 'Brother,' he said, 'sign your heart with the sign of the cross. What are you saying? Sign your heart!' Then, calling the others together, he had one of them take the lamp instead, and told the murmurer to sit down by himself and be quiet. Later, when asked what he had done wrong, the monk explained how he had given in to the spirit of pride and silently murmured against the man of God. At this the brethren all realized that nothing could be kept secret from their holy abbot, since he could hear even the unspoken sentiments of the heart.

21. During a time of famine [possibly the great famine of 537-38] the severe shortage of food was causing a great deal of suffering in Campania. At Benedict's monastery the entire grain supply had been used up and nearly all the bread was gone as well. In fact, when mealtime came, only five loaves could be found to set before the community. Noticing how downcast they were, the saint gently reproved them for their lack of trust in God and at the same time tried to raise their dejected spirits with a comforting assurance. 'Why are you so depressed at the lack of bread?' he asked 'What if today there is only a little? Tomorrow you will have more than you need.'

The next day 200 measures of flour were found in sacks at the gate of the monastery, but no one ever discovered whose services almighty God had employed in bringing them there. When they saw what had happened, the monks were filled with gratitude and learned from this miracle that even in their hour of need they must not lose faith in the bountiful goodness of God.

Peter: Are we to believe that the spirit of prophecy remained with the servant of God at all times, or did he receive it only on special occasions?

Gregory: The spirit of prophecy does not enlighten the minds of the prophets constantly, Peter. We read in sacred scripture that the Holy Spirit breathes where he pleases, and we should also realize that he breathes when he pleases. For example, when King David asked whether he could build a temple, the prophet Nathan gave his consent, but later had to withdraw it. And Eliseus once found a woman in tears without knowing the reason for her grief. That is why he told his servant who was trying to interfere, 'Let her alone, for her soul is in anguish and the Lord his hidden it from me and has not told me.'

All this reflects God's boundless wisdom and love. By granting these men the spirit of prophecy he raises their minds high above the world, and by withdrawing it again he safeguards their humility. When the spirit of prophecy is with them they learn what they are by God's mercy. When the spirit leaves them they discover what they are of themselves.

Peter: This convincing argument leaves no room for doubt about the truth of what you say. Please resume your narrative now, if you recall any other incidents in the life of blessed Benedict.

22. Gregory: A Catholic layman once asked him to found a monastery on his estate at Terracina. The servant of God readily consented and, after selecting several of his monks for this undertaking, appointed one of them abbot and another his assistant. Before they left he specified a day on which he would come to show them where to build the chapel, the refectory, a house for guests, and the other buildings they would need. Then he gave them his blessing.

After their arrival at Terracina they looked forward eagerly to the day he had set for his visit and prepared to receive the monks who would accompany him. Before dawn of the appointed day, Benedict appeared in a dream to the new abbot as well as to his prior and showed them exactly where each section of the monastery was to stand. In the morning they told each other what they had seen, but, instead of putting their entire trust in the vision, they kept waiting for the promised visit. When the day passed without any word from Benedict, they returned to him disappointed. 'Father,' they said, 'we were waiting for you to show us where to build, as you assured us you would, but you did not come.'

'What do you mean?' he replied. 'Did I not come as I promised?' 'When?' they asked. 'Did I not appear to both of you in a dream as you slept and indicate where each building was to stand? Go back and build as you were directed in the vision.' They returned to Terracina, filled with wonder, and constructed the monastery according to the plans he had revealed to them.

Peter: I wish you would explain how Benedict could possibly travel that distance and then in a vision give these monks directions which they could hear and understand while they were asleep.

Gregory: What is there in this incident that should raise a doubt in your mind, Peter? Everyone knows that the soul is far more agile than the body. Yet we have it on the authority of holy scripture that the prophet Habacuc was lifted from Judea to Chaldea in an instant, so that he might share his dinner with the prophet Daniel, and presently found himself back in Judea

again. If Habacuc could cover such a distance in a brief moment to take a
meal to his fellow prophet, is it not understandable that Abbot Benedict could
go in spirit to his sleeping brethren with the information they required? As
the prophet came in body with food for the body, Benedict came in spirit to
promote the life of the soul.

Peter: Your words seem to smooth away all my doubts. Could you tell me
now what this saint was like in his everyday speech?

23. Gregory: There was a trace of the marvelous in nearly everything he
said, Peter, and his words never failed to take effect because his heart was
fixed in God. Even when he uttered a simple threat that was indefinite and
conditional, it was just as decisive as a final verdict.

Some distance from the abbey two women of noble birth were leading
the religious life in their own home. A God-fearing layman was kind enough
to bring them what they needed from the outside world. Unfortunately, as
is sometimes the case, their character stood in sharp contrast to the nobility
of their birth, and they were too conscious of their former importance to
practise true humility toward others. Even under the restraining influence
of religious life they still had not learned to control their tongues, and the
good layman who served them so faithfully was often provoked at their harsh
criticisms. After putting up with their insults for a long time, he went to
blessed Benedict and told him how inconsiderate they were. The man of
God immediately warned them to curb their sharp tongues and added that he
would have to excommunicate them if they did not. This sentence of excommunication was not actually pronounced, therefore, but only threatened.

A short time afterward the two nuns died without any sign of amendment
and were buried in their parish church. Whenever Mass was celebrated, their
old nurse, who regularly made an offering for them, noticed that each time the
deacon announced, 'The non-communicants [the unbaptized and the excom-
municated] must now leave,' the nuns rose from their tombs and went outside.
This happened repeatedly, until one day she recalled the warning Benedict had
given them while they were still alive, when he threatened to deprive them of
communion with the Church if they kept on speaking so uncharitably.

The grief-stricken nurse had Abbot Benedict informed of what was happening. He sent her messengers back with an oblation and said, 'Have this
offered up for their souls during the Holy Sacrifice [communion], and they
will be freed from the sentence of excommunication.' The offering was made
and after that the nuns were not seen leaving the church any more at the deacon's dismissal of the non-communicants. Evidently, they had been admitted
to communion with our blessed Lord in answer to the prayers of his servant
Benedict.

Peter: Is it not extraordinary that souls already judged at God's invisible tribunal could be pardoned by a man who was still living in the mortal flesh, however holy and revered he may have been?

Gregory: What of Peter the apostle? Was he not still living in the flesh when he heard the words, 'Whatever thou shalt bind on earth shall be bound in heaven, and whatever thou shalt loose on earth shall be loosed in heaven'? All those who govern the Church in matters of faith and morals exercise the same power of binding and loosing that he received. In fact, the Creator's very purpose in coming down from heaven to earth was to impart to earthly man this heavenly power. It was when God was made flesh for man's sake that flesh received its undeserved prerogative of sitting in judgment even over spirits. What raised our weakness to these heights was the descent of an almighty God to the depths of our own helplessness.

Peter: Your lofty words are certainly in harmony with these mighty deeds.

24. Gregory: One time, a young monk who was too attached to his parents left the monastery without asking for the abbot's blessing and went home. No sooner had he arrived than he died. The day after his burial his body was discovered lying outside the grave. His parents had him buried again, but on the following day found the body unburied as before. In their dismay they hurried to the saintly abbot and pleaded with him to forgive the boy for what he had done. Moved by their tears, Benedict gave them a consecrated Host with his own hands. 'When you get back,' he said, 'place this sacred Host upon his breast and bury him once more.' They did so, and thereafter his body remained in the earth without being disturbed again. Now, Peter, you can appreciate how pleasing this holy man was in God's sight. Not even the earth would retain the young monk's body until he had been reconciled with blessed Benedict.

Peter: I assure you I do. It is really amazing.

25. Gregory: One of Benedict's monks had set his fickle heart on leaving the monastery. Time and again the man of God pointed out how wrong this was and tried to reason with him but without any success. The monk persisted obstinately in his request to be released. Finally, Benedict lost patience with him and told him to go.

Hardly had he left the monastery grounds when he noticed to his horror that a dragon with gaping jaws was blocking his way. 'Help! Help!' he cried out, trembling, 'or the dragon will devour me.' His brethren ran to the rescue, but could see nothing of the dragon. Still breathless with fright, the monk was only too glad to accompany them back to the abbey. Once safe within its walls, he promised never to leave again. And this time he kept his word, for Benedict's prayers had enabled him to see with his own eyes the invisible dragon that had been leading him astray.

26. I must tell you now of an event I heard from the distinguished Anthony. One of his father's servants had been seized with a severe case of leprosy. His hair was already falling out and his skin growing thick and swollen. The fatal progress of the disease was unmistakable. In this condition he was sent to the man of God, who instantly restored him to his previous state of health.

27. Benedict's disciple Peregrinus tells of a Catholic layman who was heavily burdened with debt and felt that his only hope was to disclose the full extent of his misfortune to the man of God. So he went to him and explained that he was being constantly tormented by a creditor to whom he owed twelve gold pieces. 'I am very sorry,' the saintly abbot replied. 'I do not have that much money in my possession.' Then, to comfort the poor man in his need, he added, 'I cannot give you anything today, but come back again the day after tomorrow.'

In the meantime the saint devoted himself to prayer with his accustomed fervor. When the debtor returned, the monks, to their surprise, found thirteen gold pieces lying on top of a chest that was filled with grain. Benedict had the money brought down at once. 'Here, take these,' he told him. 'Use twelve to pay your creditor and keep the thirteenth for yourself.'

I should like to return now to some other events I learned from the saint's four disciples who were mentioned at the beginning of this book.

There was a man who had become so embittered with envy that he tried to kill his rival by secretly poisoning his drink. Though the poison did not prove fatal, it produced horrible blemishes resembling leprosy, which spread over the entire body of the unfortunate victim. In this condition he was brought to the servant of God, who cured the disease with a touch of his hand and sent him home in perfect health.

28. While Campania was suffering from famine, the holy abbot distributed the food supplies of his monastery to the needy until there was nothing left in the storeroom but a little oil in a glass vessel. One day, when Agapitus, a subdeacon, came to beg for some oil, the man of God ordered the little that remained to be given to him, for he wanted to distribute everything he had to the poor and thus store up riches in heaven.

The cellarer listened to the abbot's command, but did not carry it out. After a while, Benedict asked him whether he had given Agapitus the oil. 'No,' he replied, 'I did not. If I had, there would be none left for the community.' This angered the man of God, who wanted nothing to remain in the monastery through disobedience, and he told another monk to take the glass with the oil in it and throw it out the window. This time he was obeyed.

Even though it struck against the jagged rocks of the cliff just below the window, the glass remained intact as if it had not been thrown at all. It was still unbroken and none of the oil had spilled. Abbot Benedict had the glass brought back and given to the subdeacon. Then he sent for the rest of the community and in their presence rebuked the disobedient monk for his pride and lack of faith.

29. After that the saint knelt down to pray with his brethren. In the room where they were kneeling there happened to be an empty oil-cask that was covered with a lid. In the course of his prayer the cask gradually filled with oil and the lid started to float on top of it. The next moment the oil was running down the sides of the cask and covering the floor. As soon as he was aware of this, Benedict ended his prayer and the oil stopped flowing. Then, turning to the monk who had shown himself disobedient and wanting in confidence, he urged him again to strive to grow in faith and humility.

This wholesome reprimand filled the cellarer with shame. Besides inviting him to trust in God, the saintly abbot had clearly shown by his miracle what marvelous power such trust possesses. In the future who could doubt any of his promises? Had he not in a moment's time replaced the little oil still left in the glass with a cask that was full to overflowing?

30. One day, on his way to the chapel of St. John at the highest point of the mountain, Benedict met the ancient Enemy of humankind, disguised as a veterinarian with medicine horn and triple shackle. 'Where are you going?' the saint asked him. 'To your brethren,' he replied with scorn. 'I am bringing them some medicine.' Benedict continued on his way and after his prayer hurried back. Meanwhile, the evil spirit had entered one of the older monks whom he found drawing water and had thrown him to the ground in a violent convulsion. When the man of God caught sight of this old brother in such torment, he merely struck him on the cheek, and the evil spirit was promptly driven out, never to return.

Peter: I should like to know whether he always obtained these great miracles through fervent prayer. Did he never perform them at will?

Gregory: It is quite common for those who devoutly cling to God to work miracles in both of these ways, Peter, either through their prayers or by their own power, as circumstances may dictate. Since we read in St. John that 'all those who did welcome him he empowered to become the children of God,' why should we be surprised if those who are the children of God use this power to work signs and wonders? Holy men can undoubtedly perform miracles in either of the ways you mentioned, as is clear from the fact that St. Peter raised Tabitha to life by praying over her, and by a simple rebuke brought death to Ananias and Sapphira for their lies. Scripture does not say that he prayed for their death, but only that he reprimanded them for the crime they had committed. Now, if St. Peter could restore to life by a prayer and deprive of life by a rebuke, is there any reason to doubt that the saints can perform miracles by their own power as well as through their prayers?

I am now going to consider two instances in the life of God's faithful servant Benedict. One of them shows the efficacy of his prayer; the other the marvelous powers that were his by God's gift.

31. In the days of King Totila one of the Goths, the Arian heretic Zalla, had been persecuting devout Catholics everywhere with the utmost cruelty. No monk or cleric who fell into his hands ever escaped alive. In his merciless brutality and greed he was one day lashing and torturing a farmer whose money he was after. Unable to bear it any longer, the poor man tried to save his life by telling Zalla that all his money was in Abbot Benedict's keeping. He only hoped his tormentor would believe him and put a stop to his brutality. When Zalla heard this, he did stop beating him, but immediately bound his hands together with a heavy cord. Then, mounting his horse, he forced the farmer to walk ahead of him and lead the way to this Benedict who was keeping his money.

The helpless prisoner had no choice but to conduct him to the abbey. When they arrived, they found the man of God sitting alone in front of the entrance reading. 'This is the abbot Benedict I meant,' he told the infuriated Goth behind him.

Imagining that this holy man could be frightened as readily as anyone else, Zalla glared at him with eyes full of hate and shouted harshly, 'Get up! Do you hear? Get up and give back the money this man left with you!' At the sound of this angry voice the man of God looked up from his reading and, as he glanced toward Zalla, noticed the farmer with his hands bound together. The moment he caught sight of the cord that held them, it fell miraculously to the ground. Human hands could never have unfastened it so quickly. Stunned at the hidden power that had set his prisoner free, Zalla fell trembling to his knees and, bending his stubborn cruel neck at the saint's feet, begged for his prayers. Without rising from his place, Benedict called for his monks and had them take Zalla inside for some food and drink. After that he urged him to give up his heartless cruelty. Zalla went away thoroughly humbled and made no more demands on this farmer who had been freed from his bonds by a mere glance from the man of God.

So you see, Peter, what I said is true. Those who devote themselves wholeheartedly to the service of God can sometimes work miracles by their own power. Blessed Benedict checked the fury of a dreaded Goth without even rising to his feet, and with a mere glance unfastened the heavy cord that bound the hands of an innocent man. The very speed with which he performed this marvel is proof enough that he did it by his own power.

And now, here is a remarkable miracle that was the result of his prayer.

32. One day, when he was out working in the fields with his monks, a farmer came to the monastery carrying in his arms the lifeless body of his son. Brokenhearted at his loss, he begged to see the saintly abbot and, on learning that he was at work in the fields, left the dead body at the entrance of the monastery and hurried off to find him. By then the abbot was already returning from his work. The moment the farmer caught sight of him he cried out, 'Give me back my son! Give me back my son!'

Benedict stopped when he heard this. 'But I have not taken your son from you, have I?' he asked. The boy's father only replied, 'He is dead. Come! Bring him back to life.' Deeply grieved at his words, the man of God turned to his disciples. 'Stand back, brethren!' he said. 'Stand back! Such a miracle is beyond our power. The holy apostles are the only ones who can raise the dead. Why are you so eager to accept what is impossible for us?' But overwhelming sorrow compelled the man to keep on pleading. He even declared with an oath that he would not leave until Benedict restored his son to life. The saint then asked him where the body was. 'At the entrance to the monastery,' he answered.

When Benedict arrived there with his monks, he knelt down beside the child's body and bent over it. Then, rising, he lifted his hands to heaven in prayer. 'O Lord,' he said, 'do not consider my sins but the faith of this man who is asking to see his son alive again, and restore to this body the soul you have taken from it.'

His prayer was hardly over when the child's whole body began once more to throb with life. No one present there could doubt that this sudden stirring was due to a heavenly intervention. Benedict then took the little boy by the hand and gave him back to his father alive and well. Obviously, Peter, he did not have the power to work this miracle himself. Otherwise he would not have begged for it prostrate in prayer.

Peter: The way facts bear out your words convinces me that everything you have said is true. Will you please tell me now whether holy men can always carry out their wishes, or at least obtain through prayer whatever they desire?

33. Gregory: Peter, will there ever be a holier man in this world than St. Paul? Yet he prayed three times to the Lord about the sting in his flesh and could not obtain his wish. In this connection I must tell you how the saintly Benedict once had a wish he was unable to fulfil.

His sister Scholastica, who had been consecrated to God in early childhood, used to visit with him once a year. On these occasions he would go down to meet her in a house belonging to the monastery, a short distance from the entrance.

For this particular visit he joined her there with a few of his disciples and they spent the whole day singing God's praises and conversing about the spiritual life. When darkness was setting in, they took their meal together and continued their conversation at table until it was quite late. Then the holy nun said to him, 'Please do not leave me tonight, brother. Let us keep on talking about the joys of heaven till morning.'

'What are you saying, sister?' he replied. 'You know I cannot stay away from the monastery.' The sky was so clear at the time that there was not a cloud in sight. At her brother's refusal Scholastica folded her hands on the table and rested her head upon them in earnest prayer. When she looked up again, there was a sudden burst of lightning and thunder, accompanied by such a downpour that Benedict and his companions were unable to set a foot outside the door.

By shedding a flood of tears while she prayed, this holy nun had darkened the cloudless sky with a heavy rain. The storm began as soon as her prayer was over. In fact, the two coincided so closely that the thunder was already resounding as she raised her head from the table. The very instant she ended her prayer the rain poured down.

Realizing that he could not return to the monastery in this terrible storm, Benedict complained bitterly. 'God forgive you, sister!' he said. 'What have you done?' Scholastica simply answered, 'When I appealed to you, you would not listen to me. So I turned to my God and he heard my prayer. Leave now if you can. Leave me here and go back to your monastery.' This, of course, he could not do. He had no choice now but to stay, in spite of his unwillingness. They spent the entire night together and both of them derived great profit from the holy thoughts they exchanged about the interior life.

Here you have my reason for saying that this holy man was once unable to obtain what he desired. If we consider his point of view, we can readily see that he wanted the sky to remain as clear as it was when he came down from the monastery. But this wish of his was thwarted by a miracle almighty God performed in answer to a woman's prayer. We need not be surprised that in this instance she proved mightier than her brother; she had been looking forward so long to this visit. Do we not read in St. John that God is love? Surely it is no more than right that her influence was greater than his, since hers was the greater love.

Peter: I find this discussion very enjoyable.

34. Gregory: The next morning Scholastica returned to her convent and Benedict to his monastery. Three days later as he stood in his room looking up toward the sky, he beheld his sister's soul leaving her body and entering the court of heaven in the form of a dove.

Overjoyed at her eternal glory, he gave thanks to God in hymns of praise.

Then, after informing his brethren of her death, he sent some of them to bring her body to the monastery and bury it in the tomb he had prepared for himself. The bodies of these two were now to share a common resting place, just as in life their souls had always been one in God.

35. At another time, the deacon Servandus came to see the servant of God on one of his regular visits. He was abbot of the monastery in Campania that had been built by the late Senator Liberius, and always welcomed an opportunity to discuss with Benedict the truths of eternity, for he, too, was a man of deep spiritual understanding. In speaking of their hopes and longings they were able to taste in advance the heavenly food that was not yet fully theirs to enjoy. When it was time to retire for the night, Benedict went to his room on the second floor of the tower, leaving Servandus in the one below, which was connected with his own by a stairway. Their disciples slept in the large building facing the tower.

Long before the night office began, the man of God was standing at his window, where he watched and prayed while the rest were still asleep. In the dead of night he suddenly beheld a flood of light shining down from above more brilliant than the sun, and with it every trace of darkness cleared away. Another remarkable sight followed. According to his own description, the whole world was gathered up before his eyes in what appeared to be a single ray of light. As he gazed at all this dazzling display, he saw the soul of Germanus, the Bishop of Capua, being carried by angels up to heaven in a ball of fire.

Wishing to have someone else witness this great marvel, he called out for Servandus, repeating his name two or three times in a loud voice. As soon as he heard the saint's call, Servandus rushed to the upper room and was just in time to catch a final glimpse of the miraculous light. He remained speechless with wonder as Benedict described everything that had taken place. Then without any delay the man of God instructed the devout Theoprobus to go to Cassino and have a messenger sent to Capua that same night to find out what had happened to Germanus. In carrying out these instructions the messenger discovered that the revered bishop was already dead [the year was 541]. When he asked for further details, he learned that his death had occurred at the very time blessed Benedict saw him carried into heaven.

Peter: What an astounding miracle! I hardly know what to think when I hear you say that he saw the whole world gathered up before his eyes in what appeared to be a single ray of light. I have never had such an experience. How is it possible for anyone to see the whole universe at a glance?

Gregory: Keep this well in mind, Peter. All creation is bound to appear small to a soul that sees the creator. Once it beholds a little of his light, it finds all creatures small indeed. The light of holy contemplation enlarges and expands the mind in God until it stands above the world. In fact, the soul that sees him rises even above itself, and as it is drawn upward in his light all its inner powers unfold. Then, when it looks down from above, it sees how small everything is that was beyond its grasp before.

Now, Peter, how else was it possible for this man to behold the ball of fire and watch the angels on their return to heaven except with light from God? Why should it surprise us, then, that he could see the whole world gathered up before him after this inner light had lifted him so far above the world? Of course, in saying that the world was gathered up before his eyes I do not mean that heaven and earth grew small, but that his spirit was enlarged. Absorbed as he was in God, it was now easy for him to see all that lay beneath God. In the light outside that was shining before his eyes, there was a brightness which reached into his mind and lifted his spirit heavenward, showing him the insignificance of all that lies below.

Peter: My difficulty in understanding you has proved of real benefit; the explanation it led to was so thorough. Now that you have cleared up this problem for me, would you return once more to your account of blessed Benedict's life?

36. Gregory: I should like to tell you much more about this saintly abbot, but I am purposely passing over some of his miraculous deeds in my eagerness to take up those of others. There is one more point, however, I want to call to your attention. With all the renown he gained by his numerous miracles, the holy man was no less outstanding for the wisdom of his teaching. He wrote a Rule for monks that is remarkable for its discretion and its clarity of language. Anyone who wishes to know more about his life and character can discover in his Rule exactly what he was like as abbot, for his life could not have differed from his teaching.

37. In the year that was to be his last, the man of God foretold the day of his holy death to a number of his disciples. In mentioning it to some who were with him in the monastery, he bound them to strict secrecy. Some others, however, who were stationed elsewhere he only informed of the special sign they would receive at the time of his death.

Six days before he died he gave orders for his tomb to be opened. Almost immediately he was seized with a violent fever that rapidly wasted his remaining strength. Each day his condition grew worse until finally, on the sixth day, he had his disciples carry him into the chapel, where he received the body and blood of our Lord to gain strength for his approaching end. Then, supporting his weakened body on the arms of his brethren, he stood with his hands raised to heaven and as he prayed breathed his last [21 March 547 is the generally accepted date of Benedict's death].

That day two monks, one of them at the monastery, the other some distance away, received the very same revelation. They both saw a magnificent road covered with rich carpeting and glittering with thousands of lights. From his monastery it stretched eastward in a straight line until it reached up into heaven. And there in the brightness stood a man of majestic appearance, who asked them, 'Do you know who passed this way?' 'No,' they replied. 'This,' he told them, 'is the road taken by blessed Benedict, the Lord's beloved, when he went to heaven.' Thus, while the brethren who were with Benedict witnessed his death, those who were absent knew about it through the sign he had promised them. His body was laid to rest in the chapel of St. John the Baptist, which he had built to replace the altar of Apollo.

38. Even in the cave at Subiaco, where he had lived before, this holy man still works numerous miracles for people who turn to him with faith and confidence. The incident I am going to relate happened only recently.

A woman who had completely lost her mind was roaming day and night over hills and valleys, through forests and fields, resting only when she was utterly exhausted. One day, in the course of her aimless wanderings, she strayed into the saint's cave and rested there without the least idea of where she was. The next morning she woke up entirely cured and left the cave without even a trace of her former affliction. After that she remained free from it for the rest of her life.

Peter: How is it that, as a rule, even the martyrs in their care for us do not grant the same great favors through their bodily remains as they do through their other relics? We find them so often performing more outstanding miracles away from their burial places.

Gregory: There is no doubt, Peter, that the holy martyrs can perform countless miracles where their bodies rest. And they do so on behalf of all who pray there with a pure intention. In places where their bodies do not actually lie buried, however, there is danger that those whose faith is weak may doubt their presence and their power to answer prayers. Consequently, it is in these places that they must perform still greater miracles. But one whose faith in God is strong earns all the more merit by his faith, for he realizes that the martyrs are present to hear his prayers even though their bodies happen to be buried elsewhere.

It was precisely to increase the faith of his disciples that the eternal Truth told them, 'If I do not go, the advocate will not come to you.' Now certainly the Holy Spirit, the advocate, is ever proceeding from the Father and the Son. Why, then, should the Son say he will go in order that the Spirit may come, when, actually, the Spirit never leaves him? The point is that as long as the disciples could see our Lord in his human flesh they would want to keep on seeing him with their bodily eyes. With good reason, therefore, did he tell them, 'If I do not go, the advocate will not come.' What he really meant was, 'I cannot teach you spiritual love unless I remove my body from your sight; as long as you continue to see me with your bodily eyes you will never learn to love me spiritually.'

Peter: That is a very satisfying explanation.

Gregory: Let us interrupt our discussion for a while. If we are going to take up the miracles of other holy men, we shall need a short period of silence to rest our voices.

4. VENANTIUS FORTUNATUS'S *LIFE OF ST. RADEGUND*

Although women saints were in the minority throughout the Middle Ages (according to the historian David Herlihy, the overall ratio up to 1500 was about one woman for every five men), from 476 to 750 they were more likely than at any other time to hold powerful positions as abbesses, and therefore to be sanctified. These women were also generally from aristocratic families. Radegund (518-87) was a Frankish queen, but it was as a nun, founder, and abbess of an important convent at Poitiers that she achieved fame. When still a child she was carried off as war booty by Clothar I, king of the Franks, after his forces had virtually annihilated her family, the ruling house of Thuringia, in a feud. Clothar sent her to his villa in Picardy until she was old enough for him to marry, in about 540. The feuding continued, however, and after Clothar killed her surviving brother ten years later, Radegund left him, as described in Fortunatus's 'life' below, and pursued her religious vocation single-mindedly until her death, though not without having to evade at least one attempt by Clothar to get her back.

Her life is well documented by Gregory of Tours, by the poet and bishop Venantius Fortunatus (c. 540-600), who was her close friend, and by a nun, Baudonivia, who lived in the convent founded by Radegund at Poitiers. There is also a poem, 'The Thuringian War,' that laments the destruction of the Thuringian royal house and that may have been written by Radegund herself. Fortunatus's account tells us little about Radegund's management of her convent; his aim was rather to prove that her great charity and extreme suffering (often self-inflicted) made her worthy of the same status as a martyr. That she herself was concerned not to let worldly affairs detract from her spiritual life is evident from the fact that she soon established one of her nuns, Agnes, as Mother Superior.

The convent at Poitiers followed the rule for nuns set down by Caesarius of Arles, which emphasized reading Scripture and meditation, constant prayer, charity to the poor, moderation in ascetic practices, and strict claustration, although the latter did not mean that the nuns could not receive visitors, including men. Later on, the convent suffered more than its share of problems, as described by Gregory of Tours in his 'History of the Franks' (9, 39-44 and 10, 15-17), and the period of Radegund's life was regarded as something of a golden age.

Source: trans. Jo Ann McNamara and John E. Halborg, with E. Gordon Whatley, *Sainted Women of the Dark Ages* (Durham and London: Duke University Press, 1992), pp. 70-86; repr. with permission. BHL 7048.

1. Our Redeemer is so richly and abundantly generous that he wins mighty victories through the female sex and, despite their frail physique, he confers glory and greatness on women through strength of mind. By faith, Christ makes them strong who were born weak so that, when those who appeared

to be imbeciles are crowned with their merits by him who made them, they garner praise for their Creator who hid heavenly treasure in earthen vessels. For Christ the king dwells with his riches in their bowels. Mortifying themselves in the world, despising earthly consort, purified of worldly contamination, trusting not in the transitory, dwelling not in error but seeking to live with God, they are united with the Redeemer's glory in Paradise. One of that company is she whose earthly life we are attempting to present to the public, though in homely style, so that the glorious memory that she, who lives with Christ, has left us will be celebrated in this world. So ends the Prologue.

Here begins the 'Life.'

2. The most blessed Radegund was of the highest earthly rank, born from the seed of the kings of the barbarian nation of Thuringia. Her grandfather was King Bassin, her paternal uncle, Hermanfred and her father, King Bertechar. But she surpassed her lofty origin by even loftier deeds. She had lived with her noble family only a little while when the victorious Franks devastated the region with barbaric turmoil and, like the Israelites, she departed and migrated from her homeland. The royal girl became part of the plunder of these conquerors and they began to quarrel over their captive. If the contest had not ended with an agreement for her disposition, the kings would have taken up arms against one another. Falling to the lot of the illustrious king Clothar, she was taken to Athies in Vermandois, a royal villa, and her upbringing was entrusted to guardians. The maiden was taught letters and other things suitable to her sex and she would often converse with other children there about her desire to be a martyr if the chance came in her time. Thus even as an adolescent, she displayed the merits of a mature person. She obtained part of what she sought, for, though the church was flourishing in peace, she endured persecution from her own household. While but a small child, she herself brought the scraps left at table to the gathered children, washing the head of each one, seating them on little chairs and offering water for their hands, and she mingled with the infants herself. She would also carry out what she had planned beforehand with Samuel, a little cleric. Following his lead, carrying a wooden cross they had made, singing psalms, the children would troop into the oratory as somber as adults. Radegund herself would polish the pavement with her dress and, collecting the drifting dust around the altar in a napkin, reverently placed it outside the door rather than sweep it away. When the aforementioned king, having provided the expenses, wished to bring her to Vitry, she escaped by night from Athies through Beralcha with a few companions. When he settled with her that she

should be made his queen at Soissons, she avoided the trappings of royalty, so she would not grow great in the world but in him to whom she was devoted and she remained unchanged by earthly glory.

3. Therefore, though married to a terrestrial prince, she was not separated from the celestial one and, the more secular power was bestowed upon her, the more humbly she bent her will – more than befitted her royal status. Always subject to God following priestly admonitions, she was more Christ's partner than her husband's companion. We will only attempt to publicize a few of the many things she did during this period of her life. Fearing she would lose status with God as she advanced in worldly rank at the side of a prince, she gave herself energetically to almsgiving. Whenever she received part of the tribute, she gave away a tithe of all that came to her before accepting any for herself. She dispensed what was left to monasteries, sending the gifts to those she could not reach on foot. There was no hermit who could hide from her munificence. So she paid out what she received lest the burden weigh her down. The voice of the needy was not raised in vain for she never turned a deaf ear. Often she gave clothes, believing that the limbs of Christ concealed themselves under the garments of the poor and that whatever she did not give to paupers was truly lost.

4. Turning her mind to further works of mercy, she built a house at Athies where beds were elegantly made up for needy women gathered there. She would wash them herself in warm baths, tending to the putrescence of their diseases. She washed the heads of men, acting like a servant. And before she washed them, she would mix a potion with her own hands to revive those who were weak from sweating. Thus the devout lady, queen by birth and marriage, mistress of the palace, served the poor as a handmaid. Secretly, lest anyone notice, at royal banquets, she fed most deliciously on beans or lentils from the dish of legumes placed before her, in the manner of the three boys [a reference to the behavior of Daniel and his companions at the court of King Nebuchadnezzar]. And if the singing of the hours [church services] started while she was still eating, she would make her excuses to the king and withdraw from the company to do her duty to God. As she went out, she sang psalms to the Lord and carefully checked what food had been provided to refresh the paupers at the door.

5. At night, when she lay with her prince she would ask leave to rise and leave the chamber to relieve nature. Then she would prostrate herself in prayer under a hair cloak by the privy so long that the cold pierced her through and through and only her spirit was warm. Her whole flesh prematurely dead, indifferent to her body's torment, she kept her mind intent on paradise and counted her suffering trivial, if only she might avoid becoming cheap in Christ's eyes. Re-entering the chamber thereafter, she could

scarcely get warm either by the hearth or in her bed. Because of this, people said that the King had yoked himself to a *monacha* [a nun] rather than a queen. Her goodness provoked him to harsher irritation but she either soothed him to the best of her ability or bore her husband's brawling modestly.

6. Indeed, it will suffice to know how she bore herself during the days of Quadragesima [the period before Easter], a singular penitent in her royal robes. When the time for fasting drew near, she would notify a *monacha* named Pia, who, according to their holy arrangement, would send a hair cloth sealed carefully in linen to Radegund. Draping it over her body through the whole of Quadragesima, the holy woman wore that sweet burden under her royal garment. When the season was over, she returned the hair cloth similarly sealed. Who could believe how she would pour out her heart in prayers when the king was away? How she would cling to the feet of Christ as though he were present with her and satiate her long hunger with tears as though she was gorging on delicacies! She had contempt for the food of the belly, for Christ was her only nourishment and all her hunger was for Christ.

7. With what piety did she care solicitously for the candles made with her own hands that burned all night long in oratories and holy places? When the king asked after her at table during the late hours, he was told that she was delayed, busy about God's affairs. This caused strife with her husband and later on the prince compensated her with gifts for the wrong he did her with his tongue.

8. If she received a report that any of God's servants was on his way to see her, either of his own accord or by invitation, she felt full of celestial joy. Hastening out in the night time, with a few intimates, through snow, mud or dust, she herself would wash the feet of the venerable man with water she had heated beforehand and offer the servant of God something to drink in a bowl. There was no resisting her. On the following day, committing the care of the household to her trusted servants, she would occupy herself wholly with the just man's words and his teachings concerning salvation. The business of achieving celestial life fixed her attention throughout the day. And if a bishop should come, she rejoiced to see him, gave him gifts and was sad to have to let him go home.

9. And how prudently she sought to devote everything possible to her salvation. If the girls attending her when she dressed praised a new veil of coarse linen ornamented with gold and gems in the barbarian fashion as particularly beautiful, she would judge herself unworthy to be draped in such fabric. Divesting herself of the dress immediately, she would send it to some holy place in the neighborhood where it could be laid as a cloth on the Lord's altar.

10. And if the king, according to custom, condemned a guilty criminal to death, wasn't the most holy queen near dead with torment lest the culprit perish by the sword? How she would rush about among his trusty men, ministers and nobles, whose blandishments might soothe the prince's temper until the king's anger ceased and the voice of salvation flowed where the sentence of death had issued before!

11. Even while she remained in her worldly palace, the blessed acts which busied her so pleased Divine Clemency that the Lord's generosity worked miracles through her. Once at her villa in Péronne, while that holiest of women was strolling in the garden after her meal, some sequestered criminals loudly cried to her from the prison for help. She asked who it might be. The servants lied that a crowd of beggars were seeking alms. Believing that, she sent to relieve their needs. Meanwhile the fettered prisoners were silenced by a judge. But as night was falling and she was saying her prayers, the chains broke and the freed prisoners ran from the prison to the holy woman. When they witnessed this, those who had lied to the holy one realized that they were the real culprits, while the erstwhile convicts were freed from their bonds.

12. If Divinity fosters it, misfortune often leads to salvation. Thus her innocent brother was killed so that she might come to live in religion. She left the king and went straight to holy Médard at Noyon. She earnestly begged that she might change her garments and be consecrated to God. But mindful of the words of the Apostle, "Art thou bound unto a wife? Seek not to be loosed," he hesitated to garb the queen in the robe of a *monacha*. For even then, nobles were harassing the holy man and attempting to drag him brutally through the basilica from the altar to keep him from veiling the king's spouse lest the priest imagine he could take away the king's official queen as though she were only a prostitute. That holiest of women knew this and, sizing up the situation, entered the sacristy, put on a monastic garb and proceeded straight to the altar, saying to the blessed Médard, "If you shrink from consecrating me, and fear man more than God, pastor, he will require his sheep's soul from your hand." He was thunderstruck by that argument and, laying his hand on her, he consecrated her as a deaconess.

13. Soon she divested herself of the noble costume which she was wont to wear as queen when she walked in procession on the day of a festival with her train of attendants. She laid it on the altar and piled the table of divine glory with purple, gems, ornaments and like gifts to honor him. She gave a heavy girdle of costly gold for the relief of the poor. Similarly, one day she ornamented herself in queenly splendor, as the barbarians would say – all decked out for *stapione* [probable meaning may be 'stepping out']. Entering

holy Jumerus's cell, she laid her frontlets, chemise, bracelets, coif and pins all decorated with gold, some with circlets of gems, on the altar for future benefit. Again, proceeding to the venerable Dato's cell one day, spectacularly adorned as she should have been in the world with whatever she could put on, having rewarded the abbot, she gave the whole from her woman's wealth to the community. Likewise going on to the retreat of holy Gundulf, later bishop of Metz, she exerted herself just as energetically to enrich his monastery.

14. From there her fortunate sails approached Tours. Can any eloquence express how zealous and munificent she showed herself there? How she conducted herself around the courts, shrines, and basilica of St. Martin, weeping unchecked tears, prostrating herself at each threshold! After mass was said, she heaped the holy altar with the clothing and bright ornaments with which she used to adorn herself in the palace. And when the handmaid of the Lord went from there to the neighborhood of Candes whence the glorious Martin, Christ's senator and confidant, migrated from this world, she gave him no less again, ever profiting in the Lord's grace.

15. From there, in decorous manner, she approached the villa of Saix near the aforesaid town in the territory of Poitiers, her journey ever prospering. Who could recount the countless remarkable things she did there or grasp the special quality of each one? At table she secretly chewed rye or barley bread which she had hidden under a cake to escape notice. For from the time she was veiled, consecrated by Saint Médard, even in illness, she ate nothing but legumes and green vegetables: not fruit nor fish nor eggs. And she drank no drink but honeyed water or perry and would touch no undiluted wine nor any decoction of mead or fermented beer.

16. Then, emulating St. Germanus's custom, she secretly had a millstone brought to her. Throughout the whole of Quadragesima, she ground fresh flour with her own hands. She continuously distributed each offering to local religious communities, in the amount needed for the meal taken every four days. With that holy woman, acts of mercy were no fewer than the crowds who pressed her; as there was no shortage of those who asked, so was there no shortage in what she gave so that, wonderfully, they could all be satisfied. Where did the exile get such wealth? Whence came the pilgrim's riches?

17. How much did she spend daily on relief? Only she who bore it to the beggars ever knew. For beyond the daily meal which she fed to her enrolled paupers, twice a week, on Thursday and Saturday, she prepared a bath. Girding herself with a cloth, she washed the heads of the needy, scrubbing away whatever she found there. Not shrinking from scurf, scabs, lice or pus, she plucked off the worms and scrubbed away the putrid flesh. Then she herself combed the hair on every head she had washed. As in the Gospel, she

applied oil to their ulcerous sores that had opened when the skin softened or that scratching had irritated, reducing the spread of infection. When women descended into the tub, she washed their limbs with soap from head to foot. When they came out, if she noticed that anyone's clothes were shoddy with age, she would take them away and give them new ones. Thus she spruced up all who came to the feast in rags. When they were gathered around the table and the dinner service laid out, she brought water and napkins for each of them and cleaned the mouth and hands of the invalids herself. Then three trays laden with delicacies would be carried in. Standing like a good hostess before the diners, she cut up the bread and meat and served everyone while fasting herself. Moreover, she never ceased to offer food to the blind and weak with a spoon. In this, two women aided her but she alone served them, busy as a new Martha [the type of active religious life, opposed to her sister Mary, symbol of the contemplative life] until the "brothers" were drunk and happily satisfied with their meal. Then, leaving the place to wash her hands, she was completely gratified with her well-served feast. And if anyone protested, she ordered that they sit still until they wished to get up.

18. Summer and winter, on Sundays, she followed a praiseworthy rule. She would provide an undiluted drink of sweet wine to the assembled paupers. First she doled it out herself and then, while she hurried off to Mass, she assigned a maid to serve everyone who remained. Her devotions completed, she would meet the priests invited to her table for it was her royal custom not to let them return home without a gift.

19. Doesn't this make one shudder, this thing she did so sweetly? When lepers arrived and, sounding a warning, came forward, she directed her assistant to inquire with pious concern whence they came or how many there were. Having learned that, she had a table laid with dishes, spoons, little knives, cups and goblets, and wine and she went in herself secretly that none might see her. Seizing some of the leprous women in her embrace, her heart full of love, she kissed their faces. Then, while they were seated at table, she washed their faces and hands with warm water and treated their sores with fresh unguents and fed each one. When they were leaving she offered small gifts of gold and clothing. To this there was scarcely a single witness, but the attendant presumed to chide her softly, "Most holy lady, when you have embraced lepers, who will kiss you?" Pleasantly, she answered, "Really, if you won't kiss me, it's no concern of mine."

20. With God's help, she shone forth in diverse miracles. For example, if anyone was in desperate straits because of pus from a wound, an attendant would bring a vine leaf to the saint speaking with her about what was to be done with it. As soon as the saint made the sign of the cross over it, the attendant would take it to the desperate one, placing it on the wound which

would soon be healed. Similarly an invalid or someone with a fever might come and say that he had learned in a dream that to be healed he should hasten to the holy woman and present one of her attendants with a candle. After it had burned through the night his disease would be killed while the invalid was healed. How often when she heard of someone lying bedridden would she sally forth like a pilgrim bearing fruit, or something sweet and warm to restore their strength? How quickly would an invalid who had eaten nothing for ten days take food when she served it herself and thus receive both food and health together? And she ordered these things herself lest anyone tell tales.

21. Weren't there such great gatherings of people on the day that the saint determined to seclude herself that those who could not be contained in the streets climbed up to fill the roofs? Anyone who spoke of all the most holy woman had fervently accomplished in fasting, services, humility, charity, suffering, and torment, proclaimed her both confessor and martyr. Truly every day, except for the most venerable day of the Lord, was a fast day for that most holy woman. Her meal of lentils or green vegetables was virtually a fast in itself for she took no fowl or fish or fruit or eggs to eat. Her bread was made from rye or barley which she concealed under the pudding lest anyone notice what she ate. And to drink she had water and honey or perry and only a little of that was poured out for her, however thirsty she was.

22. The first time she enclosed herself in her cell throughout Quadragesima, she ate no bread, except on Sundays but only roots of herbs or mallow greens without a drop of oil or salt for dressing. In fact, during the entire fast, she consumed only two *sestaria* [about four cups] of water. Consequently, she suffered so much from thirst that she could barely chant the psalms through her desiccated throat. She kept her vigils in a shift of hair cloth instead of linen incessantly chanting the offices. A bed of ashes served her for a couch which she covered with a hair cloth. In this manner, rest itself wearied her but even this was not enough to endure.

23. While all the *monachas* [nuns] were deep in sleep, she would collect their shoes, restoring them cleaned and oiled to each. On other Quadragesimas, she was more relaxed, eating on Thursday and again on Sundays. The rest of the time when health permitted, except for Easter and other high holy days, she led an austere life in sackcloth and ashes, rising early to be singing psalms when the others awoke. For no monasterial offices pleased her unless she observed them first. She punished herself if anyone else did a good deed before she did. When it was her turn to sweep the pavements around the monastery, she even scoured the nooks and crannies, bundling away whatever nasty things were there, never too disgusted to carry off what others shuddered to look upon. She did not shrink from cleaning the priv-

ies but cleaned and carried off the stinking dung. For she believed that she would be diminished if these vile services did not ennoble her. She carried firewood in her arms. She blew on the hearth and stirred the fire with tongs and did not flinch if she hurt herself. She would care for the infirm beyond her assigned week, cooking their food, washing their faces, and bringing them warm water, going the rounds of those she was caring for and returning fasting to her cell.

24. How can anyone describe her excited fervor as she ran into the kitchen, doing her week of chores? None of the *monachas* but she would carry as much wood as was needed in a bundle from the back gate. She drew water from the well and poured it into basins. She scrubbed vegetables and legumes and revived the hearth by blowing so that she might cook the food. While it was busy boiling, she took the vessels from the hearth, washing and laying out the dishes. When the meal was finished, she rinsed the small vessels and scrubbed the kitchen till it shone, free of every speck of dirt. Then she carried out all the sweepings and the nastiest rubbish. Further, she never flagged in supporting the sick, and even before she took up the Rule of Arles did her weekly tour of service preparing plenty of warm water for them all. Humbly washing and kissing their feet, the holy one prostrated herself and begged them all to forgive her for any negligence she might have committed.

25. But I shudder to speak of the pain she inflicted on herself over and above all these labors. Once, throughout Quadragesima, she bound her neck and arms with three broad iron circlets. Inserting three chains in them she fettered her whole body so tightly that her delicate flesh, swelling up, enclosed the hard iron. After the fast was ended, when she wished to remove the chains locked under her skin, she could not for the flesh was cut by the circlet through her back and breast over the iron of the chains, so that the flow of blood nearly drained her little body to the last drop.

26. On another occasion, she ordered a brass plate made, shaped in the sign of Christ. She heated it up in her cell and pressed it upon her body most deeply in two spots so that her flesh was roasted through. Thus, with her spirit flaming, she caused her very limbs to burn. One Quadragesima, she devised a still more terrible agony to torture herself, in addition to the severe hunger and burning thirst of her fast. She forced her tender limbs, already suppurating and scraped raw by the hard bristles of a hair cloth, to carry a water basin full of burning coals. Then, isolated from the rest, though her limbs were quivering, her soul was steeled for the pain. She drew it to herself so that she might be a martyr though it was not an age of persecution. To cool her fervent soul, she thought to burn her body. She imposed the glowing brass and her burning limbs hissed. Her skin was consumed and a deep furrow remained where the brand had touched her. Silently, she concealed

the holes, but the putrefying blood betrayed the pain that her voice did not reveal. Thus did a woman willingly suffer such bitterness for the sweetness of Christ! And in time, miracles told the story that she herself would have kept hidden.

27. For example, a noble matron of Gislad named Bella, who had suffered from blindness for a long time, had herself led from Francia to Poitiers into the saint's presence. Though won over with difficulty, she had her brought in during the silence of a foul night. Prostrate at the saint's knees, the woman could barely ask her to deign to sign her eyes. As soon as she impressed the sign of the cross on them in the name of Christ, the blindness fled; the light returned. Daylight shone on the orbs so long darkened beneath the shades of night. Thus she who had been led there, went home without a guide.

28. Similarly, a girl named Fraifled, whom the Enemy [Satan] vexed, was violently contorted and most wretched. Without delay, she was found worthy of a cure at the saint's hands at Saix. Nor should we omit to mention the following miracle, revealed through the blessed woman at this time. The next day a woman named Leubela, who was gravely vexed in the back by the Adversary, was publicly restored to health when the saint prayed for her and Christ worked a new miracle of healing. For a rustling sound came from under the skin of her shoulder blades and a worm emerged. Treading it underfoot, she went home liberated.

29. What she did secretly was to become known to all people. A certain *monacha* shivered with cold by day and burned with fire by night through an entire year. And when she had lain lifeless for six months, unable to move a step, one of her sisters told the saint of this infirmity. Finding her almost lifeless, she bade them prepare warm water and had the sick woman brought to her cell and laid in the warm water. Then she ordered everyone to leave, remaining alone with the sick woman for two hours as a doctor. She nursed the sick limbs, tracing the form of her body from head to foot. Wherever her hands touched, the sickness fled from the patient and she who had been laid in the bath by two persons got out of it in full health. The woman who had been revolted by the smell of wine, now accepted it, drank and was refreshed. What more? The next day, when she was expected to migrate from this world, she went out in public, cured.

30. Let us increase her praise by recounting another miracle that has rightly not been forgotten. A certain woman labored so heavily under an invasion of the Enemy that the struggling foe could scarcely be brought to the saint. She commanded the Adversary to lie prostrate on the pavement and show her some respect. The moment the blessed woman spoke, he threw himself down for she frightened him who was feared. When the saint, full of faith, trod on the nape of her neck, he left her in a flux that poured from her belly.

Also from small things great glory may accrue to the Creator. Once, a ball of thread which the saint had spun was hanging from the vault, when a shrew mouse came to nibble it. But, before he could break the thread, he hung there dead in the very act of biting.

31. Let our book include another event worthy to be called a miracle. One of the saint's men named Florius was at sea fishing when a whirlwind appeared and a mass of billows surged. The sailor had not even begun to bail when a wave came over the side, the ship filled and went under. In his extremity, he cried out, "Holy Radegund, while we obey you, keep us from shipwreck and prevail upon God to save us from the sea." When he said this, the clouds fled away, serenity returned, the waves fell and the prow arose.

32. Goda, a secular girl who later served God as a *monacha*, lay on her bed for a long time. The more she was plied with medicine, the more she languished. A candle was made to the measure of her own height, in the name of the holy woman, and the Lord took pity on her. At the hour when she expected the chills, she kindled the light and held it and as a result, the cold fled before the candle was consumed.

33. The more we omit for brevity's sake, the greater grows our guilt. Therefore, as we dispose quickly of the remainder, our relief is slowed. A carpenter's wife had been tormented by diabolic possession for many days. Jokingly, the venerable abbess [Agnes, whom Radegund had made head of the convent] said of her to the holy woman, "Believe me, Mother, I will excommunicate you if the woman is not purged of the Enemy and restored in three days." She said this publicly but she made the holy woman secretly sorry that she had been so slow to heal the afflicted. To be brief, at the saint's prayer on the next day, the Adversary went roaring out of her ear and abandoned the little vessel he had violently seized. Unhurt, the woman returned to the hospice with her husband. Nor should we neglect a similar deed. The most blessed one asked that a flourishing laurel tree be uprooted and transferred to her cell so she could enjoy it there. But when this was done all the leaves withered because the transplanted tree did not take root. The abbess jokingly remarked that she had better pray for the tree to take root in the ground, or she herself would be separated from her food [exclusion from community meals was a common monastic punishment]. She did not speak in vain for, through the saint's intercession, the laurel with the withered root grew green again in leaf and branch.

34. When one of the *monachas* closest to her suffered because her eye was flooded with a bloody humor, she laid hold of some wormwood which the saint had about her breast for refreshment. When she placed it on her eye, the pain and blood soon fled and, from the freshness of the herb, the eye was suddenly clear and bright again. And that reminds me of something I almost

passed by in silence. Children were born to the blessed one's agent, Andered, but he scarcely saw them before he lost them and the sorrowing mother had to think about burying her child even while birthing it. During the preparations, the tearful parents wrapped the lifeless babe in the saint's hair cloth. As soon as the infant's body touched that most medicinal garment and those noble rags, he came back from the dead to normal life. Blushing away his tomblike pallor, he rose from the mantle.

35. Who can count the wonders that Christ's merciful kindness performs? A *monacha* Animia suffered so with dropsical swelling that she seemed to have reached her end. The appointed sisters awaited the moment when she would exhale her spirit. While she was sleeping, however, it seemed to her that the most venerable blessed Radegund ordered her to descend nude into a bath with no water in it. Then, with her own hand, the blessed one seemed to pour oil on the sick woman's head and cover her with a new garment. After this strange ritual, when she awakened from her sleep, all trace of the disease had disappeared. She had not even sweated it away for the water was consumed from within. As a result of this new miracle, no vestige of disease was left in her belly. She who was thought to be ready for the tomb rose from her bed for the office. Her head still smelled of oil in witness of the miracle but the pernicious disease was no longer in her belly.

36. Let us now tell a tale in which the whole region may rejoice. One evening as twilight cast its shadows, the layfolk were singing noisy songs near the monastery as they danced around accompanied by musicians with cithars. The saint had spent some time exhorting two listeners. Then one *monacha* said, joking: "Lady, I recognize one of my songs being preached by the dancers." To which she responded: "That's fine if it thrills you to hear religion mingled with the odor of the world." Then the sister stated: "Truly, lady, I have heard two or three of my songs which I have bound together in this way." Then the saint said: "God witness that I have heard nothing of any worldly song." Thus it was obvious that though her flesh remained in the world, her spirit was already in Heaven.

37. In praise of Christ, let us proclaim a miracle from our own time patterned after an ancient model in the tradition of the blessed Martin. When the most blessed female was secluded in her cell, she heard a *monacha* crying. At the signal, she entered and asked what was the matter. She answered that her infant sister was dead, and though still warm she was laid out and ready to be washed in cold water. Condoling with her, the saint bade her bring the corpse to her in her cell. There she took it into her own hands, closing the door behind her and ordering the other to withdraw to a distance lest she sense what she was doing. But what she did secretly could not be concealed for long. By time the services for the dead were prepared, she had handled

the corpse of the dead little girl for seven hours. But seeing a faith he could not deny, Christ utterly restored her health. When the saint rose from prayer, the infant rose from the dead. The old woman got up when the infant revived. When the signal was repeated, she joyfully restored alive the one who was dead when she had tearfully received her.

38. And this noble deed should be commemorated. On the day the holy woman migrated from earth, a tribune of the *fisc* [treasury] named Domnolenus, who was wasting away with a suffocating disease, dreamed that he seemed to see the saint approach his town in state. He ran out and saluted her and asked what the blessed one wished. Then she said that she had come to see him. And since it was the wish of the people to establish an oratory for blessed Martin, the most blessed one seized the tribune's hand, saying, "There are venerable relics of the Confessor here with which you could build a shrine which he would consider most fitting." Behold the mystery of God! The foundation and the pavement where a basilica had been built were revealed. Then, in addition, in his slumber she drew her hand over his jaws and stroked his throat for a long time, saying: "I came that God might confer better health on you." And he dreamed she asked, "On my life, because of me, release those whom you have in prison." Waking, the tribune recounted what he had seen to his wife, saying, "Indeed, I believe that at this hour the saint has gone from this earth." He sent to the city to confirm the truth of this. He directed the prison that the seven prisoners held there should be admonished and released. The messenger, returning, reported that she had migrated from the world in that very hour. And the saint's oracle was proved by a triple mystery: the relief of the prisoners, the restoration of the tribune's health, and the temple building.

39. But let this small sample of the blessed one's miracles suffice, lest their very abundance arouse contempt. And even this should in no way be reckoned a small amount, since from these few tales we may recognize in the miracles the greatness with which she lived in such piety and self-denial, affection and affability, humility and honor, faith and fervor, with the result that after her death wonders also ensued upon her glorious passing.

5. THEFT OF RELICS: *THE TRANSLATION OF SS. MARCELLINUS AND PETER*

The veneration of relics – bodily parts of the saints, or objects connected with them such as cloths dipped in the blood of a martyr – began as early as the second century. By the fifth century the cult of relics had spread to northern Europe, and there was a brisk traffic in bodily parts between Rome and Gaul. Because the saints were understood to be actually present in their bodily remains, and thus able to act as powerful mediators in human affairs on a continuing basis, both secular and religious authorities saw in miracle-working relics a means of promoting their political aims and their prestige. The custom of placing relics in church altars as a condition of consecration gave further impetus to the trade and enhanced the appeal of relics among wealthy and powerful individuals who wished to obtain them. Relics might be purchased, given as gifts, included in war booty, or simply stolen. Their miraculous powers were intensely coveted by most members of society.

Einhard (c. 770-840), the Frankish courtier and scholar at the court of Charlemagne and his successor, Louis the Pious, has left us (besides his famous biography of Charlemagne) a startling account of the relics trade as it was practised in early ninth-century Europe. Charlemagne and his immediate successors emphasized the cult of the saints and the role of relics, re-invoking the original decree that altars should contain them, and requiring that all oaths, whether secular or religious, should be sworn upon them. There was official encouragement for the adoption of the saints as a focus of devotion, for the discovery of relics to place in new churches, and for pilgrimages in their honor. Relics were therefore at a premium, in particular the corporeal relics of martyrs that were mostly available in Rome, where many martyrdoms had occurred. The need for relics was made more acute by an increase in the number of religious foundations and by the competition among them (inspired by both spiritual and economic interests) to obtain prestigious relics. This in turn created a need for documents authenticating the movement of relics from one place to another, known as 'translations.' Such documents both honored the saints and commemorated a particular historical event, for example, the movement of their remains from a lowly tomb to a more elevated one, or from one place to another. In some cases this was given the express approval of the bishop; in others the translation was effected by more furtive and elaborate means, as in the following account. Only the first two books of Einhard's account are presented here; two further books detail the miracles performed by the saints through their relics.

Source: trans. Paul Edward Dutton, "The Translation and Miracles of the Blessed Martyrs, Marcellinus and Peter," in *Charlemagne's Courtier: the Complete Einhard* (Peterborough, ON: Broadview, 1998), pp. 69-91. repr. with permission. BHL 5233.

Preface

Einhard, a sinner, [sends greetings] to the true worshippers and genuine lovers of the true God, of our Lord Jesus Christ, and of his saints.

Those who have set down in writing and recorded the lives and deeds of the just [that is, the saved] and of people living according to divine commands, seem to me to have wanted to accomplish nothing but to inspire by means of examples of this sort the spirits of all people to emend their evil ways and to sing the praises of God's omnipotence. These [writers] did this, not only because they lacked envy, but because they were completely full of charity, which seeks the improvement of all. Since their praiseworthy intention was so obviously to accomplish nothing other than those [goals] I described, I do not see why their [plan] should not be imitated by many other [writers]. Therefore, since I am aware that the books I have written, with what skill I could, concerning the translation of the bodies of the blessed martyrs of Christ, Marcellinus and Peter, and concerning the signs and miracles the Lord wished to bring about through them for the salvation of believers, were composed with the same wish and purpose [in mind], I have decided to disseminate these books and to offer them to the lovers of God to read. For I suppose that this book will not only seem deep and meaningful to the faithful, but I also assume that I will have worked productively and usefully if I am able to move the spirit of [even] one person reading these things to rise up in praise of its Creator.

Book One

1. When I was resident at the palace and occupied with the business of the world, I used to give much thought to the retirement I hoped one day to enjoy. Due to the generosity of Louis, the ruler whom I then served, I [had] obtained a certain remote piece of property that was well out of most people's way. This estate is in Germany in the forest that lies halfway between the Neckar and Main rivers, which in these days is called Odenwald by both its inhabitants and those living nearby. I had constructed there, as far as my resources would allow, not only permanent houses and dwellings, but also a well-built church that was suitable for holding divine services. Then I became very concerned, wondering in whose name and honor – to which saint or martyr – that church should be dedicated.

After I had passed quite some time unsure what to do, it [so] happened that a certain deacon of the Roman church by the name of Deusdona came to the palace to appeal to the king for help in some pressing problems of his own. He remained there for some time and, when he had finished the business for which he had come, he was preparing to return to Rome. One day, to show courtesy to the traveler, I invited him to share a meager meal with us. Then, after we had spoken of many things over dinner, we came to a point in our conversation where the translation of the body of the blessed Sebastian was mentioned [Hilduin of St-Denis had acquired the relics of Sebastian in 826]. [We also spoke] of the neglected tombs of the martyrs, for there are many of those in Rome. When the conversation came to the [question of the] dedication of my new church, I began to inquire how I might arrange to obtain some particle of the genuine relics of the saints buried in Rome. At first, in fact, he hesitated, and stated that he did not know how it could be done. Then, when he saw that I was both distressed and intrigued by this business, he promised that he would respond to my inquiry on another day.

After that I invited him [to my place] again and he [then] produced a document from his purse and handed it to me. He asked me to read it thoroughly when I was alone and to be sure to tell him whether I liked what it said. I took the document and, as requested, read it carefully when I was alone. It said that he possessed many saints' relics at home and that he wished to give them to me, if [only] I could help him return to Rome. He knew that I had two mules [and said that], if I gave one to him and sent along one of my faithful men to receive the relics from him and bring them back to me, he would immediately send those [relics] to me. The plan he suggested was very appealing to me, and I hastily decided to check out the truth of his uncertain claim.

As a result, after giving him the animal he requested and even adding [some] money for his daily expenses, I ordered my notary, Ratleig, who had made a vow to travel to Rome to pray, to accompany him. Therefore, they set out from the palace at Aachen, where the emperor [Louis] was then holding court, and traveled to Soissons. There they spoke with Hilduin, the abbot of the monastery of St-Médard, because the deacon [Deusdona had] promised him that he could arrange for the body of the holy martyr Tiburtius to come into his possession. Seduced by these promises, [Hilduin] sent a certain priest, a cunning man by the name of Hunus, with them and ordered him to bring him back the body of the martyr [Tiburtius] once he had received it from [Deusdona]. And so having started out on their journey, they made their way as quickly as they could toward Rome.

2. After they had entered Italy, however, it happened that my notary's servant, whose name was Reginbald, was seized by a tertian fever [malaria]. His sickness led to a serious delay in their progress, since during those times when he was gripped by bouts of fever they could not continue their journey, for their number was small and they did not want to be separated from each other. Although their journey had been considerably delayed because of this

trouble, they nevertheless tried to hurry as fast as they could. Three days before they reached [Rome], the feverish man had a vision in which a man in a deacon's clothes appeared to him and asked him why his master was rushing to Rome. When [Reginbald] revealed to him, as much as he knew, about the deacon's promises to send saints' relics to me and about what he had promised Abbot Hilduin, [the figure] said: "[Events] will not turn out as you think [they will], but quite differently, and yet the goal of your mission will [still] be achieved. For that deacon, who asked you to come to Rome, will bring about few or none of the things he promised you. For that reason, I want you to come with me and to pay careful attention to the things I am about to reveal and describe to you."

Then grasping him by the hand, which is how it seemed to him, he made him ascend with him to the peak of an extremely high mountain. When they stood on the summit together, he said: "Turn to the east and look down upon the landscape before your eyes!" When he had done that and had seen the landscape [the figure] had mentioned, he saw buildings of immense size rising up there like some great city. When he was asked if he knew what that was, he answered that he did not. Then [the figure] said, "That is Rome you see." He also added: "Direct your gaze to the more distant parts of the city and see if any church is visible to you there." And when he had said that, [Reginbald] did [in fact] see a certain church, and [his guide] said: "Go and tell Ratleig that in the church you just saw is hidden the very thing that he should carry to his lord. Let him strive to acquire it as soon as possible and then return to his lord." When he said that none of his companions would believe an account of this sort, [his guide] answered, saying: "You know that everyone making this journey with you is aware that you have struggled with a tertian fever for many days [now] and that you have not yet been released from it." He said: "It is just as you say." His [guide] said, "For that reason, I wish [to provide] a sign to you and to those to whom you will recount what I have said, for from this [very] hour you will be so cured, by the mercy of God, from the fever that has gripped you until now, that it will no longer bother you on this journey." [Reginbald] awoke at these words, and made sure to recount everything he thought he had seen and heard to Ratleig. When Ratleig had revealed these things to the priest traveling with him, it seemed [prudent] to both of them to accept [as true] the experience of the dream if [Reginbald regained] his health as promised. On that very day, according to the usual nature of the fever he was suffering from, the one who had seen the dream should have become feverish [again]. But [the dream] was shown to have been a true revelation rather than a vain illusion, since he perceived no sign of the usual fever in his body on that day or on the ones that followed. Thus, they came to believe in the vision and [now] had no faith in the promises of the deacon [Deusdona].

3. When they arrived in Rome, they took up residence near the church of the blessed Apostle Peter that is called [St-Peter] in Chains, in the house of the very deacon with whom they had come. They stayed with him for some time, waiting for him to fulfill his promises. But that man, like those not able to carry out their promises, concealed his inability by procrastinating. Finally, they spoke to him and asked him why he wished to deceive them like that. At the same time they asked him not to detain them any longer by trickery or by delaying their return home with false hopes. When he had heard them out, and realized that he could now no longer take advantage of them with cunning of this sort, he first let my notary know that he could not [at present] obtain the relics I had been promised, because his brother, to whom he had entrusted his house and all his possessions while he was away, had left for Benevento on business and he had no idea when he would return. He had given him those relics to watch over, along with his other moveable property, but he was entirely unable to determine what he had done with them, since he had not found them in the house. Hence he did [not] see what he could do, since there remained nothing on his part that he could hope for.

After he said that to my notary, [Ratleig] complained that he had been deceived and badly treated by him. I do not know with what empty and meaningless words [Deusdona] spoke to Hilduin's priest, [but] he sent him away filled with little hope. The very next day, when he saw how sad they were, he urged them all to come with him to the saints' cemeteries, for it seemed to him that something could be discovered there that would satisfy their desires, and that there was no need for them to go home empty-handed. Since this plan appealed to them, they wanted to begin what he had urged them to do as soon as possible, [but] in his usual manner he neglected the matter and threw those men, whose spirits had been high a short while before, into such a state of despair by this postponement, that they gave up on [Deusdona] and resolved to return home, even though their business had not been accomplished.

4. But my notary, recalling the dream his servant had seen, began to press his partner [the priest Hunus] to go [with him] to the cemeteries without their host. [Deusdona had] promised that he wanted to take them there to see those [cemeteries]. Thus, after they had found and hired a guide to the [holy] places, they first traveled three miles outside the city to the church of the blessed martyr Tiburtius on the Via Labicana. There they investigated the tomb of the martyr with as much care as they could, and cautiously inspected whether it could be opened in such a way that others would not detect [it]. Then they descended into the crypt connected to the same church, in which

the bodies of the blessed martyrs of Christ, Marcellinus and Peter, were entombed. After they had also examined the condition of this monument, they departed. They thought that they could hide their activity from their host, but it turned out otherwise than they supposed. Word of their activity quickly reached him, though they were unsure how. Since [Deusdona] was worried that they might achieve their goal without him, he was determined to thwart their plan and so rushed to them. He spoke to them seductively and advised them that, since he had a complete and detailed knowledge of those holy places, they should visit them together and, if God chose to answer their prayers, they would do [together and] as agreed upon by all whatever they thought they needed to do. They gave in to his plan and together set a time for carrying out [this business].

Then, after a fast of three days, they traveled by night to that place without any Roman citizens noticing them. Once in the church of St. Tiburtius, they first tried to open the altar under which it was believed his holy body was located. But the strenuous nature of the job they had started foiled their plan, for the monument was constructed of extremely hard marble and easily resisted the bare hands of those trying to open it. Therefore, they abandoned the tomb of that martyr and descended to the tomb of the blessed Marcellinus and Peter. There, once they had called on our Lord Jesus Christ [for help] and had adored the holy martyrs, they were able to lift the tombstone from its place covering the top of the sepulcher. Once it had been lifted off, they saw the most sacred body of Saint Marcellinus set in the upper part of that sepulcher and a marble tablet placed near his head. It contained an inscription clearly indicating which martyr's limbs lay there. They lifted up the body, treating it, as was proper, with the greatest reverence. After they had wrapped it in a clean linen shroud, they handed it over to the deacon [Deusdona] to carry and hold for them. Then they put the tombstone back into place, so that no trace of the body's removal would remain, and they returned to their dwelling place in Rome. The deacon, however, asserted that he could and would keep the body of the most holy martyr, which he had received, in that house where he lived, [which was located] near the church of the blessed Apostle Peter that is called [St. Peter] in Chains. He entrusted it to the care of his own brother Luniso. [Deusdona] thought that this [relic] would satisfy my notary [and so] began to urge him to return to his own country, now that he had obtained the body of the blessed Marcellinus.

5. But [Ratleig] was contemplating and considering something very different. For, as he told me later, it seemed wrong to him to return home with only the body of the blessed Marcellinus. [Indeed] it would almost be a crime for the body of the blessed martyr Peter, who had been his companion in death and who had for more than five hundred years rested with him in the

same sepulcher, to remain there after his [friend] had left. Once this thought had occurred to him, his mind labored under such great anxiety and torment that he could neither eat nor sleep with any pleasure until the martyrs' bodies were joined together again on the trip they were about to make far from home, just as they had been joined together in death and in their tomb. He was in great doubt, however, about how this [reunification of the relics] could be achieved. For he realized that he could not find any Roman to help him in this affair, nor in fact was there [a Roman] to whom he dared reveal his secret thoughts. While wrestling with this worry in his heart, he happened to meet a foreign monk by the name of Basil who two years before had traveled from Constantinople to Rome. He resided in Rome with four of his students on the Palatine hill in a house occupied by other Greek [monks]. [Ratleig] went to him and revealed the [nature of the] anxiety troubling him. Then, encouraged by [the monk's] advice and confident of his prayers, he discovered such strength in his own heart that he was determined to attempt the deed as soon as he could, despite the danger to himself. He sent for his partner, Hilduin's priest, and suggested to him that they should return in secret to the church of the blessed Tiburtius, just as they had before, and try once again to open the tomb in which the body of the martyr was thought to be buried. This plan pleased [them] and [so], in the company of the servants they had brought with them [to Rome], they set out secretly at night. Their host had no idea where they were going. After this band had come to that place and prayed for success in their mission before the doors of the church, they entered. The group [then] split up. The priest stayed with some of them to search for the body of the blessed Tiburtius in his church. Ratleig [descended] with the rest into the crypt connected to the church and approached the body of the blessed Peter. They opened the sepulcher with no trouble and [Ratleig] removed the sacred limbs of the holy martyr without any resistance and carefully placed the recovered [bones] on the silk cushion he had prepared for this purpose.

In the meantime, the priest who was looking for the body of the blessed Tiburtius had expended a great deal of energy without success. When he saw that he could accomplish nothing [there], he abandoned his efforts and descended into the crypt [to join] Ratleig. He started to ask him what he should do. [Ratleig] answered that he thought that the relics of Saint Tiburtius had [already] been found, and showed him what he meant by this. Not long before the priest had joined him in the crypt, he had discovered [something] in the very tomb in which the sacred bodies of the saints Marcellinus and Peter lay. For a hole, which was round in shape, almost three feet deep and one foot wide, had been excavated there and a substantial quantity of fine dust had been stored in it. It seemed to both of them that this dust could have been left there by the body of the blessed Tiburtius, if his bones had been removed from there. Perhaps, [at one time] his body had been placed in that tomb between the blessed Marcellinus and Peter to make it more difficult to discover. They agreed that the priest should collect that dust and take it away as the relics of the blessed Tiburtius. When they had settled and arranged things in this way, they returned to their dwelling with the objects they had discovered.

6. After this, Ratleig spoke to his host and asked him to return the sacred ashes of the blessed Marcellinus that he had entrusted to his care. He also requested that, since he wished to return to his own country, that [Deusdona] not detain him with any unnecessary delay. He not only restored immediately what was demanded, but also presented [Ratleig with] a substantial quantity of saints' relics collected together in a parcel that was supposed to be carried to me. When he was asked the names of these saints, he said that he would supply them to me after he had visited me. Nevertheless, he advised [Ratleig] that these relics should be cherished with the same veneration as the other relics of the holy martyrs, since they were worthy of the same respect before God as the blessed Marcellinus and Peter, and that I would realize this as soon as I knew their names. [Ratleig] accepted the gift he was offered and, as he had agreed, placed it alongside the bodies of the holy martyrs. After hitting upon a plan with his host [for secreting away the relics], he arranged for that sacred and deeply desired treasure to be sealed and hidden in chests and for them to be carried as far as Pavia by Luniso, [Deusdona's] brother, whom I mentioned before, and also by Hilduin's priest with whom he had come. [Ratleig] himself stayed with his host in Rome, waiting and listening for seven consecutive days to determine whether any news of the removal of the bodies of the saints had come to the attention of the people [of Rome]. After he observed that no mention was made of this deed by any stranger and he judged that this business was still unknown, he started out after those whom he had sent in advance and took along his host [Deusdona]. They found them awaiting their arrival in Pavia in the church of the blessed John the Baptist that is commonly called Domnanae and that was then under my possession through a benefice of the kings [Louis and Lothar]. They too [Ratleig and company] decided to stop there for a few days, in order to give the horses on which they were riding a rest and to ready themselves for the longer journey ahead.

7. During this delay, a rumor arose that representatives of the holy Roman church, sent by the pope to the emperor, would shortly arrive there. Since [Ratleig and company] feared that, if they were found there when [the papal party] arrived, they might experience some inconvenience or even some obstacle [to their return], they decided that some of their party by leaving at

once could depart [with the relics] before their arrival. The rest of the party, [however], would remain there and after the business they were concerned about had been carefully investigated and those representatives [of the pope] had departed, they would hurry to follow their companions, whom they had sent on in advance. After they had agreed upon [this plan] among themselves, Deusdona and Hilduin's priest departed before the representatives from Rome arrived. They traveled with as much speed as they could to Soissons, where Hilduin was believed to be. But Ratleig stayed in Pavia with the treasure he was holding, waiting for the representatives of the Apostolic See to come and go, so that when they had crossed the Alps he could make his own way with more safety. Still he feared that Hilduin's priest, who had gone ahead with Deusdona and who had a full and complete knowledge of everything they had done and decided, and who seemed so cunning and slimy, had probably plotted to place some obstacle for him along the route by which he had chosen to travel. [So Ratleig] decided to travel by a different route. First he sent the servant of my steward Ascolf to me with a letter apprising me of his own return and of the treasure that he had discovered with divine assistance and was [now] carrying to me. After calculating the number of stops made ready for the [other party], he thought that they must have already crossed the Alps and [so] he left Pavia and reached St. Maurice in six days [a distance of approximately 240 kms or 150 miles]. There he purchased the things he needed [to construct a bier] and placed the sacred bodies, which were enclosed in a reliquary, upon the bier. From that point on, and with the help of the people flocking to them, he began to carry the relics publicly and openly.

8. When, however, he had gone by that place known as the Head of Lake [that is, Villeneuve in Switzerland], he reached the point where the way leading into Francia splits into two. He took the path to the right and came via the territory of the Alemannians to Solothurn, a town of the Burgundians. There he encountered the people I had sent from Maastricht to meet him after word of his return had reached me. For when the letter of my notary was brought to me by my steward's servant, the one I mentioned before, I was at the monastery of St. Bavo on the Scheldt River. After reading that letter I learned about the approach of the saints and I immediately ordered a member of my household to go to Maastricht to collect priests, other clergymen, and also laymen there, and then to hasten to meet the oncoming saints at the first possible place. With no delay, he and the group he brought with him met up in a few days with those who were carrying the saints at the place I mentioned above [Solothurn]. They joined forces at once and were accompanied from that point on by an ever increasing crowd of chanting people. Soon they came, to the great joy of everyone, to the city of Argentoratus, which is now called Strasbourg. From there they sailed down the Rhine until they

came to a place called Portus [the port at Sandhofen] where they disembarked on the eastern shore of the river, and, after a trip lasting five days and with a great crowd of people reveling in the praise of God they came to that place called Michelstadt. It lies in the German forest known today as Odenwald and is located about six leagues from the Main River. In that place they found the church I had recently built, but had still not dedicated, and they carried those sacred ashes into it and deposited them as though they were destined to stay there forever.

9. When that news reached me, I immediately hurried to that place as quickly as I could. Three days after my arrival, at the end of the evening service, a certain servant of Ratleig, who was acting on his [master's] orders, remained alone in the church, which was empty and had its doors closed. He took up a position on a small stool next to those holy bodies, as though he would keep watch [over them]. Suddenly he fell asleep and seemed to see two doves fly through a choir window on the right side [of the church] and come to rest on the top of the bier above the saints' bodies. One of the doves appeared to be entirely white, the other to be variously colored grey and white. After they had walked back and forth on the top [of that bier] for a long time and had made again and again the cooing sound normally made by doves, as if they were talking to each other, they [finally] flew out through the same window and were not to be seen [any more]. Then, all at once, a voice spoke above the servant's head: "Go and tell Ratleig to announce to his master [Einhard] that these holy martyrs of his do not want their bodies to rest in this place, because they have selected another place to which they intend to move very soon." He could not see the one who spoke in this way, but when the sound stopped he awoke. Now awake, he told Ratleig, who had returned to the church, what he had seen. [Ratleig] was anxious to relate to me the very next day, as soon as he could see me, what his servant had reported to him. For my part, although I did not dare to spurn the sacred secret of this vision, I nevertheless decided to await evidence of some more certain sign [of its truth]. In the meantime I arranged for those sacred ashes to be removed from the linen shroud in which they had been bound up and carried and to be sewn up in new silk cushions. Upon inspecting them, I noticed that the relics of the blessed Marcellinus were smaller in quantity than those of Saint Peter. I thought that [perhaps Saint Marcellinus] had been of smaller size than Saint Peter in the stature of his body. But the discovery of a theft later on proved that this was not so. Where, when, by whom, and how this theft was committed and [finally] uncovered I shall describe at the proper time. For now the sequence of the story as I have begun to relate it must be laid out and consistently followed.

10. After I had inspected that great and wonderful treasure, which was

more valuable than gold, the reliquary in which it was held began to displease me a great deal, because of the poorness of the material out of which it was made. I wanted to improve it, [and so] one day at the end of the evening service I directed one of the sacristans to find out for me the dimensions of the reliquary as measured by a ruler. When he was about to do this he lit a candle and raised the cloth covering the reliquary; then he noticed that the reliquary was dripping all over in an amazing fashion with a bloody liquid. Frightened by the strangeness of this phenomenon, he immediately made sure to tell me what he had seen. I went there at once with the priests who were present and I [too] with wonder observed that awesome and true miracle. For just as columns, tiles, and marble statues commonly sweat and drip when rain is coming on, so that reliquary containing those most sacred bodies was drenched with blood and was dripping all over. The unusual nature of this miracle, which had never been heard of before, terrified us. Thus, we devised a plan and decided to spend three days fasting and praying, in order to be worthy of learning by a divine revelation what that great and ineffable sign meant and what it wanted done. When the three days of fasting had passed and twilight was coming on, that liquid of frightening blood suddenly began to dry up. It was amazing, but that liquid, which had dripped for seven straight days without stopping like some incessant stream, dried up so quickly in a few hours that when the bell called us to the night service, for it was Sunday and we celebrated before dawn, and we entered the church, no trace of blood could still be found on the reliquary. But I ordered that the linen cloth hanging around the reliquary, which had been splashed with that liquid and so was stained with bloody spots, should be saved. To this day considerable evidence of that unique portent remains on those linens. Indeed, it is agreed that that liquid had a somewhat salty taste similar to that of tears and had the consistency of water, but that it possessed the color of real blood.

11. On that same night, in a dream, one of our servants by the name of Roland saw two young men standing at his side. They commanded him, as he himself reported, to tell me many things about the necessity of translating the bodies of the saints. They revealed to him both to what place and how this transfer ought to take place. They menaced him in frightening ways, demanding that this must be announced to me at once. As soon as he could, he carefully told me everything that he had been ordered to tell me. When I had learned of these things, I was very troubled and began to wonder what I should do. Should I again order fasts and prayers and should God once again be asked to resolve my doubt? Or should I seek out some individual serving God with perfect devotion, to whom I could reveal the worry in my heart and the plaintive nature of my troubles, and whom I could ask to

pray to God to reveal the meaning of this thing to us? But where and when could I find such a servant of the Lord Christ, particularly in this region? For although it was known that some monasteries had been founded not far from us, nevertheless, because of the crude regulation of [religious] life in those places, there was no one, or few men, about whose holiness anything, even the slightest rumor, was spoken. In the meantime, while I was troubled by these worries and had prayed for the intercession of the holy martyrs and had eagerly advised everyone around me to do the same, it happened that for twelve straight days no night passed in which it was not revealed in dreams to one, two, or even three of our companions that the bodies of the saints should be transferred from that place [Michelstadt] to another.

On the last night, a certain man in the dress of a priest, who was distinguished by the venerable whiteness of his hair and who was dressed all in white, appeared in a vision to a certain priest from our church by the name of Hiltfrid. He himself reported that [this man] addressed him in words like these: "Why is Einhard so hard-hearted and so stubborn that he refuses to believe these many revelations and supposes that he should scorn these many warnings sent to him from heaven? Go and tell him that what the blessed martyrs want done with their bodies cannot remain undone, even though until now he has put off satisfying their wishes in this matter. But let him now hurry, if he does not want the reward for this deed to pass to another, to fulfill their command and not fail to transport their bodies to the place they have selected."

12. After these and other warnings of various kinds had been brought to my attention, it seemed to me that the translation of the sacred ashes should not be postponed any longer. And so, after we had devised a plan, I decided to try to achieve [the transfer] as quickly as possible. Therefore, after everything that seemed necessary for transporting [the relics] was rapidly and with greatest care readied, we lifted up that sacred and priceless treasure at dawn after the completion of the morning Mass and started on our way. There was great sadness and grief among those who were to remain behind [at Michelstadt], as we started on our journey. As we began to carry [the relics] we were accompanied by a throng of poor people, who had gathered there from one place or another at that time to receive charity. The people who lived nearby were entirely ignorant about what we were doing. The sky was full of dark clouds that could soon turn into a heavy rain unless divine power prevented it. Indeed, it [had] rained so hard without stopping the [previous] night, that it had almost not seemed possible for us to begin our journey that day. But that doubt of ours sprang from the weakness of our faith, for divine grace, because of the saints' merits, arranged something very different from what we had expected. We found that the way through which we were

traveling had been changed into another condition than the anticipated one. For we found that there was little mud and that the streams that usually rise after so much and such steady rain as there had been that night had hardly risen at all. When we left the forest and approached the nearest villages, we were intercepted by constant crowds of people praising God. These people accompanied us for a distance of almost eight leagues. They were committed to helping me and my party carry the sacred burden and they actively joined with us in singing divine praises.

13. But when we saw that we could not reach our destination that day, we stopped at a village called Ostheim, which we could see from the road. With night now falling, we carried those holy bodies into the church of St. Martin located in that village. While our companions were left there to act as guards [of the relics], I and a few others hurried on toward our final destination. During the night, I prepared those things that ritual stipulates for the reception of saints' bodies.

But a partially paralyzed nun by the name of Ruodlang was brought to the church in which we had left that very holy treasure. She belonged to the convent of Mosbach that lies about one league from that church and had been brought there on a cart by her friends and relatives. After she had spent the entire night along with others awake and praying beside the bier of the saints, health was restored to all her limbs. With no one helping her or propping her up in any way, she walked the next day on her own feet all the way back to the place she had come from.

14. Now we rose at daybreak and went out to meet our approaching companions. We had with us a huge throng of our neighbors, who were excited by the rumor of the arrival of the saints. For this reason, they had gathered before our [church] doors at the first light of dawn, in order to travel out with us to meet the saints. We encountered them at the spot where the small river Gersprinz flows into the Main River [near Aschaffenburg]. From there we traveled on together and, praising in unison the mercy of our Lord Jesus Christ, we carried, to the great happiness and joy of all who were there, the sacred remains of the most blessed martyrs to Upper Mulinheim [later renamed Seligenstadt], for that is how that place is called in our day. But, because a great throng of people preceded us and had blocked every way [forward], we were unable to reach the church or to carry the bier into it. And so in a nearby field, which was on higher ground, we erected an altar in the open air. After depositing the bier behind the altar, we celebrated the solemn rights of the Mass. When the service was finished and the crowd had gone home, we carried those most sacred bodies into the church [as] specified by the blessed martyrs [themselves]. There we placed the bier beside the altar and celebrated the Mass once again.

While the Mass was being celebrated there, a boy about fifteen years old by the name of Daniel, from the Portian region, who had come there with other poor people to beg and who was so bent over that if he did not lay on his back he could not see the sky, approached the bier. Suddenly he collapsed as if he had been struck by someone. After he had lain there a long time like someone sleeping, all his limbs were made straight and he regained the strength of his muscles. He got up before our eyes and was healthy. This happened on the sixteenth [day before the] Kalends of February [17 January 828] and the light that day was so great and so clear that it rivaled the brilliance of the summer sun and the air was so calm and gentle that it seemed, along with the warming sunshine, milder than spring.

15. The next day [18 January] we placed the sacred bodies of the blessed martyrs, now enclosed in a new reliquary, in the apse of the church, and, as is the practice in Francia, we erected over it a wooden structure and, in order to beautify it, covered it with linen and silk cloth. Beside it, we placed an altar and erected on either side the two standards of the Lord's passion that had been carried before the bier on its journey. I tried within the extent of my limited means to make that place suitable and appropriate for the celebration of divine services. Clerics were appointed to keep permanent watch there and to devote themselves constantly and willingly to chanting the praises of the Lord. These men were summoned [to this task] not just by me, but by a royal charter that reached me on the road. The Lord made my journey a successful one and I returned to the palace [at Aachen] in an extremely joyful spirit.

Book Two

1. Quite a few days later after arriving at court, I went to the palace early one morning, since it was the habit of courtiers to rise very early. After entering, I found Hilduin there, of whom I had spoken in the previous book. He was sitting before the doors of the royal bedchamber waiting for the ruler to come out. After greeting him in the usual way, I asked him to get up and come over to a certain window with me, from which one could look [down] into the lower parts of the palace. Standing side by side while leaning on the window, we spoke with great wonder of the translation of the holy martyrs Marcellinus and Peter and also about the miracle revealed by the stream of blood with which, as I recorded, their reliquary sweated for seven days. When we had reached that point in our conversation where the subject of the garments found with their bodies was raised, I observed that the garment of the blessed Marcellinus was remarkably fine. [Hilduin], like one who had observed the same thing I had, responded that I had spoken the truth about

that garment. I was astonished and surprised at this, [and so] I began to ask him how he had acquired his knowledge of garments he had never seen. He stared at me, but remained silent for a time. Then he said, "I suppose it would be better for you to hear this from me, since [even] if I don't tell you, you will soon learn of it from others [anyway]. I myself should be the direct betrayer of this [news], since should anyone else betray it, he would not report [it to you] as directly [as I can]. Nor, indeed, could he [report it], since it is only natural that no one can tell the whole truth about something if he gained his knowledge of it not by himself, but from the stories told by others. Thus, I am counting on your good faith as to how you will act toward me after you have heard from me the whole truth about this incident." When I had responded briefly that I would not act other than as we had agreed, he said: "That priest, who traveled to Rome on my orders to bring back the relics of the blessed Tiburtius, discovered that he could not accomplish the goal for which he had come. So, after your notary had taken up the relics of the holy martyrs we have been talking about and had decided to return home, [Hunus] devised a plan with him whereby [Ratleig] would remain in Rome for a short time. He himself and Luniso, Deusdona's brother, along with the men who were assigned to carry those sacred ashes would proceed to Pavia and wait there for the arrival of [Ratleig] and Deusdona. This agreement suited both of them, and so, while [Ratleig and Deusdona] remained in Rome, my priest along with Luniso and the servants carrying the relics started out for Pavia. After they arrived there, they placed the cases containing the sacred ashes behind the altar. These were watched with constant attention by vigilant clerics and laymen. But one night while the priest himself was on watch along with others in the church, it happened, as he himself maintains, that around the middle of the night sleep gradually stole over every single person who had gathered in the church to guard [the relics], except the priest. Then the thought occurred to him that it was unlikely that sleep would have so suddenly overcome so many people without some powerful cause. He thought that he should seize the opportunity offered [to him] and so he arose and by candlelight proceeded quietly to the cases [containing the relics]. Then he burned the strings of the seals with the candle's flame and hurriedly opened the cases without [using] a key. He removed what seemed to him a [moderate] portion of each body and [then] he refastened the seals with the ends of the burned strings as though they were intact. Since no one was aware of his action, he returned to his place. Later on, after he had returned to me, he presented me with the saints' relics he had removed by this theft. At first he claimed that they were not the relics of Saint Marcellinus or Peter, but of Saint Tiburtius. Then, although I don't know what he was afraid of, he spoke to me in secret and fully disclosed to which saints the relics belonged and also how he had acquired them. I am holding those collected relics honorably at St-Médard in a prominent place where they are cherished with great veneration by all the faithful. But whether it is right for us to keep them [or not] is for you to decide."

After I heard this, I recalled what I had heard from a certain host of mine on my recent trip to the palace. Among the other things he told me, he said, "Have you not heard the rumor about the holy martyrs Marcellinus and Peter that is spreading throughout this area?" When I said that I was unaware of it, he said, "Those coming from Saint Sebastian say that some priest of Abbot Hilduin traveled to Rome with your own notary. While they were returning from there and were sharing lodgings at a certain spot, all your people were overcome with drink and sleep and were entirely unaware of what happened. For [that priest] opened the cases containing the saints' bodies and removed them. When he returned [home], he delivered [the relics] to Hilduin, and now they are at St-Médard. Apparently little of the sacred dust was left in your own cases, the ones carried to you by your notary." When I had remembered this story and compared it to the one related by Hilduin, I was extremely upset, particularly since I have not as yet found a way to do away with that horrible rumor that was spread everywhere by the cunning of the devil or to drive it out of the hearts of the deceived masses. Nevertheless, I thought it best to ask Hilduin to restore to me what had been removed from my cases. After his voluntary confession, he could not deny that the relics had been brought to him and that he had received them. In fact I tried to bring about this [recovery] as quickly as I could. And although [Hilduin] was slightly more stubborn and difficult in agreeing to this than I might have wished, he was eventually won over by my persistent request. [Hilduin] had a little while before proclaimed that in this matter in particular he would submit to the judgment of no one, but he [finally] gave in to my censure.

2. In the meantime I sent a letter to Ratleig and Luniso, who were in the place [Seligenstadt] where I had deposited the bodies of the martyrs. I made sure to inform them of the sort of rumor about those holy martyrs that was spreading throughout most of Gaul. And I urged them in the strongest possible terms to ponder whether they could remember or identify some such event or something like those events that Hilduin claimed were committed on their journey by his priest. They immediately came to me at the palace and told a story very different from Hilduin's. They especially declared that everything that the priest had told Hilduin was false. After they had left Rome, there had never been an opportunity for that priest or for anyone else to commit a crime of that sort. But they agreed that the [theft] of the sacred ashes of the martyrs had occurred in another way, for it had happened in Rome at the house of Deusdona through the greed of Luniso and the

trickery of Hilduin's priest. For it had occurred during that time when the body of the blessed Marcellinus, after it had been lifted from its tomb, was being kept in the house of Deusdona. They said that it had happened in this way. That priest of Hilduin had been so thwarted in his hope of gaining the body of Saint Tiburtius, that he was determined, in order not to return to his lord with nothing, to acquire by fraud what he had not been able to acquire honorably. Since he knew that Luniso was poor and, consequently, greedy, [Hunus] approached him and offered him four gold coins and five silver pieces, [and so] lured him into committing this act of betrayal. After receiving the proffered money, [Luniso] opened the chest in which the body of the blessed Marcellinus had been laid and locked up by Deusdona, and he gave that worthless rascal [Hunus] permission, just as he had hoped he would, to take from it what he wanted. He was not moderate in his theft, for it seemed that he removed as much of the sacred ashes of the blessed martyr as a pint container could hold. That the theft was committed in this way, Luniso himself, who had engineered the scheme with the priest, confessed in tears and threw himself at my feet. With the truth of the matter now known, I ordered Ratleig and Luniso back to the place they had come from [that is, Seligenstadt].

3. After I had spoken with Hilduin and we had reached an agreement about when the sacred relics would be returned to me, I sent two clerics from my household, Hiltfrid and Filimar – one was a priest and the other a subdeacon – to Soissons to receive the relics. I sent along with them 100 gold coins as a gift to the place from which the relics were to be carried away. After [my men] had arrived on Palm Sunday [29 March 828] at the monastery of St-Médard, they stayed there for three days. Once they had received that incomparable treasure they had been sent [to retrieve], they returned to the palace as quickly as they could in the company of two monks from the same monastery. But they gave the relics not to me, but to Hilduin. When he received them, he arranged for them to be held in the chapel of his house, until after the many engagements of Easter [which fell on 5 April] were over and he would have the free time in which to show me what was to be returned before he [actually] returned it. When eight days or even more had passed after holy Easter and the king had left the palace to go hunting, Hilduin, according to what we had agreed, removed those relics from his oratory where they had been held, and carried them into the church of the Holy Mother of God [Charlemagne's chapel at Aachen], and set them down upon the altar. He arranged for me to be summoned to receive those relics. Then he opened the box containing the relics and showed them to me, so that I could see what it was that he was returning and what it was that I was receiving. Next he lifted up that same box from the altar and set it in my hands. Once a

fitting prayer had been given, he even took on the role of choirmaster and called upon clerics, who were skilled in singing psalms, to sing an appropriate antiphon for the praise of the martyrs. And so, with everyone singing, he followed us to the door of the church as we withdrew with that priceless treasure. Praising the mercy of God, we moved slowly from [the church] with crosses and candles [in front of us] to the chapel that had been crudely constructed in my house. I carried the sacred relics into that [chapel], since no other [suitable] place was available there.

4. But on that procession we made, as I said, from the church to my chapel, something of a miracle occurred that I don't think I should neglect to mention. For as we were leaving the church and singing with raised voices to our Lord God, a great and sweet smell filled that part of the city of Aachen that lies west of the church. Almost all the residents of that part [of the city] and also everyone who happened to be there for some reason or for some business were so divinely affected by that fragrance that they dropped the work they were doing and all quickly raced first to the church and, then, as if [by following] the smell, to my chapel, for they had heard that those relics had been carried there. A great crush of people who were both full of joy and wonder gathered within the walls [of my house]. Although a great part of the crowd that collected there didn't know what was happening, they were nevertheless filled with great excitement and together they praised the mercy of almighty God.

5. After the rumor had spread far and wide that the relics of the martyr, Saint Marcellinus, had been carried [into my chapel], a huge crowd [of people] constantly collected there. They came not only from the city of Aachen itself and the neighboring and nearby towns, but also from more distant places and districts. Indeed, there was no easy way for us to enter that chapel to celebrate a divine service except during the evening or night hours. Sick people were brought there from all parts and friends and relatives deposited those suffering from various illnesses near the walls of the chapel. You would have seen there that almost every kind of infirmity, affecting both sexes and people of all ages, was cured by means of the power of the Lord Christ and the merit of that most blessed martyr. Sight was restored to the blind, the ability to walk to the lame, hearing to the deaf, and speech to the speechless. Even the paralyzed and those who had completely lost control over their bodies were carried forward by the hands of strangers. Once cured, they returned home on their own [two] feet.

6. When Hilduin brought these things to the attention of the king, [Louis] at first planned, after he had returned to the palace, to come to my chapel, in which these [miracles] were occurring, to venerate the martyr. But he was stopped from doing that by Hilduin himself who suggested that [the king should instead] order the relics brought to the larger church [of St. Mary].

When they had been carried there, he venerated them and prayed humbly. After the solemn celebration of the Mass, he granted to the blessed martyrs, Marcellinus and Peter, a small estate named Ludolvesthorp [near Sinzig] located close to the River Ahr; it has fifteen homesteads and nine arpents [an arpent was 120 square feet] of vineyards. And the queen [Judith] presented a belt made of gold and jewels that weighs three pounds. After the conclusion of these events, the relics were returned to their own place, namely in my chapel, and there they stayed for forty days or more until the emperor left the palace to go hunting in the forest, as was his annual practice. After that, I too, after purchasing the things needed for our journey [to Seligenstadt], left the town of Aachen with the relics.

7. At the very point of our departure, however, a certain old woman well-known around the palace, who was around eighty years old and suffering from a tightening of her tendons, was cured in front of us. I learned from her own account that she had suffered from this affliction for fifty years and had managed to walk by crawling around like a four-legged animal on her hands and knees.

8. After that we began our journey and, thanks to the merits of the saints, we came at last on the sixth day, with the Lord's help, to the village of Mulinheim [Seligenstadt], where I had left the sacred ashes of the blessed martyrs when I had departed for court [in January]. I must report how much joy and happiness the arrival of those relics brought to the people living along [our] route, but it cannot be related or described in all its richness. Nevertheless, I must try to describe it, so that it not seem that something that brought forth so much praise of God was buried in silence because of my laziness. To begin with, I am anxious to report what I and many others remember having seen after we left the palace. A stream called the Wurm [which flows into the Ruhr] lies about two miles from the palace of Aachen and has a bridge across it. When we reached it, we stopped for a short time so that the crowd that had followed us all the way from the palace and now wanted to turn back might have an opportunity to pray. One of the men who was praying there approached the relics with another man and, turning to his companion, said, "For the love and honor of this saint, I release you from the debt you know you owe me." For he owed him, as that man admitted, half a pound of silver. Likewise, another man led a companion by the hand to the relics, and said, "You killed my father and for that reason we have been enemies. But now, for the love and honor of God and this saint, I want to end our feud and to make and enter into an agreement with you that henceforth we shall maintain a lasting friendship between us. Let this saint be a witness to the reconciliation we have promised each other and let him punish the first person tempted to destroy this peace."

9. At this point the crowd that had left the palace with us, after adoring and kissing the sacred relics and after shedding many tears, which they could not restrain because everyone was filled with so much joy, returned home. Then another crowd met us and these people joined us in singing the *Kyrie eleison* without stopping until we reached another place where we were overtaken by others also hurrying to meet us. Then, just as before, the [second] crowd said prayers and returned home. In this way, we were joined every day from dawn to dusk by crowds of people praising the Lord Christ, and, with the Lord watching over our journey, we traveled from the palace at Aachen to Mulinheim [Seligenstadt]. Then we placed those relics [of Marcellinus], which were stored in a bejeweled box, upon the altar behind which was the reliquary containing the [rest of the] sacred ashes of the martyrs.

10. The relics remained in that position until November [828], when, as I was getting ready to travel to the palace, I was warned by a vision not to leave there before I had rejoined those relics to the body from which they had been removed. But how it was revealed that this should be done must be related, since it was made manifest not only through a dream, where it normally occurs, but even through some signs and frightening incidents experienced by those guarding [the relics] that the blessed martyrs wanted their commands followed down to the last detail in this business.

11. One of the clerics assigned to stand guard in the church was a man by the name of Landulf. His bed was near the eastern door of the church and he was in charge of ringing the bell. [Once] he had risen as usual and had solemnly rung the bell as usual for the evening and morning services, but then with his duty done before dawn, he wished to go back to sleep. He closed the doors of the church and prostrated himself in prayer before the holy ashes of the martyrs. Then, as he himself claims, when he had begun to say the fiftieth Psalm, he heard close to him the sound of footsteps on the ground, as if a man was walking back and forth there. He was very afraid and raised himself up a little onto his knees and began to look all around, thinking that one of the poor had stayed behind after the doors had been closed and was [now] lurking in some corner of the church. When he realized that he was the only person inside the church, he kneeled down again in prayer and resumed the psalm that he had begun earlier. But before he could complete even one verse of it, the box containing the sacred relics of the blessed Marcellinus, which had been set upon the altar, suddenly began to shake and make such a loud noise that it was as if it had flown open after being struck by a hammer. Two of the church's doors, the western and the southern ones, also made a similar racket, as though someone was shaking and pounding them.

He was so terrified and shocked by this, not knowing what to do, that he got up from the altar and threw himself trembling upon his bed. Almost immediately he was overcome by sleep and saw a man whose face he didn't recognize standing beside him. He addressed him with words like these: "Is it the case," he said, "that Einhard wishes to rush so quickly to the palace that he may not first restore the relics of Saint Marcellinus, which he brought here, to the place from which they were removed?" When he answered that he did not know anything about this, he said, "Get up at dawn and command him on the authority of the martyrs not to dare to leave here or to go anywhere before he has returned those relics to their proper place." Startled from his sleep he arose and, as soon as he could, he saw me and urgently told me what he had been ordered to relate. Indeed, I did not think that a matter of this [importance] should be acted upon slowly, but rather I judged that what the saints had ordered must be carried out at once. In fact, on that very day I ordered the preparation of those things that seemed necessary [for the task]. On the following day, I delicately joined those sacred relics to the body from which they had been removed.

That the blessed martyrs were grateful for this is proved by the clear evidence of the following miracle. For the very next night, while we were solemnly seated in the church for the morning service, an old man, who was not able to walk, came forward with great difficulty to pray, crawling on his hands and knees. Before all of us and within an hour of entering the church he was so completely cured by God's power and the merits of the blessed martyrs that in fact he no longer required the support of a crutch in order to walk. He also stated that he had been deaf for five straight years, but that his hearing had been restored to him at the same time as his ability to walk.

After these events had transpired, I proceeded to court, as I said before I had intended to. I would spend the winter there thinking over these many events.

6. THE PILGRIM'S GUIDE TO ST. JAMES OF COMPOSTELLA

The importance of pilgrimage as an institution deriving from the cult of the saints can hardly be overestimated for its influence on medieval trade, communications, art, architecture, and spirituality. Most pilgrims probably were inspired by hopes of receiving a healing miracle at the saint's shrine, but pilgrimages were also undertaken in order to visit the holy places of the Bible, or from a desire to renounce the world, or as an act of expiation for sin, either one's own or another's. Compulsory pilgrimages were sometimes imposed on members of the clergy or nobility who were found guilty of serious crimes. Of course, many people also went on pilgrimage for less legitimate purposes: curiosity to see new places, a desire to enjoy the company of other travelers, or simply to escape the dullness of daily life. Pilgrim accounts range from simple logs and practical travel guides to literature of the highest imaginative order.

Among the most famous shrines in Europe was that of St. James the Great in Compostella ('the field of the star') in north-western Spain. As early as the sixth century, the tradition arose that the body of St. James was returned to Spain, where the Apostle was thought to have preached the Gospel. Then in the early ninth century a hermit claimed to have had a vision in which the tomb of the saint was revealed to him by a bright star. The local bishop, Theodomir, searched for the tomb on the strength of the hermit's vision and found it in the place indicated by the star; a church was built above it, a town grew up around it, and pilgrims began to arrive in great numbers. Later the shrine was linked with the legendary names of Charlemagne and Roland as the great bulwark of Christianity against the Mozarabic domination of Spain.

'The Pilgrim's Guide,' from which the following excerpt is taken, is found in the famous 'Codex Callixtinus,' a twelfth-century compilation of materials that promoted pilgrimage to Compostella. 'The Guide' is usually ascribed to Aimery Picaud, a French cleric from Poitou who may also have served as a papal chancellor. The detailed description of the four sanctioned routes to the shrine may appear unnecessary to modern readers, but it was a matter of some controversy in the Middle Ages. We tend to be more interested in the writer's lively concerns for the health and safety of travelers, including his racial prejudices. He is also very interested in the shrines encountered on the four routes, as demonstrated by his long lists of them and by his inclusion of a fully-fledged though dubious 'life,' omitted here, of St. Eutrope of Saintes.

Source: trans. James Hogarth, *The Pilgrim's Guide: A 12th-century Guide for the Pilgrim to St. James of Compostella* (London: Confraternity of St. James, 1992), pp. 3–88; abridged and repr. with permission.

1. *Of the Roads to St. James.*

There are four roads leading to St. James which join to form one road at Puente la Reina, in the territory of Spain. One runs by way of St. Giles [St-Gilles du Gard] and Montpellier and Toulouse and the Somport pass; another by St. Mary of Le Puy and St. Faith of Conques and St. Peter of Moissac; the third by St. Mary Magdalene of Vézelay and St. Leonard of Limousin [St-Léonard de Noblat] and the town of Perigueux; and the fourth by St. Martin of Tours and St. Hilary of Poitiers and St. John of Angély [St-Jean d'Angély] and St. Eutropius of Saintes and the town of Bordeaux.

The roads which go by St. Faith, by St. Leonard and by St. Martin join at Ostabat and after crossing the pass of Cize [through the Pyrenees] meet the road over the Somport pass at Puente la Reina; and from there a single road leads to St. James.

[*Chapters 2 and 3 list the stages and places encountered on the road "so that pilgrims setting out for St. James may be able to estimate the expenses involved in their journey."*]

4. *Of the World's Three Hospices.*

The Lord established in this world three columns most necessary for the support of the poor: the hospice in Jerusalem, the hospice of Mont-Joux [on the Great St. Bernard pass] and the hospice of Santa Cristina on the Somport pass. These hospices were sited in places where they were necessary: they are holy places, houses of God, places of refreshment for holy pilgrims, of rest for the needy, of comfort for the sick, of salvation for the dead, of help for the living. Those who built these most holy places will without doubt possess the kingdom of God.

5. *Of the Names of those who repaired the Road to St. James.*

These are the names of those who, in the time of Diego [Gelmirez] archbishop of St. James, and Alfonso, emperor of Spain and Galicia, and Pope Callistus, repaired the road to St. James, from Rabanal to Puertomarin, for the love of God and his apostle, before the year 1120, in the reign of Alfonso [I] of Aragon and Louis [VI] the Fat, king of France: Andrew, Roger, Avitus, Fortus, Arnold, Stephen and Peter, who rebuilt the bridge over the Mino which had been demolished by Queen Urraca. May the souls of these men and those who worked with them rest in eternal peace!

6. *Of the Good and the Bad Rivers on the Road to St. James.*

These are the rivers on the road to St. James from the Pass of Cize and the Somport pass. From the Somport pass there flows down a river of pure water, the Aragon, which irrigates Spain. From the Pass of Cize there flows a river of pure water which many call the Runa and which flows down towards Pamplona. At Puente la Reina there are both the Arga and the Runa. At a place called Lorca, to the east, there flows a stream known as the Salt River. Beware of drinking from it or of watering your horse in it, for this river brings death. On its banks, while we were going to St. James, we found two Navarrese sitting there sharpening their knives; for they are accustomed to flay pilgrims' horses which die after drinking the water. In answer to our question they lied, saying that the water was good and drinkable. Accordingly we watered our horses in the river, and at once two of them died and were forthwith skinned by the two men.

Through Estella flows the river Ega, the water of which is sweet, pure and excellent. At the village of Los Arcos is a stream which is death, and between Los Arcos and the first hospice beyond the village is another stream which is fatal to both horses and men who drink it. At the village of Torres del Rio, in Navarrese territory, is a river which also is fatal to horses and men, and there is another river that brings death at the village of Cuevas.

At Logrono is a large river called the Ebro, with pure water and an abundance of fish. All the rivers between Estella and Logrono have water which brings death to men and beasts who drink it, and the fish in these streams are likewise poisonous. Do not eat, in Spain or Galicia, the fish commonly known as *barbus* [barbel] or the one which the Poitevins call *alose* [shad] and the Italians *clipia,* or an eel or a tench: if you do you will assuredly die or fall sick. And anyone who eats any great quantity of these and does not fall sick must have a stronger constitution than other people or must have lived in the country for a long time; for all kinds of fish, beef and pork in Spain and Galicia make foreigners ill.

Those rivers which are sweet and good for drinking are the following: the Pisuerga, which flows at the Puente de Itero; the Carrion, at Carrion de los Condes; the Cea at Sahagun; the Elsa at Mansilla de las Mulas; the Porma, at the large bridge [the Puente de Villarente] between Mansilla and Leon, the Torio, which flows through Leon, below the Jewish quarter; the Bernesga, on the far side of Leon in the direction of Astorga; the Sil at Ponferrada, in a green valley; the Cua at Cacabelos; the Burbia at the bridge of Villafranca del Bierzo; the Valcarce, which flows down the valley of that name; the Mino at Puertomarin; and a river in wooded country two miles from the city of St. James, at a place called Lavacolla, in which French pilgrims traveling to

St. James are accustomed, for love of the apostle, to take off their clothes and cleanse not only their private parts but the whole of their body. The river Sar, which flows between the Mount of Joy [Monte del Gozo] and the city of St. James, is held to be clean; so too is the Sarela, which flows on the other side of the town, to the west.

I have described these rivers so that pilgrims going to St. James may take care to avoid drinking bad water and may choose water that is good for them and for their horses.

7. Of the Names of the Countries and the Characteristics of the Peoples on the Road to St. James.

Going to St. James on the Toulouse road we come first, after crossing the Garonne, into Gascony, and then, going over the Somport pass, enter Aragon and then Navarre, which extends as far as the bridge over the Arga [Puente la Rienna] and beyond. If, however, we take the road over the Pass of Cize we come, after Tours, into Poitou, a fertile and excellent region, full of all delights. The men of Poitou are strong and warlike, skilled in the use of bows and arrows and of lances in war, valiant in battle, swift runners, elegant in their attire, handsome of face, ready of tongue, generous and hospitable. Then comes Saintonge; and from there, after crossing an arm of the sea and the river Garonne, we come into the territory of Bordeaux, which has excellent wine and an abundance of fish but an uncouth manner of speech. The speech of Saintonge is also uncouth, but that of Bordeaux is more so.

Then, for travelers who are already tired, there is a three days' journey through the Landes of Bordeaux. This is a desolate country, lacking in everything: there is neither bread nor wine nor meat nor fish nor water nor any springs. There are few villages on this sandy plain, though it has honey, millet, panic [a kind of millet] and pigs in plenty. If you are going through the Landes in summer be sure to protect your face from the huge flies, called *guespe* [wasps] and *tavones* [horse flies], which are particularly abundant in this region. And if you do not watch your feet carefully you will sink up to your knees in the sea sand which is found everywhere here.

After passing through this region you come into Gascony, a land well supplied with white bread and excellent red wine, woods and meadows, rivers and springs of pure water. The Gascons are loud-mouthed, talkative, given to mockery, libidinous, drunken, greedy eaters, clad in rags and poverty stricken; but they are skilled fighters and notable for their hospitality to the poor. They take their meals without a table, sitting round the fire, and all drink out of the same cup. They eat and drink a great deal and are ill clad; nor do they scruple to sleep all together in a scanty litter of rotting straw, the servants along with the master and mistress.

Leaving this country, the road to St. James crosses two rivers near the village of St-Jean de Sorde, one on the right and the other on the left; one is called a *gave,* the other a river, and they must both be crossed by boat. Accursed be their boatmen! For although the rivers are quite narrow these men are in the habit of taking a piece of money for each person, rich or poor, whom they ferry across, and for a horse they exact four, unworthily and by force. Their boat is small, made from a single tree-trunk, ill-suited to carry horses; and so when you get into the boat you must take care not to fall into the water. You will do well to hold on to your horse's bridle and let it swim behind the boat. Nor should you go into a boat that has too many passengers, for if it is overloaded it will at once capsize.

Often, too, having taken their passengers' money, the boatmen take such a number of other pilgrims on board that the boat overturns and the pilgrims are drowned; and then the wicked boatmen are delighted and appropriate the possessions of the dead.

Then, round the pass of Cize is the Basque country with the town of Bayonne, on the coast to the north. Here a barbarous tongue is spoken; the country is wooded and hilly, short of bread, wine and all other foodstuffs, except only apples, cider and milk. In this country there are wicked toll-collectors – near the pass of Cize and at Ostabat and St-Jean and St-Michel-Pied-de Port – may they be accursed. They come out to meet pilgrims with two or three cudgels to exact tribute by improper use of force; and if any traveler refuses to give the money they demand they strike him with their cudgels and take the money, abusing him and rummaging in his very breeches. They are ruthless people, and their country is no less hostile, with its forests and its wildness; the ferocity of their aspect and the barbarousness of their language strike terror into the hearts of those who encounter them. Although they should levy tribute only on merchants they exact it unjustly from pilgrims and all travelers. When custom requires that the duty to be paid on a particular object is four or six pieces of money they charge eight or twelve – double the proper amount.

We urge and demand, therefore, that these toll-collectors, together with the king of Aragon and the other rich men who receive the proceeds of the tolls and all those who are in league with them, to wit Raymond de Soule, Vivien d'Aigremont and the Vicomte de St-Michel, with all their posterity, and also the ferrymen already mentioned and Arnauld de la Guigne, with his posterity, and the other lords of the two rivers, who unjustly receive the money collected by the ferrymen, and also the priests who, knowing what they do, admit them to confession and the Eucharist, celebrate divine service for them and receive them in church – we demand that all these men should be excommunicated until they have expiated their offences by a long and public penance and have moderated their demands for tribute, and that the sentence of excommunication should be made public not only in their own episcopal see but also in the basilica of St. James, in presence of the pilgrims. And if any prelate should pardon them, either from benevolence or for his own profit, may he be struck with the sword of anathema!

It should be said that the toll-collectors are not entitled to levy any kind of tribute on pilgrims and that the ferrymen are properly entitled to charge only an *obol* [half a penny] for taking over two men – that is, if they are rich – and for a horse a piece of money; for a poor man they may charge nothing at all. Moreover the ferrymen are required to have boats amply large enough to accommodate both men and horses.

Still in the Basque country, the road to St. James goes over a most lofty mountain known as the Portus Cisere tribute [Pass of Cize], so called either because it is the gateway of Spain or because necessary goods are transported over the pass from one country to the other. It is a journey of eight miles up to the pass and another eight down from it. The mountain is so high that it seems to touch the sky, and a man who has climbed it feels that he could indeed reach the sky with his hand. From the summit can be seen the Sea of Brittany and the Western Sea, and the bounds of the three countries of Castile, Aragon and France. On the highest point of the mountain is the place known as the Cross of Charles, because it was here that Charlemagne, advancing into Spain with his armies, cleared a passage with the aid of axes and picks and mattocks and other implements, set up the Lord's cross and, kneeling with his face turned towards Galicia, prayed to God and St. James. And so pilgrims are accustomed to kneel here in prayer, looking towards the country of St. James, and each then sets up a cross. Sometimes as many as a thousand crosses are to be seen here, and so the place is known as the first station for prayer on the road to St. James.

On this mountain, before Christianity was fully established in Spain, the impious Navarrese and the Basques were accustomed not only to rob pilgrims going to St. James but to ride them like asses and kill them. Near the mountain, to the north, is a valley known as the Valley of Charles [Valcarlos] in which Charlemagne was encamped with his armies when his warriors were killed at Roncesvalles. This is the road used by many pilgrims who do not wish to climb the mountain.

Below the pass on the other side of the mountain are the hospice and the church containing the rock which Roland, that most valiant hero, split from top to bottom with a triple stroke of his sword. Beyond this is Roncesvalles, scene of the great battle in which King Marsile [the Moslem king of Spain in the French poem *Chanson de Roland*], Roland, Oliver and forty thousand other warriors, both Christians and Saracens, were killed.

After this valley comes Navarre which is well supplied with bread and wine, milk and livestock. The Navarrese and the Basques resemble one another in appearance, diet, dress and language; but the Basques have a fairer complexion than the Navarrese. The Navarrese wear short black garments reaching only to the knee, after the manner of the Scots. Their shoes, which they call *lavarcas*, are made of hairy untanned leather; they are tied on with thongs, and cover only the sole of the foot, leaving the upper part bare. They wear dark-colored woollen cloaks, fringed like traveling cloaks, which reach to the elbow and are known as *saias*. Coarsely dressed, they also eat and drink coarsely: in Navarre the whole household – master and servant, mistress and maid – eat from the same pot, in which all the food is mixed together, using their hands instead of spoons, and drink from the same cup. Watching them eat, you are reminded of dogs or pigs greedily gulping down their food; and when you hear them speaking it is like the barking of dogs. Their language is utterly barbarous: they call God *Urcia*, the Mother of God *Andrea Maria*, bread *orgui*, wine *ardum*, meat *aragui*, fish *araign*, a house *echea*, the master of the house *iaona*, the mistress *Andrea*, a church *elicera*, the priest *belaterra* (which means 'good earth'), corn *gari*, water *uric*, the king *ereguia* and St. James *Jaona domne Jacue*.

This is a barbarous people, different from all other peoples in customs and in race, malignant, dark in color, ugly of face, debauched, perverse, faithless, dishonorable, corrupt, lustful, drunken, skilled in all forms of violence, fierce and savage, dishonest and false, impious and coarse, cruel and quarrelsome, incapable of any good impulses, past masters of all vices and iniquities. They resemble the Getae [the people who lived around the mouth of the Danube, and whose name was synonymous in Roman times for ferocity] and the Saracens in their malignance, and are in every way hostile to our French people. A Navarrese or a Basque will kill a Frenchman for a penny if he can. In some parts of the region, in Biscay and Alava, when the Navarrese are warming themselves, men show their private parts to women and women to men. The Navarrese fornicate shamelessly with their beasts, and it is said that a Navarrese will put a padlock on his she-mule and his mare lest another man should get at them. He also libidinously kisses the vulva of a woman or a she-mule.

The Navarrese, therefore, are condemned by all right-minded people. But they are good in battle, though not in besieging fortresses; and they are regular in the payment of tithes and accustomed to make offerings to the altar. Every day, when a Navarrese goes to church, he makes an offering to

God of bread, wine, corn or some other substance. Wherever a Navarrese or Basque goes he has a horn round his neck like a hunter and carries two or three javelins, which he calls *auconas*. When he goes into his house or returns there he whistles like a kite; and when he is hiding in secret places or in some solitary spot with robbery in mind and wants to summon his companions without attracting notice he hoots like an owl or howls like a wolf.

It is commonly said that the Basques are descended from the Scots; for they resemble them in customs and in appearance. Julius Caesar is said to have sent three peoples – the Nubians [perhaps the Numiani, another British tribe], the Scots, and the tailed men of Cornwall – into Spain to make war on the peoples of Spain who refused to pay him tribute, telling them to kill all males and to spare only the women. These peoples came to Spain by sea and after destroying their ships devastated the country by fire and sword, from Barcelona to Saragossa and from Bayonne to Mount Oca. They were unable to advance any further, for the Castilians united and drove them out of their territory. In their flight they came to the coastal mountains between Najera and Pamplona and Bayonne, on the seaward side in Biscay and Alava, where they settled down and built many fortresses. Having killed all the men, they took their wives by violence and had children by them, who later became known as Navarrese – the name being interpreted as *non verus* ['not true'], that is not engendered of a pure race or legitimate stock. The Navarrese also used to derive their name from a town called Naddaver [possibly Nadabar, in Ethiopia] in the country from which they originally came: a town which was converted to the Lord in early times by the preaching of Matthew, the apostle and evangelist. Leaving Navarre, the route runs through the forest of Oca and continues through Spanish territory – Castile and the Campos – in the direction of Burgos. This is a country full of treasures, of gold and silver, fortunate in producing fodder and sturdy horses and with an abundance of bread, wine, meat, fish, milk and honey. It is, however, lacking in trees and the people are wicked and vicious.

Then, after crossing the territory of Leon and going over the passes of Monte Irago [Foncebadon] and Cebrero, you come into Galicia, a well wooded and well watered region with rivers and meadows and fine orchards, excellent fruit and clear springs, but with few towns and villages or cultivated fields. There is little wheaten bread or wine but ample supplies of rye bread and cider, cattle and horses, milk, honey, and sea fish both large and small. The country is rich in gold, silver, cloths, animal furs from the forests, and other riches, as well as precious Saracen wares.

The Galicians are more like our French people in their customs than any other of the uncultivated races of Spain, but they have the reputation of being violent-tempered and quarrelsome.

8. Of the Bodies of Saints which rest on the Road to St. James and are to be visited by Pilgrims.

Pilgrims going to St. James by way of St-Gilles must in the first place pay honor to the body of the blessed Trophimus the Confessor in Arles [Trophime, first-century bishop, but not the one referred to by St. Paul]. St. Paul refers to him in his epistle to Timothy; he was consecrated as a bishop by Paul and sent by him to preach the Gospel in Arles for the first time. It was from this most clear spring, we are told by Pope Zosimus, that the whole of France received the waters of the faith. His feast is celebrated on 29th December.

Also to be visited in Arles is the body of the blessed Caesarius [the sixth-century archbishop of Arles], bishop and martyr, who instituted a Rule for nuns in that city. His feast is celebrated on 1st November. In the cemetery of Arles pilgrims should seek out the relics of the blessed bishop Honoratus [of Arles, d. 429], whose feast is celebrated on 16th January. In his venerable and magnificent basilica rests the body of the Blessed Genesius, that most precious martyr [d. Arles, 303 or 308]. In the village of Trinquetaille near Arles, between two arms of the Rhône, is a magnificent tall marble column, standing behind the church of St. Genesius, to which it is said he was tied by the faithless people before being beheaded; it is still stained red with his blood. Immediately after his execution the saint took his head and threw it into the Rhône; his body was carried down by the river to the basilica of St. Honoratus, where it was given honorable burial. His head floated down the river to the sea and was conveyed under angelic guidance to Cartagena in Spain, where it now gloriously rests, performing numerous miracles. The saint's feast is celebrated on 25th August.

The pilgrim must then visit the cemetery near Arles known as Aliscamps and, as the custom is, intercede for the dead with prayers, psalms and alms. The cemetery is a mile long and a mile wide, and in no other cemetery can be found so many and such large marble tombs. They are of different forms and bear ancient inscriptions in Latin script but in unintelligible language. The further you look the more sarcophagi you see. In this cemetery there are seven churches. If, in any one of them, a priest celebrates the Eucharist for the dead, or a layman has a mass said for them, or a clerk reads the Psalter, they will be sure on the day of resurrection before God to find these pious dead helping them to obtain salvation; for many are the holy martyrs and confessors who rest here, and whose souls dwell amid the joys of Paradise. Their memory is celebrated, according to custom, on the Monday after the Easter octave. A visit must also be paid, with a most attentive eye, to the venerable body of the blessed Aegidius the most pious confessor and abbot

[St. Giles, an eighth-century hermit and one of the most popular saints of the Middle Ages]; for this most blessed saint, famed in all the countries of the world, must be venerated by all, worthily honored by all and loved, invoked and supplicated by all. After the prophets and the apostles none among the blessed is worthier than he, none is more holy, none is more glorious, none is readier to help. It is he, more than any of the other saints, who comes most rapidly to the help of the needy and the afflicted and the suffering who call on his aid. What a fine and profitable act it is to visit his tomb! Anyone who prays to him with all his heart will assuredly be granted his help that very day. I have had personal experience of what I say: once in this saint's town I saw a man who, on the very day that he had invoked this blessed confessor, escaped from a house belonging to a cobbler named Peyrot just before it collapsed and was reduced to rubble. Who will spend most time at his place of burial? Who will worship God in his most holy basilica? Who will most frequently embrace his sarcophagus? Who will kiss his venerable altar or tell the story of his most pious life?

[*A detailed description of the shrine follows.*]

Such is the tomb of the blessed Aegidius, confessor, in which his venerable body rests with honor. May they blush with shame, those Hungarians who claim to have his body; may they be dismayed, those monks of Chamalières, who think they have his whole body; may they be confounded, those men of St-Seine who assert that they possess his head; may they be struck with fear, those Normans of Coutances who boast that they have his whole body; for his most holy bones, as many have borne witness, could not be removed from his own town. Certain men once attempted by fraud to carry off the venerable arm of the blessed confessor to distant lands, but were quite unable to remove it....

Those Burgundians and Germans who go to St. James by the Le Puy road should venerate the relics of the blessed Faith [Foy], virgin and martyr, whose soul, after her beheading on the hill town of Agen, was borne up to heaven in the form of a dove by choirs of angels and crowned with the laurels of immortality. When the blessed Caprasius [Caprais], bishop of Agen, heard this, while hiding in a cave to escape the rage of persecution, he found the courage to face martyrdom, hastened to the place where the blessed virgin had suffered and himself gained the palm of martyrdom, bearing himself most valiantly and even reproaching his executioners for their slowness.

Thereafter the most precious body of the blessed Faith, virgin and martyr, was honorably buried by Christians in the valley commonly known as Conques [in fact, her remains were stolen from Agen in the late ninth century]. Over her tomb was built a handsome basilica, in which the Rule of St. Benedict is strictly observed to this day for the glory of God. Many benefits are granted both to the sick and to those who are in good health. In front of the basilica is an excellent spring, the virtues of which are too great to be told. The saint's feast is celebrated on 6th October. Then, on the road to St. James by way of St-Léonard [de Noblat], the most holy body of the blessed Mary Magdalene is above all to be venerated [at Vézelay]. This is that glorious Mary who in the house of Simon the Leper watered the Savior's feet with her tears, wiped them with her hair, kissed them and anointed them with a precious ointment. Accordingly her many sins were forgiven her, for she had greatly loved Jesus Christ her redeemer, who loves all men. It was she who after the Lord's ascension left Jerusalem with the blessed Maximinus and other disciples of the Lord, sailed to Provence and landed at the port of Marseilles. She lived the life of a hermit in that country for some years and was then buried in Aix by Maximinus, who had become bishop of the town. Much later a sanctified monk named Badilo translated her most precious relics to Vézelay where they now rest in an honorable tomb. There a large and beautiful basilica and an abbey were built; there sinners have their faults remitted by God for love of the saint, the blind have their sight restored, the tongues of the dumb are loosed, the lame are cured of their lameness, those possessed by devils are delivered and ineffable benefits are granted to many of the faithful. The saint's feast is celebrated on 22nd July....

Pilgrims traveling on this road should also pay honor, on the banks of the Loire to the venerable body of the blessed Martin [of Tours], bishop and confessor, who gloriously brought three dead men back to life and is reported to have restored lepers, men possessed by devils, the sick, the lunatic and the demoniac, and sufferers from other diseases, to the health they desired. The shrine containing his most sacred remains, in the city of Tours, is resplendent with a profusion of gold, silver, and precious stones and is graced by numerous miracles. Over it a great and splendid basilica, in the likeness of the church of St. James, has been built. The sick come to it and are made well, the possessed are delivered, the blind see, the lame stand upright, all kinds of sickness are cured and all those who ask for the saint's intercession are fully satisfied. His glorious renown, therefore, is spread throughout the world in well merited eulogies, for the honor of Christ. His feast is celebrated on 11th November....

Also to be visited is the venerable head of the blessed John the Baptist, which was brought by certain religious men from Jerusalem to a place called Angély in Poitou. There a great and magnificent basilica was built and dedicated to him, and in this his most sacred head is venerated night and day by a choir of a hundred monks and has wrought countless miracles. While the head was being transported by sea and by land it gave many proofs of its miraculous power: on the sea it warded off numerous perils, and on land it brought dead men back to life. Accordingly it is believed to be indeed the head of the venerable Forerunner. It was found on 24th February in the time of the emperor Marcian, when the Forerunner first revealed to two monks the place where his head was concealed....

[*An account of the life and martyrdom of Eutropius of Saintes follows, and a continuing list of other saints to be honored on the way to St. James.*]

Finally, and above all, pilgrims are to visit and pay the greatest veneration to the most holy body of the blessed apostle James in the city of Compostella.

May the saints mentioned here and all the other saints of God intercede for us, through their merits and their prayers, with our Lord Jesus Christ, who lives and reigns with the Father and the Holy Ghost, God from eternity to eternity.

Amen....

9. *Of the body and the altar of St James.*

... So far we have spoken of the characteristics of the church: we must now consider the venerable altar of the apostle. In this venerable basilica, according to tradition, the revered body of the blessed James rests under the magnificent altar set up in his honor. It is enclosed in a marble tomb which lies within a fine vaulted sepulcher of admirable workmanship and fitting size. That the body is immutably fixed there we know from the evidence of St. Theodomir, bishop of the city, who discovered it and was unable to move it from the spot. May they blush for shame, therefore, those envious people beyond the mountains who claim to have some part of it or to possess relics of it [Toulouse, and a number of places in France and Italy claimed such possession]! For the body of the saint is here in its entirety – divinely illuminated by paradisiac carbuncles, constantly honored by divine fragrances, radiant in the light of celestial candles and devoutly attended by watching angels....

11. *Of the Reception to be given to Pilgrims of St. James.*

Pilgrims, whether poor or rich, returning from St. James or going there must be received with charity and compassion; for whosoever receives them and gives them hospitality has for his guest not only St. James but our Lord himself. As the Lord says in his Gospel, 'He that receiveth you receiveth me.' Many are those who have incurred the wrath of God because they would not take in the pilgrims of St. James and the needy.

A weaver in Nantua, a town between Geneva and Lyons, refused bread to a pilgrim of St. James who asked for it; and at once he saw his cloth fall to the ground, rent asunder. At Villeneuve a poor pilgrim of St. James asked for alms, for the love of God and the blessed James, from a woman who was keeping bread under hot ashes. She told him that she had no bread: whereupon the pilgrim said, 'May the bread that you have turn into stone!' The pilgrim had left the house and gone some distance on his way when the wicked woman went to take her bread out of the ashes and found a round stone in the place where the bread had been. Struck with remorse, she set out to look for the pilgrim, but could not find him.

At Poitiers two valiant French pilgrims, returning from St. James in great need, asked for hospitality, for the love of God and St. James, in the street running from the house of Jean Gautier to the church of St-Porchaire, but found none. Finally, at the last house in the street, by the church, they were taken in by a poor man; and that night, by the operation of divine vengeance, a fierce fire broke out and quickly destroyed the whole street, beginning with the house where they had first asked for hospitality and going right up to the house where they were taken in. Some thousand houses were destroyed, but the one where the servants of God were taken in was, by grace, spared.

Thus we learn that the pilgrims of St. James, whether rich or poor, should be given hospitality and a considerate reception.

Here ends the fourth book of the apostle St James. Glory be to him who has written it and to him who reads it.

7. ST. FRANCIS OF ASSISI: HIS CONVERSION AND STIGMATA

In the eleventh and twelfth centuries, increasing numbers of lay people were recognized as saints, and there was a growing awareness among people from many walks of life that it was possible to follow the way of perfection outside established ecclesiastical institutions. This movement had several aspects: the growth of lay initiatives, the rise of mysticism, increased opportunities for women to live spiritual lives, and a revival of the eremitical tradition. People looked back to the lives of the apostles, with their emphasis on poverty, manual labor, and care of the sick and the indigent, as well as to the lives of the desert fathers and mothers with their emphasis on withdrawal from society. The individualistic approach of the new hermits, mystics, and spiritual women gave rise both to suspicion and admiration, and to a number of efforts on the part of the Church to regulate them. The innovative directions also coincided with the centralization of canonization procedures in the Vatican, and thus many of the new lay 'saints,' lacking powerful supporters, received only local recognition.

One who certainly received both popular and official recognition – and who is arguably still the best-known medieval saint – is Francis of Assisi (1181-1226). The impact of his personality on the church and on popular spirituality was so great that no fewer than three 'lives' were authorized within forty years of his death. In addition to these and to some writings by Francis himself, there is a complex manuscript tradition comprising a large body of material by Francis's companions: most familiar is the collection compiled early in the fourteenth century and entitled 'The Little Flowers of St. Francis.'

The writer of the first 'life,' Thomas of Celano, had entered the Franciscan order in about 1215, and although he was not one of the saint's close companions, he may have known him personally. He was an elegant Latin stylist, given to using the kind of rhetorical ornamentation that modern readers find less appealing than his contemporaries did, and he was well versed in the standard forms of hagiography. Probably because of his scholarly reputation, he was commissioned by Pope Gregory IX to write the first 'life' at the time of Francis's canonization in 1228, two years after his death. Fifteen years later the Franciscan order asked him to write a second 'life' that would include further material collected by Francis's companions, presumably not available when the first 'life' was written. The following account of Francis's conversion and the founding of the Friars Minor (as the Franciscans were called) is taken from Thomas's first 'life.'

In 1256 the General Chapter of the Franciscan Order commissioned yet a third 'life' from their minister general, St. Bonaventure. His suppression of some material in the earlier ' lives' reflects the controversies that had developed both within the order, concerning Francis's intentions for his followers, and outside it, between the monastic orders, jealous of their ancient prerogatives, and the friars, eager to assert their new privileges. St. Bonaventure's 'life' of the saint was both an attempt to make peace among the factions and an assertion of what he felt to be the true spirit of the Order. The famous story of the stigmata (St. Francis's culminating mystical experience in which he received the marks of Christ's crucifixion imprinted in his own flesh) is included in all three 'lives,' but by the time St. Bonaventure wrote, it was more essential than ever to give a convincing version of this event, since its veracity was being called into question by the Order's critics. His account is given here following the excerpt from the first 'life.'

Sources: trans. Placid Hermann, *St. Francis of Assisi: First and Second Life of St. Francis by Thomas of Celano* (Chicago: Franciscan Herald Press, 1963), pp. 5-38, abridged; repr. with permission. BHL 3096. Trans. Benen Fahy, "Major and Minor Life of St. Francis with excerpts from other works by St. Bonaventure," in *St. Francis of Assisi: Writings and Early Biographies; English Omnibus of the Sources for the Life of St. Francis,* ed. Marion A. Habig (4th ed. rev.; Quincy, IL: Franciscan Press, 1991), pp. 729-35; repr. with permission. BHL 3107.

Thomas of Celano: How Francis lived in the world before his conversion.

I, I. In the city of Assisi, which lies at the edge of the Spoleto valley, there was a man by the name of Francis, who from his earliest years was brought up by his parents proud of spirit, in accordance with the vanity of the world; and imitating their wretched life and habits for a long time, he became even more vain and proud. For this very evil custom has grown up everywhere among those who are considered Christians in name, and this pernicious teaching has become so established and prescribed, as though by public law, that people seek to educate their children from the cradle on, very negligently and dissolutely. For, indeed, when they first begin to speak or stammer, children, just hardly born, are taught by signs and words to do certain wicked and detestable things; and when they come to be weaned, they are forced not only to speak but also to do certain things full of lust and wantonness. Impelled by a fear that is natural to their age, none of them dares to conduct himself in an upright manner, for if he were to do so he would be subjected to severe punishments. Therefore, a secular poet [Seneca] says well: "Because we have grown up amid the practices of our parents, we therefore pursue all evil things from our childhood on." This testimony is true, for so much the more injurious to their children are the desires of the parents, the more successfully they work out. But when the children have progressed a little in age, they always sink into worse deeds, following their own impulses. For from a corrupt root a corrupt tree will grow, and what has once become wickedly depraved can hardly ever be brought into harmony with the norms of uprightness. But when they begin to enter the portals of adolescence, how do you think they will turn out? Then, indeed, tossed about amid every kind of debauchery, they give themselves over completely to shameful practices, in as much as they are permitted to do as they please. For once they have become the slaves of sin by a voluntary servitude, they give over all their members to be instruments of wickedness; and showing forth in themselves nothing of the Christian religion either in their lives or in their conduct, they take refuge under the mere name of Christianity. These miserable people very often pretend that they have done even worse things than they have actually done, lest they seem more despicable the more innocent they are.

2. These are the wretched circumstances among which the man whom we venerate today as a saint, for he is truly a saint, lived in his youth; and almost up to the twenty-fifth year of his age, he squandered and wasted his time miserably. Indeed, he outdid all his contemporaries in vanities and he came to be a promoter of evil and was more abundantly zealous for all kinds of foolishness. He was the admiration of all and strove to outdo the rest in the pomp of vainglory, in jokes, in strange doings, in idle and useless talk, in songs, in soft and flowing garments, for he was very rich, not however avaricious but prodigal, not a hoarder of money but a squanderer of his possessions, not a cautious business man but a very unreliable steward. On the other hand, he was a very kindly person, easy and affable, even making himself foolish because of it; for because of these qualities many ran after him, doers of evil and promoters of crime. And thus overwhelmed by a host of evil companions, proud and high-minded, he walked about the streets of Babylon until the Lord looked down from heaven and for his own name's sake removed his wrath far off and for his praise bridled Francis lest he should perish. The hand of the Lord therefore came upon him and a change was wrought by the right hand of the most high, that through him an assurance might be granted to sinners that they had been restored to grace and that he might become an example to all of conversion to God.

How God touched the heart of Francis by sickness and by a vision.

3. For, indeed, while this man was still in the glow of youthful passion, and the age of wantonness was urging him on immoderately to fulfil the demands of youth; and while, not knowing how to restrain himself, he was stirred by the venom of the serpent of old, suddenly the divine vengeance, or, perhaps better, the divine unction, came upon him and sought first to recall his erring senses by visiting upon him mental distress and bodily suffering, according to the saying of the prophet: "Behold I will hedge up thy way with thorns and I will stop it up with a wall." Thus, worn down by a long illness, as man's stubbornness deserves when it can hardly be corrected except by punishments, he began to think of things other than he was used to thinking

upon. When he had recovered somewhat and had begun to walk about the house with the support of a cane to speed the recovery of his health, he went outside one day and began to look about at the surrounding landscape with great interest. But the beauty of the fields, the pleasantness of the vineyards, and whatever else was beautiful to look upon, could stir in him no delight. He wondered therefore at the sudden change that had come over him, and those who took delight in such things he considered very foolish.

4. From that day on, therefore, he began to despise himself and to hold in some contempt the things he had admired and loved before. But not fully or truly, for he was not yet freed from the cords of vanity nor had he shaken off from his neck the yoke of evil servitude. It is indeed very hard to give up things one is accustomed to, and things that once enter into the mind are not easily eradicated; the mind, even though it has been kept away from them for a long time, returns to the things it once learned; and by constant repetition vice generally becomes second nature. So Francis still tried to flee the hand of God, and, forgetting for a while his paternal correction, he thought, amid the smiles of prosperity, of the things of the world; and, ignorant of the counsel of God, he still looked forward to accomplishing great deeds of worldly glory and vanity. For a certain nobleman of the city of Assisi was preparing himself in no mean way with military arms, and, puffed up by a gust of vainglory, vowed that he would go to Apulia to increase his wealth and fame. Upon hearing this, Francis, who was flighty and not a little rash, arranged to go with him; he was inferior to him in nobility of birth, but superior in generosity, poorer in the matter of wealth, but more lavish in giving things away.

5. On a certain night, therefore, after he had given himself with all deliberation to the accomplishment of these things, and while, burning with desire, he longed greatly to set about the journey, he who had struck him with the rod of justice visited him in the sweetness of grace by means of a nocturnal vision; and because Francis was eager for glory, he enticed him and raised his spirits with a vision of the heights of glory. For it seemed to Francis that his whole home was filled with the trappings of war, namely, saddles, shields, lances, and other things; rejoicing greatly, he wondered silently within himself what this should mean. For he was not accustomed to see such things in his home, but rather piles of cloth to be sold. When, accordingly, he was not a little astonished at this sudden turn of events, the answer was given him that all these arms would belong to him and to his soldiers. When he awoke, he arose in the morning with a glad heart, and considering the vision an omen of great success, he felt sure that his journey to Apulia would come out well. He did not know what to say and he did not as yet recognize the task given him from heaven. Nevertheless, he might have understood that his interpretation of the vision was not correct, for while the vision bore

some resemblance to things pertaining to war, his heart was not filled with his usual happiness over such things. He had to use some force on himself to carry out his designs and to complete the proposed journey. It is indeed quite fitting that mention be made of arms in the beginning and it is quite opportune that arms should be offered to the soldier about to engage one strongly armed, that like another David he might free Israel from the long-standing reproach of its enemies in the name of the Lord God of hosts.

How, changed in mind but not in body, Francis spoke of the treasure he had found and of his spouse in allegory.

6. Changed, therefore, but in mind, not in body, he refused to go to Apulia and he strove to bend his own will to the will of God. Accordingly, he withdrew for a while from the bustle and the business of the world and tried to establish Jesus Christ dwelling within himself. Like a prudent business man, he hid the treasure he had found from the eyes of the deluded, and, having sold all his possessions, he tried to buy it secretly. Now since there was a certain man in the city of Assisi whom he loved more than any other because he was of the same age as the other, and since the great familiarity of their mutual affection led him to share his secrets with him, he often took him to remote places, places well-suited for counsel, telling him that he had found a certain precious and great treasure. This one rejoiced and, concerned about what he heard, he willingly accompanied Francis whenever he was asked. There was a certain grotto near the city where they frequently went and talked about this treasure. The man of God, who was already holy by reason of his holy purpose, would enter the grotto, while his companion would wait for him outside; and filled with a new and singular spirit, he would pray to his Father in secret. He wanted no one to know what he did within, and taking the occasion of the good to wisely conceal the better, he took counsel with God alone concerning his holy proposal. He prayed devoutly that the eternal and true God would direct his way and teach him to do his will. He bore the greatest sufferings in mind and was not able to rest until he should have completed in deed what he had conceived in his heart; various thoughts succeeded one another and their importunity disturbed him greatly. He was afire within himself with a divine fire and he was not able to hide outwardly the ardor of his mind; he repented that he had sinned so grievously and had offended the eyes of God's majesty, and neither the past evils nor those present gave him any delight. Still he had not as yet won full confidence that he would be able to guard himself against them in the future. Consequently, when he came out again to his companion, he was so exhausted with the strain, that one person seemed to have entered, and another to have come out.

7. One day, however, when he had begged for the mercy of God most earnestly, it was shown to him by God what he was to do. Accordingly, he was so filled with joy that he could not contain himself, and, though he did not want to, he uttered some things to the ears of men. But, though he could not keep silent because of the greatness of the joy that filled him, he nevertheless spoke cautiously and in an obscure manner. For, while he spoke to his special friend of a hidden treasure, as was said, he tried to speak to others only figuratively; he said that he did not want to go to Apulia, but he promised that he would do noble and great things in his native place. People thought he wished to take to himself a wife, and they asked him, saying: "Francis, do you wish to get married?" But he answered them, saying: "I shall take a more noble and more beautiful spouse than you have ever seen; she will surpass all others in beauty and will excel all others in wisdom." Indeed, the immaculate spouse of God is the true religion which he embraced; and the hidden treasure is the kingdom of heaven, which he sought with such great desire; for it was extremely necessary that the Gospel calling be fulfilled in him who was to be the minister of the Gospel in faith and in truth.

Francis sold all his goods and despised the money given him.

8. Behold, when the blessed servant of the Most High was thus disposed and strengthened by the Holy Spirit, now that the opportune time had come, he followed the blessed impulse of his soul, by which he would come to the highest things, trampling worldly things under foot. He could not delay any longer, because a deadly disease had grown up every where to such an extent and had so taken hold of all the limbs of many that, were the physician to delay even a little, it would snatch away life, shutting off the life-giving spirit. He rose up, therefore, fortified himself with the sign of the cross, got his horse ready and mounted it, and taking with him some fine cloth to sell, he hastened to the city called Foligno [about 10 miles or 16 km from Assisi]. There, as usual, he sold everything he had with him, and, successful as a merchant, he left behind even the horse he was riding, after he had received payment for it; and, free of all luggage, he started back, wondering with a religious mind what he should do with the money. Soon, turned toward God's work in a wondrous manner, and accordingly feeling that it would be a great burden to him to carry that money even for an hour, he hastened to get rid of it, considering the advantage he might get from it as so much sand. When, therefore, he neared the city of Assisi, he discovered a certain church along the way that had been built of old in honor of St. Damian but which was now threatening to collapse because it was so old.

9. When this new soldier of Christ came up to this church, moved with

pity over such great need, he entered it with fear and reverence. And when he found there a certain poor priest, he kissed his sacred hands with great faith, and offered him the money he had with him, telling him in order what he proposed to do. The priest was astonished and, wondering over a conversion so incredibly sudden, he refused to believe what he heard. And because he thought he was being deceived, he refused to keep the money offered him. For he had seen him just the day before, so to say, living in a riotous way among his relatives and acquaintances and showing greater foolishness than the rest. But Francis persisted obstinately and tried to gain credence for what he said, asking earnestly and begging the priest to suffer him to remain with him for the sake of the Lord. In the end the priest acquiesced to his remaining there, but out of fear of the young man's parents, he did not accept the money; whereupon this true contemner of money threw it upon a window sill, for he cared no more for it than for the dust. He wanted to possess that wisdom that is better than gold and to acquire that prudence that is more precious than silver.

How his father persecuted Francis and put him in chains.

10. So while the servant of the most high God was staying in the aforesaid place, his father [Pietro Bernardone, a rich cloth merchant] went about everywhere, like a persistent spy, wanting to learn what had happened to his son. And when he learned that he was living in such a way at that place, being touched inwardly with sorrow of heart, he was troubled exceedingly at the sudden turn of events, and calling together his friends and neighbors, he hurried to the place where the servant of God was staying. But he, the new athlete of Christ, when he heard of the threats of those who were pursuing him and when he got knowledge of their coming, wanting to give place to wrath, hid himself in a certain secret pit which he himself had prepared for just such an emergency. That pit was in that house and was known probably to one person alone; in it he hid so continuously for one month that he hardly dared leave it to provide for his human needs. Food, when it was given to him, he ate in the secrecy of the pit, and every service was rendered to him by stealth. Praying, he prayed always with a torrent of tears that the Lord would deliver him from the hands of those who were persecuting his soul, and that he would fulfil his pious wishes in his loving kindness; in fasting and in weeping he begged for the clemency of the Savior, and, distrusting his own efforts, he cast his whole care upon the Lord. And though he was in a pit and in darkness, he was nevertheless filled with a certain exquisite joy of which till then he had had no experience; and catching fire there from, he left the pit and exposed himself openly to the curses of his persecutors.

11. He arose, therefore, immediately, active, eager, and lively; and, bearing the shield of faith to fight for the Lord, armed with a great confidence, he took the way toward the city; aglow with a divine fire, he began to accuse himself severely of laziness and cowardice. When those who knew him saw this, they compared what he was now with what he had been; and they began to revile him miserably. Shouting out that he was mad and demented, they threw the mud of the streets and stones at him. They saw that he was changed from his former ways and greatly worn down by mortification of the flesh, and they therefore set down everything he did to exhaustion and madness. But since a patient man is better than a proud man, the servant of God showed himself deaf to all these things and, neither broken nor changed by any of these injuries, he gave thanks to God for all of them. In vain does the wicked man persecute one striving after virtue, for the more he is buffeted, the more strongly will he triumph. As someone says, indignity strengthens a generous spirit.

12. Now, when the noise and the shouting of this kind concerning Francis had been going on for a long time through the streets and quarters of the city, and the sound of it all was echoing here and there, among the many, to whose ears the report of these things came, was finally his father. When he heard the name of his son mentioned, and understood that the commotion among the citizens turned about his son, he immediately arose, not indeed to free him but rather to destroy him; and, with no regard for moderation, he rushed upon him like a wolf upon a sheep, and looking upon him with a fierce and savage countenance, he laid hands upon him and dragged him shamelessly and disgracefully to his home. Thus, without mercy, he shut him up in a dark place for several days, and thinking to bend his spirit to his own will, he first used words and then blows and chains. But Francis became only the more ready and more strong to carry out his purpose; but he did not abandon his patience either because he was insulted by words or worn out by chains. For he who is commanded to rejoice in tribulation cannot swerve from the right intention and position of his mind or be led away from Christ's flock, not even by scourgings and chains; neither does he waver in a flood of many waters whose refuge from oppression is the Son of God, who, lest our troubles seem hard to us, showed always that those he bore were greater.

How Francis's mother freed him and how he stripped himself before the bishop of Assisi.

13. It happened, however, when Francis's father had left home for a while on business and the man of God remained bound in the basement of the house, his mother, who was alone with him and who did not approve of what her

husband had done, spoke kindly to her son. But when she saw that he could not be persuaded away from his purpose, she was moved by motherly compassion for him, and loosening his chains, she let him go free. He, however, giving thanks to Almighty God, returned quickly to the place where he had been before. But now, after he had been proved by temptations, he allowed himself greater liberty, and he took on a more cheerful aspect because of the many struggles he had gone through. From the wrongs done him he acquired a more confident spirit, and he went about everywhere freely with higher spirits than before. Meanwhile, his father returned, and not finding Francis, he turned to upbraid his wife, heaping sins upon sins. Then, raging and blustering, he ran to that place hoping that if he could not recall him from his ways, he might at least drive him from the province. But, because it is true that in the fear of the Lord is confidence, when this child of grace heard his carnally minded [i.e., worldly] father coming to him, confident and joyful he went to meet him, exclaiming in a clear voice that he cared nothing for his chains and blows. Moreover, he stated that he would gladly undergo evils for the name of Christ.

14. But when his father saw that he could not bring him back from the way he had undertaken, he was roused by all means to get his money back. The man of God had desired to offer it and expend it to feed the poor and to repair the buildings of that place. But he who had no love for money could not be misled by any aspect of good in it; and he who was not held back by any affection for it was in no way disturbed by its loss. Therefore, when the money was found, which he who hated the things of this world so greatly and desired the riches of heaven so much had thrown aside in the dust of the windowsill, the fury of his raging father was extinguished a little, and the thirst of his avarice was somewhat allayed by the warmth of discovery. He then brought his son before the bishop of the city, so that, renouncing all his possessions into his hands, he might give up everything he had. Francis not only did not refuse to do this, but he hastened with great joy to do what was demanded of him.

15. When he was brought before the bishop, he would suffer no delay or hesitation in anything; indeed, he did not wait for any words nor did he speak any, but immediately putting off his clothes and casting them aside, he gave them back to his father. Moreover, not even retaining his trousers, he stripped himself completely naked before all. The bishop, however, sensing his disposition and admiring greatly his fervor and constancy, arose and drew him within his arms and covered him with the mantle he was wearing. He understood clearly that the counsel was of God, and he understood that the actions of the man of God that he had personally witnessed contained a mystery. He immediately, therefore, became his helper and cherishing him

and encouraging him, he embraced him in the bowels of charity. Behold, now he wrestles naked with his naked adversary, and having put off everything that is of this world, he thinks only about the things of the Lord. He seeks now so to despise his own life, putting off all solicitude for it, that he might find peace in his harassed ways, and that meanwhile only the wall of flesh should separate him from the vision of God.

How Francis was seized by robbers and cast into the snow, and how he served the lepers.

16. He who once wore fine garments now went about clad only in scanty garments. As he went through a certain woods singing praises to the Lord in the French language, robbers suddenly rushed out upon him. When they asked him in a ferocious tone who he was, the man of God replied confidently in a loud voice: "I am the herald of the great King. What is that to you?" But they struck him and cast him into a ditch filled with deep snow, saying: "Lie there, foolish herald of God!" But he rolled himself about and shook off the snow; and when they had gone away, he jumped out of the ditch, and, glad with great joy, he began to call out the praises of God in a loud voice throughout the grove. At length, coming to a certain cloister of monks, he spent several days there as a scullion, wearing a ragged shirt and being satisfied to be filled only with broth. But, when all pity was withdrawn from him and he could not get even an old garment, he left the place, not moved by anger, but forced by necessity; and he went to the city of Gubbio, where he obtained a small tunic from a certain man who once had been his friend. Then, after some time had elapsed, when the fame of the man of God was beginning to grow and his name was spread abroad among the people, the prior of the aforementioned monastery recalled and realized how the man of God had been treated and he came to him and begged pardon for himself and for his monks out of reverence for the Savior.

17. Then the holy lover of complete humility went to the lepers and lived with them, serving them most diligently for God's sake; and washing all foulness from them, he wiped away also the corruption of the ulcers, just as he said in his Testament: "When I was in sins, it seemed extremely bitter to me to look at lepers, and the Lord himself led me among them and I practiced mercy with them." So greatly loathsome was the sight of lepers to him at one time, he used to say, that, in the days of his vanity, he would look at their houses only from a distance of two miles and he would hold his nostrils with his hands. But now, when by the grace and the power of the most high he was beginning to think of holy and useful things, while he was still clad in secular garments, he met a leper one day and, made stronger than himself, he

kissed him. From then on he began to despise himself more and more, until, by the mercy of the Redeemer, he came to perfect victory over himself. Of other poor, too, while he yet remained in the world and still followed the world, he was the helper, stretching forth a hand of mercy to those who had nothing, and showing compassion to the afflicted. For when one day, contrary to his custom, for he was a most courteous person, he upbraided a certain poor man who had asked an alms of him, he was immediately sorry; and he began to say to himself that it was a great reproach and a shame to withhold what was asked from one who had asked in the name of so great a King. He therefore resolved in his heart never in the future to refuse any one, if at all possible, who asked for the love of God. This he most diligently did and carried out, until he sacrificed himself entirely and in every way; and thus he became first a practicer before he became a teacher of the evangelical counsel: "To him who asks of thee," he said, "give; and from him who would borrow of thee do not turn away."

How Francis built the church of St. Damian; and of the life of the Ladies who dwelt in that place.

18. The first work that blessed Francis undertook after he had gained his freedom from the hand of his carnally minded father was to build a house of God. He did not try to build one anew, but he repaired an old one, restored an ancient one. He did not tear out the foundation, but he built upon it, ever reserving to Christ his prerogative, though he was not aware of it, for other foundation no one can lay but that which has been laid which is Christ Jesus. When he had returned to the place where, as has been said, the church of St. Damian had been built in ancient times, he repaired it zealously within a short time with the help of the grace of the most high. This is the blessed and holy place, where the glorious religion and most excellent order of Poor Ladies and holy virgins had its blessed origin about six years after the conversion of St. Francis and through that same blessed man. Of it, the Lady Clare, a native of the city of Assisi, the most precious and the firmest stone of the whole structure, was the foundation. For when, after the beginning of the Order of Brothers, the said lady [who had run away from home to join Francis at the age of about eighteen] was converted to God through the counsel of the holy man, she lived unto the advantage of many and as an example to a countless multitude. She was of noble parentage, but she was more noble by grace; she was a virgin in body, most chaste in mind; a youth in age, but mature in spirit; steadfast in purpose and most ardent in her desire for divine love; endowed with wisdom and excelling in humility; Clare by name, brighter in life, and brightest in character.

19. Over her arose a noble structure of most precious pearls [her followers, including her sister Agnes] whose praise is not from men but from God, since neither is our limited understanding sufficient to imagine it, nor our scanty vocabulary to utter it. For above everything else there flourishes among them that excelling virtue of mutual and continual charity, which so binds their wills into one that, though forty or fifty of them dwell together in one place, agreement in likes and dislikes molds one spirit in them out of many. Secondly, in each one there glows the gem of humility, which so preserves the gifts and good things bestowed from heaven, that they merit other virtues too. Thirdly, the lily of virginity and chastity so sprinkles them with a wondrous odor that, forgetful of earthly thoughts, they desire to meditate only on heavenly things; and so great a love for their eternal Spouse arises in their hearts from the fragrance of that lily that the integrity of that holy affection excludes from them every habit of their former life. Fourthly, they have all become so conspicuous by the title of the highest poverty that their food and clothing hardly at all or never come together to satisfy extreme necessity....

How Francis having changed his habit rebuilt the church of St. Mary of the Portiuncula and how upon hearing the Gospel he left all things and how he designed and made the habit the brothers wear.

21. Meanwhile the holy man of God, having put on a new kind of habit and having repaired the aforesaid church, went to another place near the city of Assisi, where he began to rebuild a certain dilapidated and well-nigh destroyed church, and he did not leave off from his good purpose until he had brought it to completion. Then he went to another place, which is called the Portiuncula [about a mile south-west of Assisi, deep in the woods] where there stood a church of the Blessed Virgin Mother of God that had been built in ancient times, but was now deserted and cared for by no one. When the holy man of God saw how it was thus in ruins, he was moved to pity, because he burned with devotion toward the mother of all good; and he began to live there in great zeal. It was the third year of his conversion when he began to repair this church. At this time he wore a kind of hermit's dress, with a leather girdle about his waist; he carried a staff in his hands and wore shoes on his feet.

22. But when on a certain day the Gospel was read in that church, how the Lord sent his disciples out to preach, the holy man of God, assisting there, understood somewhat the words of the Gospel; after Mass he humbly asked the priest to explain the Gospel to him more fully. When he had set forth for him in order all these things, the holy Francis, hearing that the disciples of Christ should not possess gold or silver or money; nor carry along the way

scrip, or wallet, or bread, or a staff; that they should not have shoes, or two tunics; but that they should preach the kingdom of God and penance, immediately cried out exultingly: "This is what I wish, this is what I seek, this is what I long to do with all my heart." Then the holy father, overflowing with joy, hastened to fulfil that salutary word he had heard, and he did not suffer any delay to intervene before beginning devoutly to perform what he had heard. He immediately put off his shoes from his feet, put aside the staff from his hands, was content with one tunic, and exchanged his leather girdle for a small cord. He designed for himself a tunic that bore a likeness to the Cross, that by means of it he might beat off all temptations of the devil; he designed a very rough tunic so that by it he might crucify the flesh with all its vices and sins; he designed a very poor and mean tunic, one that would not excite the covetousness of the world. The other things that he had heard, however, he longed with the greatest diligence and the greatest reverence to perform. For he was not a deaf hearer of the Gospel, but committing all that he had heard to praiseworthy memory, he tried diligently to carry it out to the letter.

Of his preaching of the Gospel and his announcing peace and of the conversion of the first six brothers.

23. From then on he began to preach penance to all with great fervor of spirit and joy of mind, edifying his hearers with his simple words and his greatness of heart. His word was like a burning fire, penetrating the inmost reaches of the heart, and it filled the minds of all the hearers with admiration. He seemed completely different from what he had been, and, looking up to the heavens, he disdained to look upon the earth. This indeed is wonderful, that he first began to preach where as a child he had first learned to read and where for a time he was buried amid great honor, so that the happy beginning might be commended by a still happier ending. Where he had learned he also taught, and where he began he also ended. In all his preaching, before he proposed the word of God to those gathered about, he first prayed for peace for them, saying: "The Lord give you peace." He always most devoutly announced peace to men and women, to all he met and overtook. For this reason many who had hated peace and had hated also salvation embraced peace, through the cooperation of the Lord, with all their heart and were made children of peace and seekers after eternal salvation.

24. Among these, a certain man from Assisi, of pious and simple spirit, was the first to devoutly follow the man of God. After him, Brother Bernard, embracing the delegation of peace, ran eagerly after the holy man of God to purchase the kingdom of heaven. He had often given the blessed father hos-

pitality, and, having had experience of his life and conduct and having been refreshed by the fragrance of his holiness, he conceived a fear and brought forth the spirit of salvation. He noticed that Francis would pray all night, sleeping but rarely, praising God and the glorious Virgin Mother of God, and he wondered and said: "In all truth, this man is from God." He hastened therefore to sell all his goods and gave the money to the poor, though not to his parents; and laying hold of the title to the way of perfection, he carried out the counsel of the holy Gospel: 'If thou wilt be perfect, go, sell what thou hast, and give to the poor, and thou shalt have treasure in heaven; and come, follow me.' When he had done this, he was associated with St. Francis by his life and by his habit, and he was always with him until, after the number of the brothers had increased, he was sent to other regions by obedience to his kind father. His conversion to God was a model to others in the manner of selling one's possessions and giving them to the poor. St. Francis rejoiced with very great joy over the coming and conversion of so great a man, in that the Lord was seen to have a care for him by giving him a needed companion and a faithful friend.

25. But immediately another man of the city of Assisi followed him; he deserves to be greatly praised for his conduct, and what he began in a holy way, he completed after a short time in a more holy way. After a not very long time, Brother Giles followed him; he was a simple and upright man and one fearing God. He lived a long time, leading a holy life, justly and piously, and giving us examples of perfect obedience, manual labor, solitary life, and holy contemplation. After another one had been added to these, Brother Philip brought the number to seven. The Lord touched his lips with a purifying coal, that he might speak pleasing things of him and utter sweet things. Understanding and interpreting the sacred Scriptures, though he had not studied, he became an imitator of those whom the leaders of the Jews alleged to be ignorant and unlearned.

Of the spirit of prophecy of St. Francis and of his admonitions.

27.... And then ... he said with joy to his brothers: "Be strengthened dear brothers, and rejoice in the Lord, and do not be sad because you seem so few; and do not let either my simplicity or your own dismay you, for, as it has been shown me in truth by the Lord, God will make us grow into a very great multitude and will make us increase to the ends of the world. For your profit I am compelled to tell you what I have seen, though I would much rather remain silent, were it not that charity urges me to tell you. I saw a great multitude of men coming to us and wanting to live with us in the habit of our way of life and under the rule of our blessed religion. And behold, the sound of them is in my ears as they go and come according to the command of holy obedience. I have seen, as it were, the roads filled with their great numbers coming together in these parts from almost every nation. Frenchmen are coming, Spaniards are hastening, Germans and Englishmen are running, and a very great multitude of others speaking various tongues are hurrying." When the brothers had heard this, they were filled with a salutary joy, both because of the grace the Lord God gave to his holy one and because they were ardently thirsting for the advantages to be gained by their neighbors, whom they wished to grow daily in numbers and to be saved thereby....

How Francis first wrote a rule when he had eleven brothers, and how the lord pope confirmed it; and how he had a vision of a a great tree.

32. When blessed Francis saw that the Lord God was daily adding to their number, he wrote for himself and his brothers, present and to come, simply and with few words, a form of life and rule, using for the most part the words of the holy Gospel, for the perfection of which alone he yearned. But he did insert a few other things that were necessary to provide for a holy way of life. He then came to Rome with all the aforementioned brothers, desiring very much that what he had written should be confirmed by the Lord Pope Innocent. At that time the venerable bishop of Assisi was at Rome, Guido by name, who honored Francis and all his brothers in all things and venerated them with special affection. When he saw St. Francis and his brothers, he was grievously annoyed at their coming, not knowing the reason for it; for he feared that they might wish to leave their native region where the Lord had already begun to work very great things through his servants. He rejoiced greatly to have such great men in his diocese, on whose life and conduct he was relying greatly. But when he had heard the reason for their coming and understood their purpose, he rejoiced greatly in the Lord, promising to give them his advice and help in these things. St. Francis also approached the lord bishop of Sabina, John of St. Paul by name, who of all the other princes and great ones at the Roman curia was seen to despise earthly things and love heavenly things. He received Francis kindly and charitably, and praised highly his will and purpose.

33. Indeed, because he was a prudent and discreet man, he began to ask Francis about many things and urged him to turn to the life of a monk or hermit. But St. Francis refused his counsel, as humbly as he could, not despising what was counseled, but in his pious leaning toward another life, he was inspired by a higher desire. The lord bishop wondered at his fervor, and, fearing that he might decline from so great a purpose, he showed him ways

that would be easier to follow. In the end, overcome by Francis's constancy, he acquiesced to his petition and strove from then on to further his aims before the lord pope. It was Pope Innocent III who was at that time at the head of the Church, a famous man, greatly learned, renowned in discourse, burning with zeal for justice in the things that the cause of the Christian faith demanded. When he had come to know the wishes of these men of God, he first examined the matter, then gave assent to their request and carried out all that had to be done; exhorting them concerning many things and admonishing them, he blessed St. Francis and his brothers and said to them: "Go with the Lord, brothers, and as the Lord will deign to inspire you, preach penance to all. Then, when the almighty Lord shall give you increase in number and in grace, return to me with joy, and I will add many more things to these and entrust greater things to you with greater confidence."

In all truth the Lord was with St. Francis wherever he went, cheering him with revelations and encouraging him by his gifts. For one night after he had given himself to sleep, it seemed to him that he was walking along a certain road, at the side of which stood a tree of great height. The tree was beautiful and strong, thick and exceedingly high. It happened as he drew near to it, and was standing beneath it, admiring its beauty and its height, that suddenly the holy man himself grew to so great a height that he touched the top of the tree, and taking hold of it with his hand, he bent it to the ground. And so indeed it happened, for the lord Innocent, the highest and loftiest tree in the world, graciously stooped to Francis' petition and desire....

Concerning the fame of the blessed Francis and the conversion of many to God; how the order was called the Order of Friars Minor and how blessed Francis formed those entering religion.

36. Francis, therefore, the most valiant knight of Christ, went about the towns and villages announcing the kingdom of God, preaching peace, teaching salvation and penance unto the remission of sins, not in the persuasive words of human wisdom, but with the learning and power of the Spirit. He acted boldly in all things, because of the apostolic authority granted to him, using no words of flattery or seductive blandishments. He did not know how to make light of the faults of others, but he knew well how to cut them out; neither did he encourage the life of sinners, but he struck hard at them with sharp reproof, for he had first convinced himself by practising himself what he wished to persuade others to do by his words; and fearing not the censurer, he spoke the truth boldly, so that even the most learned men, men enjoying renown and dignity, wondered at his words and were struck with wholesome fear by his presence. Men ran, and women too ran, clerics hur-

ried, and the religious hastened that they might see and hear the holy man of God who seemed to all to be a man of another world. Every age and every sex hurried to see the wonderful things that the Lord was newly working in the world through his servant. It seemed at that time, whether because of the presence of St. Francis or through his reputation, that a new light had been sent from heaven upon this earth, shattering the widespread darkness that had so filled almost the whole region that hardly anyone knew where to go. For so profound was the forgetfulness of God and the sleep of neglect of his commandments oppressing almost everyone that they could hardly be aroused even a little from their old and deeply rooted sins....

38. But our first concern here is with the order of which he was the founder and preserver both by charity and by profession. What shall we say? He himself first planted the Order of Friars Minor and accordingly gave it this name. For he wrote in the rule, "and let them be lesser brothers," and when these words were spoken, indeed in that same hour, he said: "I wish that this fraternity should be called the Order of Friars Minor." And indeed they were lesser brothers, who, being subject to all, always sought a place that was lowly and sought to perform a duty that seemed in some way to be burdensome to them so that they might merit to be founded solidly in true humility and that through their fruitful disposition a spiritual structure of all virtues might arise in them. Truly, upon the foundation of constancy a noble structure of charity arose, in which the living stones, gathered from all parts of the world, were erected into a dwelling place of the Holy Spirit. O with what ardor of charity the new disciples of Christ burned! How great was the love that flourished in the members of this pious society! For whenever they came together anywhere, or met one another along the way, as the custom is, there a shoot of spiritual love sprang up, sprinkling over all love the seed of true affection. What more shall I say? Chaste embraces, gentle feelings, a holy kiss, pleasing conversation, modest laughter, joyous looks, a single eye, a submissive spirit, a peaceable tongue, a mild answer, oneness of purpose, ready obedience, unwearied hand, all these were found in them.

39. And indeed, since they despised all earthly things and did not love themselves with a selfish love, pouring out their whole affection on all the brothers, they strove to give themselves as the price of helping one another in their needs. They came together with great desire; they remained together with joy; but separation from one another was sad on both sides, a bitter divorce, a cruel estrangement. But these most obedient knights dared put nothing before holy obedience; before the command of obedience was even uttered, they prepared themselves to fulfil the order; knowing not how to misinterpret the commands, they put aside every objection and hastened to fulfil what was commanded. Followers of most holy poverty, because they

had nothing, loved nothing, they feared in no way to lose anything. They were content with one tunic, patched at times within and without; in it was seen no refinement, but rather abjectness and cheapness, so that they might seem to be completely crucified to the world. Girt with a cord, they wore poor trousers, and they had the pious intention of remaining like this, and they wished to have nothing more. They were, therefore, everywhere secure, kept in no suspense by fear; distracted by no care, they awaited the next day without solicitude, nor were they in anxiety about the night's lodging, though in their journeyings they were often placed in great danger. For, when they frequently lacked the necessary lodging amid the coldest weather, an oven sheltered them, or at least they lay hid for the night humbly in grottos or caves. During the day, those who knew how labored with their hands, staying in the houses of lepers, or in other decent places, serving all humbly and devotedly. They did not wish to exercise any position from which scandal might arise, but always doing what is holy and just, honest and useful, they led all with whom they came into contact to follow their example of humility and patience.

St. Francis Receives the Stigmata [taken from St. Bonaventure's 'Life'].

2, 1. St. Francis never failed to keep himself occupied doing good; like the angels Jacob saw on the ladder, he was always busy, either raising his heart to God in prayer, or descending to his neighbor. He had learned how to distribute the time in which he could gain merit wisely, devoting part of it to his neighbor by doing good, and part to the restful ecstasy of contemplation. According to the demands of time or circumstances he would devote himself wholly to the salvation of his neighbor, but when he was finished, he would escape from the distracting crowds and go into solitude in search of peace. There he was free to attend exclusively to God and he would cleanse any stain he had contracted while living in the midst of the world. Two years before his death, after a period of intense activity, he was led by divine providence to a high mountain called La Verna, where he could be alone. There he began a forty-day fast in honor of St. Michael the Archangel, as was his custom, and he soon experienced an extraordinary in-pouring of divine contemplation. He was all on fire with heavenly desires and he realized that the gifts of divine grace were being poured out over him in greater abundance than ever. He was borne aloft not as one who would search curiously into the divine majesty and be crushed by its glory, but as a faithful and wise servant, anxious only to discover God's will, which he wanted to obey with all his heart and soul.

2. By divine inspiration he learned that if he opened the Gospels, Christ

would reveal to him what was God's will for him and what God wished to see realized in him. And so Francis prayed fervently and took the Gospel book from the altar, telling his companion, a devout and holy friar, to open it in the name of the blessed trinity. He opened the Gospel three times, and each time it opened at the passion, and so, Francis understood that he must become like Christ in the distress and the agony of his passion before he left the world, just as he had been like him in all that he did during his life. His body had already been weakened by the austerity of his past life and the fact that he had carried our Lord's Cross without interruption, but he was not afraid and he felt more eager than ever to endure any martyrdom. The unquenchable fire of love for Jesus in his goodness had become a blazing light of flame, so that his charity could not succumb even before the floodwaters of affliction.

3. The fervor of his seraphic longing raised Francis up to God and, in an ecstasy of compassion, made him like Christ who allowed himself to be crucified in the excess of his love. Then, one morning about the feast of the exaltation of the Holy Cross, while he was praying on the mountainside, Francis saw a seraphim with six fiery wings coming down from the highest point in the heavens. The vision descended swiftly and came to rest in the air near him. Then he saw the image of a man crucified in the midst of the wings, with his hands and feet stretched out and nailed to a cross. Two of the wings were raised above his head and two were stretched out in flight, while the remaining two shielded his body. Francis was dumbfounded at the sight and his heart was flooded with a mixture of joy and sorrow. He was overjoyed at the way Christ regarded him so graciously under the appearance of a seraphim, but the fact that he was nailed to a cross pierced his soul with a sword of compassionate sorrow.

He was lost in wonder at the sight of this mysterious vision; he knew that the agony of Christ's passion was not in keeping with the state of a seraphic spirit which is immortal. Eventually, he realized by divine inspiration that God had shown him this vision in his providence, in order to let him see that, as Christ's lover, he would resemble Christ crucified perfectly not by physical martyrdom, but by the fervor of his spirit. As the vision disappeared, it left his heart ablaze with eagerness and impressed upon his body a miraculous likeness. There and then the marks of nails began to appear in his hands and feet, just as he had seen them in his vision of the man nailed to the Cross. His hands and feet appeared pierced through the center with nails, the heads of which were in the palms of his hands and on the instep of each foot, while the points stuck out on the opposite side. The heads were black and round, but the points were long and bent back, as if they had been struck with a hammer; they rose above the surrounding flesh and stood out from it. His right side seemed as if it had been pierced with a lance and was marked with a livid scar which often bled, so that his habit and trousers were stained.

4. When he realized that he could not conceal the stigmata which had been imprinted so plainly on his body from his intimate companions, he was thrown into an agony of doubt; he was afraid to make God's secret publicly known, and he did not know whether he should say what he had seen, or keep it quiet. He called some of the friars and asked them in general terms what he should do. One of them, who was called Illuminatus, was enlightened by God and he realized that some miracle had taken place because the saint was still completely dazed. He said to him, "Brother, remember that when God reveals his secrets to you, it is not for yourself alone; they are intended for others too. If you hide something which was intended to do good to many others, then you have every reason to fear that you will be condemned for burying the talent given to you." Francis often said, "It is for me to keep my secret to myself," but when he heard these words, he described the vision he had just seen apprehensively, adding that the person who had appeared to him had told him a number of secrets which he would never reveal to anyone as long as he lived.

We can only conclude from this that the message given him by the seraphim who appeared to him on the Cross was so secret that it could not be communicated to any human being.

5. True love of Christ had now transformed his lover into his image, and when the forty days which he had intended spending in solitude were over and the feast of St. Michael had come, St. Francis came down from the mountain. With him he bore a representation of Christ crucified which was not the work of an artist in wood or stone, but had been reproduced in the members of his body by the hand of the living God. "Kings have their counsel that must be kept secret," and so Francis who realized that he shared a royal secret did his best to conceal the sacred stigmata. However, it is for God to reveal his wonders for his own glory; he had impressed the stigmata on St. Francis in secret, but he publicly worked a number of miracles by them, so that their miraculous, though hidden, power might become clearly known.

6. In the province of Rieti a fatal disease had attacked cattle and sheep and carried great numbers of them off so quickly that nothing could be done for them. Then a devout man was told in a vision at night to go immediately to the friars' hermitage where St. Francis was staying and get the water with which he had washed his hands and feet and sprinkle it over the livestock. He got up in the morning and went to the hermitage and got the water secretly from the saint's companions. Then he sprinkled the sick cattle and sheep. The animals were lying on the ground exhausted, but the moment that a mere drop of the water touched them, they immediately recovered

their normal strength and stood up and hurried off to pasture, as if there had never been anything wrong with them. The miraculous power of water which had touched the stigmata banished the disease and saved the livestock from the fatal sickness.

7. Before St. Francis went to stay on La Verna it often happened that clouds would form over the mountain and violent hailstorms would devastate the crops. After his vision, however, the hail stopped, much to the amazement of the local people. The unusually clear skies proclaimed the extraordinary nature of his vision and the power of the stigmata which he received there.

One wintertime, because he was weak and the road was bad, the saint was riding an ass belonging to a poor man. It was snowing and the approach of darkness made it impossible for them to reach shelter, so that they had to spend the night under the lee of an overhanging cliff. Francis heard his benefactor grumbling to himself and turning this way and that; he was wearing only a few clothes and he could not fall asleep in the biting cold. He himself was ablaze with the fervor of divine love and he stretched out his hand and touched him. At the touch of his hand, which was warm with the heat of the coal used to purify the lips of the prophet Isaias, the cold disappeared and the man felt as warm as if he had been hit with a blast of hot air from an oven. He immediately felt better in body and soul and he slept more soundly in the rocks and the blizzard until morning than he had ever slept in his own bed, as he used to say afterwards.

It is certain, therefore, that the stigmata were impressed upon St. Francis by God's power, because it is God who purifies, illuminates, and inflames by the intervention of the seraphim. These sacred wounds purified animals of disease and granted clear skies, as well as physical warmth. This was proved more clearly than ever after Francis's death by the miracles which we shall describe in their own place.

8. Francis was very careful to try and hide the treasure he had found in the field, but he could not prevent everybody from seeing the stigmata in his hands and feet, although he always kept his hands covered and wore shoes. A number of the friars saw them during his lifetime, and to put the matter beyond all doubt they testified to this under oath, although they were good religious and deserved to be believed. Some of the cardinals who were close friends of the saint also saw them and celebrated their praise in various hymns and antiphons which they composed in his honor, thus bearing witness to the truth in their words and writings. In a sermon which he preached in public and at which I was present with a number of other friars, his holiness Pope Alexander asserted that he had seen the stigmata with his own eyes during the saint's lifetime. More than fifty friars with St. Clare and her nuns and innumerable lay people saw them after his death. Many of them kissed the

stigmata and felt them with their own hands, to prove the truth, as we shall describe later.

However, Francis succeeded in covering the wound in his side so carefully that no one could get more than a glimpse of it during his lifetime. A friar who used to wait on him carefully gently prevailed upon him to take off his habit and have it shaken out, and as he watched closely he saw the wound. He put three of his fingers on it immediately so that he was able to feel as well as see how big it was. The friar who was Francis's vicar at that time managed to see the wound by a similar subterfuge. Another of his companions, a man of extraordinary simplicity, put his hand in under his capuche to massage his chest because he was not feeling well, and accidentally touched the wound, causing the saint great pain. As a result, Francis always wore trousers which reached up to his armpits, in order to cover the scar on his side. The friars who washed his trousers or shook out his habit found them stained with blood. This clear proof left them with no doubt of the existence of the wound which they afterwards contemplated and venerated with others on his death.

9. O valiant knight of Christ! You are armed with the weapons of your invulnerable Leader. They will mark you out and enable you to overcome all your enemies. It is for you to bear aloft the standard of the High King, at the sight of which the rank and file of God's army take heart. And you bear, nonetheless, the seal of the supreme High Priest Christ, so that your words and example must be regarded by everyone as genuine and sound beyond all cavil. You bear the scars of the Lord Jesus in your body, so that no one should dare oppose you. On the contrary, all Christ's disciples are bound to hold you in devout affection. God's witness in your favor is beyond all doubt; the sacred stigmata were witnessed not just by two or three, which would have been enough, but by a whole multitude, which is more than enough, and they leave those who are unbelieving without excuse. The faithful, on the other hand, are confirmed in their faith and raised up by confident hope and inflamed with the fire of divine love.

8. FOUR 'LIVES' FROM *THE GOLDEN LEGEND*

Many improbable stories of saints, some of whom were later removed from the Roman Calendar, circulated widely in medieval Europe and were among the most popular hagiographies. They are characterized by a practical didacticism, by lively narrative relying on direct discourse and plenty of action, by the absence of historical context, and by the use of plots and motifs found in mythology and folk tales. The popularity of this type of hagiography was a major cause of attacks on the cult of the saints in the Renaissance and led indirectly to the great work of the Bollandists, beginning in the seventeenth century, when a small group of Jesuit scholars headed by Heribert Rosweyde and John Bolland developed scientific methods of historical research aimed at separating hagiographical fact from fiction.

Undoubtedly the most important medieval collection of popular hagiography is the 'Legenda Aurea' ('The Golden Legend') compiled about 1260 by Jacobus de Voragine, a Dominican who became archbishop of Genoa in 1292. A compilation of many Latin hagiographies, it was probably intended as a convenient source book for clerics in need of material for sermons and readings for saints' days. It is organized according to the order of the saints' feast days within the liturgical year, with additional material included for other major celebrations such as Advent, the Passion, and the Resurrection. Jacobus's work became the major source for vernacular saints' 'lives' in the later Middle Ages and was one of the first books printed, in 1483, by William Caxton.

Although many of the 'lives' in this collection are legitimate retellings of accounts of major saints, the emphasis on the miraculous and the extraordinary in the hagiographic 'romances' nevertheless made it difficult for Roman Catholics to defend the cult of the saints during the Reformation and rendered it an easy object of attack by both Protestants and Catholic reformers. In the four 'lives' given below, 'Agnes' is typical of stories about virgin martyrs; 'Mary of Egypt' is a summary of a much older account of a famous desert mother who represents the type of reformed sinner; 'Christopher' is based on folk tales of giants; and 'James the Dismembered' exemplifies both the violence that characterizes many of Jacobus's accounts and his incorporation of doctrine in his narratives.

Source: trans. William Granger Ryan, *Jacobus de Voragine: The Golden Legend. Readings on the Saints* (Princeton, NJ: Princeton University Press, 1993), I, 101-4, 227-29; 2, 10-14, 343-46; repr. with permission.

1. St. Agnes, Virgin (BHL 164)

The name Agnes comes from *agna*, a lamb, because Agnes was as meek and humble as a lamb. Or her name comes from the Greek word *agnos*, pious, because she was pious and compassionate; or from *agnoscendo*, knowing, because she knew the way of truth. Truth, according to Augustine, is opposed to vanity and falseness and doubting, all of which she avoided by the virtue of truth that was hers.

Agnes was a virgin most sensible and wise, as Ambrose, who wrote the story of her martyrdom, attests. When she was thirteen years old, she lost death and found life. Childhood is computed in years, but in her immense wisdom she was old; she was a child in body but already aged in spirit. Her face was beautiful, her faith more beautiful.

One day she was on her way home from school when the prefect's son saw her and fell in love. He promised her jewels and great wealth if she consented to be his wife. Agnes answered: "Go away, you spark that lights the fire of sin, you fuel of wickedness, you food of death! I am already pledged to another lover!" She began to commend this lover and spouse for five things that the betrothed look for in the men they are to wed, namely, nobility of lineage, beauty of person, abundance of wealth, courage and the power to achieve, and love transcendent. She went on: "The one I love is far nobler than you, of more eminent descent. His mother is a virgin, his father knows no woman, he is served by angels; the sun and the moon wonder at his beauty; his wealth never lacks or lessens; his perfume brings the dead to life, his touch strengthens the feeble, his love is chastity itself, his touch holiness, union with him, virginity."

In support of these five claims, she said: "Is there anyone whose ancestry is more exalted, whose powers are more invincible, whose aspect is more beautiful, whose love more delightful, who is richer in every grace?" Then she enumerated five benefits that her spouse had conferred on her and confers on all his other spouses: he gives them a ring as an earnest of his fidelity, he clothes and adorns them with a multitude of virtues, he signs them with the blood of his passion and death, he binds them to himself with the bond of his love, and endows them with the treasures of eternal glory. "He has placed a wedding ring on my right hand," she said, "and a necklace of precious stones around my neck, gowned me with a robe woven with gold and jewels, placed a mark on my forehead to keep me from taking any lover but himself, and his blood has tinted my cheeks. Already his chaste embraces hold me close, he has united his body to mine, and he has shown me incomparable treasures, and promised to give them to me if I remain true to him."

When the young man heard all this, he was beside himself and threw himself on his bed, and his deep sighs made it clear to his physicians that lovesickness was his trouble. His father sought out the maiden and told her of his son's condition, but she assured him that she could not violate her covenant with her betrothed. The prefect pressed her to say who this betrothed was, whose power over her she talked about. Someone else told him that it was Christ whom she called her spouse, and the prefect tried to win her over with soft words at first, and then with dire threats. Agnes met this mixture of cajolery and menace with derision, and said: "Do whatever you like, but you will not obtain what you want from me." The prefect: "You have just two choices. Either you will sacrifice to the goddess Vesta with her virgins, since your virginity means so much to you, or you will be thrown in with harlots and handled as they are handled." Because she was of the nobility, the prefect could not bring force to bear upon her, so he raised the charge of her Christianity. Agnes said: "I will not sacrifice to your gods, and no one can sully my virtue because I have with me a guardian of my body, an angel of the Lord." Then the prefect had her stripped and taken nude to a brothel, but God made her hair grow so long that it covered her better than any clothing. When she entered the house of shame, she found an angel waiting for her. His radiance filled the place with light and formed a shining mantle about her. Thus the brothel became a place of prayer, and anyone who honored the light came out cleaner than he had gone in.

The prefect's son now came with other young men, and invited them to go in and take their pleasure with her, but they were terrified by the miraculous light and hurried back to him. He scorned them as cowards and in a fury rushed in to force himself upon Agnes, but the same light engulfed him, and, since he had not honored God, the devil throttled him and he expired. When the prefect heard of this, he went to Agnes, weeping bitterly, and questioned her closely about the cause of his son's death. "The one whose will he wanted to carry out," she said, "thus got power over him and killed him, whereas his companions, frightened by the miracle they saw, retreated unharmed." The prefect persisted: "You can prove that you did not do this by some magical art, if you are able to bring him back to life by your prayer." So Agnes prayed, and the youth came to life and began to preach Christ publicly. At this the priests of the temples stirred up a tumult in the populace, shouting: "Away with the witch, away with the sorceress who turns people's heads and befuddles their wits!" On the other hand the prefect, impressed by the miracle, wished to set her free but, fearing that he would be outlawed, put a deputy in charge and went away sadly.

The deputy, Aspasius by name, had Agnes thrown into a roaring fire, but the flames divided and burned up the hostile crowd on either side, leaving the maiden unscathed. Aspasius finally had a soldier thrust a dagger into her throat, and thus her heavenly spouse consecrated her his bride and martyr. It is believed that she suffered in the reign of Constantine the Great, which began in AD 309. Her kinsmen and other Christians buried her joyfully and barely escaped the pagans who tried to stone them.

Saint Agnes had a foster sister named Emerentiana, a holy virgin who had not yet received baptism. She stood by the grave and continued to berate the pagans, who proceeded to stone her to death. At once God sent an earthquake with lightning and thunder, and a large number of pagans perished; and from that time on they did not harm those who came to the virgin's tomb. The saint's parents and relatives, watching beside her grave on the eighth day, saw a chorus of angels clothed in shining gold garments, and in their midst Agnes, similarly clad and with a lamb whiter than snow standing at her right hand. Agnes consoled them: "Do not mourn my death but rejoice and be glad with me, because I now have a throne of light amidst all these holy ones." In memory of this, the octave of the feast of Saint Agnes is observed.

Constance, Constantine's daughter and a virgin, was stricken with leprosy, and when she heard of the vision just described, she went to the saint's grave. While praying there she fell asleep and saw Saint Agnes, who said to her: "Be constant, Constance! If you believe in Christ, you will be freed of your disease." Awakening at the sound of the voice she found herself completely cured. She received baptism and had a basilica erected over the saint's grave. There she continued to live a virginal life and by her example gathered many virgins around her.

Paulinus, a priest serving the church of Saint Agnes, was tormented by a violent temptation of the flesh and, not wishing to offend God, sought permission of the supreme pontiff to contract marriage. The pope, knowing the priest's goodness and simplicity, gave him a ring set with an emerald and ordered him to go before a beautiful statue of Saint Agnes that stood in her church, and to command her, in the pope's name, to allow herself to become his betrothed. When the priest delivered this order, the statue immediately extended the ring finger, accepted the ring, and withdrew the hand, and the priest was delivered of his temptation. It is said that this ring can still be seen on the finger of the statue. Elsewhere, however, we read that the pope told a priest that he wanted him to commit himself to a certain spouse, to take care of her and nourish her, and that this spouse was the church of Saint Agnes, which was falling into ruins. The pope gave him a ring that would mark his espousal to the aforesaid statue, and the statue extended its finger and withdrew it. Thus the priest espoused the statue.

In his book *On Virgins*, Ambrose says of Saint Agnes: "The old, the young, the children sing of her! No one is more worthy of praise than the one who is praised by all! All men are her heralds, who by speaking of her proclaim her martyrdom. Marvel, all of you, that she stood forth as God's witness although at her age she could not yet decide about herself! So it came about that what she said regarding God was believed, although what she said about man was not yet believed, because what is beyond nature is from the author of nature. This is a new kind of martyrdom! One hardly capable of suffering is already ripe for victory, one unready to fight is yet able to win the crown, one masters virtue before reaching the age of judgment! Bride hastens not to the bridal chamber as the virgin marched to the place of torture, joyous her approach, swift her stride!" And, from Ambrose's *Preface*: "Saint Agnes, disdaining the advantages of noble birth, merited heavenly honors; caring nothing for what human society desires, she won the society of the eternal king; accepting a precious death for professing Christ, she at the same time was conformed to his likeness."

2. St. Mary of Egypt (BHL 5421)

Mary the Egyptian, who is called the Sinner, led a most austere life in the desert for forty-seven years, beginning about the year of the Lord in the time of Claudius. A priest named Zozimus crossed the Jordan and began to wander through the broad forest, hoping to find some holy father there, and saw a figure walking about naked, the body blackened and burned by the fiery sun. It was Mary the Egyptian. She immediately took flight, and Zozimus ran after her as fast as he could. She said to him: "Father Zozimus, why are you pursuing me? Forgive me, I cannot face you because I am a woman and naked, but lend me your mantle so that I may see you without being ashamed." Astonished at being called by name, he gave her his mantle and prostrated himself on the ground, asking her to bless him. "It behooves you, father," she said, "to give the blessing, since you are adorned with the dignity of priesthood." When he heard that she knew both his name and his office, he marveled still more and urgently besought her to bless him. Then she said: "Blessed be God, the redeemer of our souls!" She extended her hands in prayer, and he saw her lifted some feet above the earth. The old man began to suspect that this might be a spirit pretending to pray. "May God forgive you," she said, "for thinking that I, a sinful woman, might be an unclean spirit."

Now Zozimus adjured her in God's name to tell him about herself. Her answer was: "Excuse me, father, because if I tell you who and what I am, you will flee as if frightened by a serpent, your ears will be contaminated by my words, the air will be polluted with filth."

The old man forcefully insisted nonetheless, so she began: "I was born in Egypt, brother, and went to Alexandria when I was twelve years old. There, for seventeen years, I plied my trade as a public woman and never refused my body to anyone. But there came a time when some people of that region were going up to Jerusalem to pay homage to the holy cross, and I asked the sailors to allow me to go with them. When they asked me for my fare, I said: 'Brothers, I have no other fare, but take my body in payment for the passage.' So they took me aboard and I paid my fare with my body.

"I arrived at Jerusalem and went to the church with the others to worship the holy cross, but suddenly, by an invisible force, I was pushed back from the door and not allowed to enter. Again and again I got to the threshold of the entrance and suffered the pain of being repulsed, while the others went in freely and encountered no obstacle. Then I came to myself and realized that this was happening to me because of my dreadful crimes. I began to beat my breast, I shed bitter tears and sighed from the bottom of my heart. Then, looking up, I saw there an image of the Blessed Virgin Mary. I began to pray tearfully to her, asking her to obtain pardon for my sins and to let me go in and worship the holy cross, promising that I would renounce the world and thenceforth live chastely. Having offered this prayer and putting my trust in the name of the Blessed Virgin, I went again to the door of the church and entered without difficulty.

"When I had worshiped the cross with the utmost devotion, someone gave me three coins with which I bought three loaves of bread, and I heard a voice saying to me: 'If you go across the Jordan, you will be saved.' I therefore crossed the Jordan and came into this desert, where I have stayed for forty-seven years without seeing a single human being. The loaves I had brought with me turned hard as stone, but they have sufficed me for food all these years. My clothes fell to pieces in time. For seventeen years I was troubled by temptations of the flesh, but now by the grace of God I have conquered them all. There now, I have told you my whole story, and I beseech you to pray to God for me."

The priest knelt and blessed the Lord in his handmaid. She said: "I beg you to come back to the Jordan on the day of the Lord's Supper and to bring with you the Body of the Lord, and I will meet you there and receive the sacred Body from your hand, because since the day I came here I have not received the communion of the Lord." The old man returned to his monastery, and the following year, when Holy Thursday was drawing near, he took the sacred Host and went to the bank of the Jordan. He saw the woman standing on the other bank, and she made the sign of the cross over the river and walked across the water. Marveling at this, the priest prostrated himself at her feet. She said: "Do not do that! You have the sacrament of the Lord on your person and you shine with the dignity of priesthood. But I pray you, father, that you may deign to come again to me next year." Then, once again making the sign of the cross over Jordan waters, she went over and returned to the solitude of the desert.

The father went back to his monastery and a year later sought the place where he had first spoken to the woman. He came to the place and found her lying there dead. He began to weep and did not dare to touch her, saying to himself "I wish I could bury the saint's body, but I fear this might displease her." As he was thinking about this, he noticed something written in the sand beside her head, and read: "Zozimus, bury Mary's little body, return her dust to the earth, and pray for me to the Lord, at whose command I left this world on the second day of April." Thus the old man knew for certain that she had reached the end of her days immediately after receiving the Lord's sacrament and returning to the desert, and that she had crossed this expanse of desert in one hour and migrated to God, whereas it took him thirty days to cover the same distance.

Zozimus tried to dig a grave but could not. Then he saw a lion meekly coming toward him and said to the lion: "This holy woman commanded me to bury her body here, but I am old and cannot dig, and anyway I have no shovel. Therefore you do the digging and we will be able to bury this holy body." The lion began to dig and prepared a suitable grave, and when that was finished went away like a gentle lamb, while the old man made his way back to his monastery, glorifying God.

3. St. Christopher (BHL 1779)

Before Christopher was baptized, he was called Reprobus, meaning outcast, but afterwards he was called Christophoros, the Christ-bearer. He bore Christ in four ways, namely, on his shoulders when he carried him across the river, in his body by mortification, in his mind by devotion, and in his mouth by confessing Christ and preaching him.

Christopher was a Canaanite by birth, a man of prodigious size – he was twelve feet tall – and fearsome of visage. According to some accounts of his life it happened one day, when he was in the presence of a certain Canaanite king, that the idea came to him of going in quest of the greatest prince in the world and staying with him. He came to a mighty king who was regarded generally as the world's greatest ruler. When this king saw Christopher, he received him gladly and made him a member of his court.

Then one day the court jester sang some ditty before the king, in which frequent mention was made of the devil. The king was a Christian and made the sign of the cross on his forehead when he heard the devil spoken of. Christopher noticed this, and wondered why the king did it and what the sign meant. He asked the king about it and, when the ruler did not answer, said to him: "Unless you answer my question I will not stay with you any longer!" The king, thus pressed, told him: "Whenever I hear the devil mentioned, I defend myself with this sign, for fear the devil might get some power over me and do me harm!" Christopher: "If you're afraid of being harmed by the devil, this proves that he is greater and more powerful than you are, or you wouldn't be afraid of him. Therefore I am frustrated in my hope that I had found the greatest and most powerful lord in the world. So now farewell! I'll go and look for the devil, accept him as my master, and become his servant!"

Christopher left that king and went in search of the devil. He was going through a desert when he saw a great host of soldiers, and one of them, fiercer and more terrible than the rest, came to him and asked where he was going. Christopher answered: "I'm looking for the lord devil! I want to take him as my master." The other said to him: "I'm the one you're looking for!" Christopher was happy to hear this and pledged himself to serve him forever, acknowledging him as his lord and master.

They marched along the highway until they came to a cross erected at roadside. When the devil saw it, he was terror-stricken, left the road, and led Christopher over a wild and desolate tract before returning to the road. Christopher was surprised at this, and asked the devil what made him so afraid that he left the highroad and took another way through a rough wilderness. The devil refused to state his reason, and Christopher said: "Unless you tell me what this is about, I shall leave you immediately!" The demon, no longer able to evade the question, said: "There was a man named Christ who was nailed to a cross, and when I see the sign of his cross, I am filled with terror and run away!" Christopher: "Well, then, this Christ, whose sign you dread so much, is greater and more powerful than you are! Therefore I have labored in vain and have not yet found the greatest prince in the world! So good-bye to you! I'm leaving you and going in search of Christ!"

He looked long and far for someone who could give him word of Christ. Finally he came upon a hermit who preached Christ to him and instructed him diligently in the Christian faith. He said to Christopher: "This king whom you wish to serve requires that you do his will in many ways. For instance, you will have to fast frequently." Christopher: "Let him require some other form of obedience! That one I just can't do!" Again the hermit: "You will also have to offer him many prayers." Christopher: "I don't even know what that means, so I can't perform that kind of service!" The hermit then asked him: "Do you know the famous river, where many people, trying to get across, go under and perish?" "Yes I do!" said Christopher. The hermit: "You're big enough and strong enough! Go dwell by the river, and if you help those who wish to cross it, that will greatly please Christ the king whom you wish to serve, and I hope he might show himself to you there!" Christopher: "Good! That kind of service I can give, and I promise to serve him that way!"

He went to the river and built himself a shelter to live in. Instead of a staff he used a long pole to steady himself in the water, and carried across all those who wished to go. Many days later he was resting in his shelter when he heard a child's voice calling him: "Christopher, come out and carry me across!" He jumped to his feet and went out, but found no one. He went indoors and again heard the same voice calling him, but ran out and again saw no one. The third time he responded to the same call and found a child standing on the riverbank. The child begged him to carry him across the river, and Christopher lifted him to his shoulders, grasped his great staff, and strode into the water. But little by little the water grew rougher and the child became as heavy as lead: the farther he went, the higher rose the waves, and the weight of the child pressed down upon his shoulders so crushingly that he was in dire distress. He feared that he was about to founder, but at last he reached the other bank.

Setting the child down he said to him: "My boy, you put me in great danger, and you weighed so much that if I had had the whole world on my back I could not have felt it a heavier burden!" The child answered him: "Don't be surprised, Christopher! You were not only carrying the whole world, you had him who created the world upon your shoulders! I am Christ your king, to whom you render service by doing the work you do here. And if you want proof that what I am saying is true, when you get back to your little house, plant your staff in the earth, and tomorrow you will find it in leaf and bearing fruit!" With that the child vanished. Christopher crossed over and thrust his staff into the earth near his shelter. The next morning he rose and found the staff bearing leaves and fruit like a palm tree.

After that, Christopher went to Samos, a city in Lycia. He did not understand the language spoken there, and prayed the Lord to make him able to understand it. As he prayed, the judges thought he was insane and left him alone; but when the favor he had prayed for was granted, he covered his face and went to the place where Christians were being tortured and executed, to speak to them and give them courage in the Lord. One of the judges struck him in the face, and Christopher, uncovering his face, said: "If I were not a Christian, I would quickly have revenge for this insult!" Then he planted his staff in the earth and prayed the to Lord that it might burst into leaf and thus help to convert the people. Leaves sprouted instantly, and eight thousand men believed and became Christians.

The king now sent two hundred soldiers to bring Christopher to him, but they found him at prayer and were afraid to tell him why they had come. The king sent as many more, but they, when they found him praying, prayed with him. Christopher rose and said to them: "For whom are you looking?" Seeing his face, they said: "The king sent us to bring you to him in bonds!"

Christopher: "If I did not wish to go, you could not take me, bound or not!" They said: "Well, then, if you don't want to come, take your leave and go wherever you wish, and we'll tell the king that we could not find you anywhere." "Not so!" he replied, "I will go with you!"

So Christopher converted the soldiers to the faith, and had them tie his hands behind his back and present him, thus bound, to the king. The sight of him terrified the king, who fell from his seat. His servitors raised him, and he asked Christopher his name and country of origin. Christopher replied: "Before baptism I was called Reprobus but now am called Christopher." The king: "You have taken a foolish name, calling yourself after Christ, who was crucified and could do nothing to save himself, and now can do nothing for you! Now, then, you trouble-making Canaanite, why do you not sacrifice to our gods?" Christopher: "You are rightly called Dagnus, because you are the death of the world and the devil's partner, and your gods are the work of men's hands!" The king: "You were brought up among wild beasts, and you can do only the works of savages and talk only of things unknown to men! Now, however, if you are ready to sacrifice, I will bestow great honors upon you. If not, you will be tortured to death!" Christopher refused to sacrifice, and the king put him in jail. As for the soldiers whom he had sent after Christopher, he had them beheaded for the name of Christ.

Now the king had two shapely young women, one named Nicaea and the other Aquilina, put into the cell with Christopher, promising them large rewards if they succeeded in seducing him. Christopher quickly saw through the stratagem and knelt to pray. When the women tried to arouse him by stroking him and putting their arms around him, he stood up and said to them: "What are you trying to do and for what reason were you sent in here?" The two were frightened by the radiance of his face and said: "Saint of God, pity us! Make us able to believe in the God to whom you preach!"

Word of this reached the king, who had the women brought to him, and said: "So you too have been seduced! I swear by the gods that unless you sacrifice to the gods, you will die an awful death!" They answered: "If your will is that we offer sacrifice, have the streets cleared and order all the people into the temple!" This done, they went into the temple, loosened their girdles, and threw them around the necks of the idols, pulling them to the ground and reducing them to dust. Then they said to the assistants: "Call your doctors and let them heal your gods!"

By order of the king, Aquilina was then hung up by the wrists and a huge stone was tied to her feet, thus breaking all her limbs. When she had breathed her last in the Lord, her sister Nicaea was thrown into the fire, but when she emerged unscathed, she was beheaded at once.

Christopher was then brought before the king, who ordered him to be beaten with iron rods, and to have an iron helmet, heated in the fire, placed on his head. Then he had an iron chair made. The saint was bound into it, then a fire was lighted underneath and pitch thrown on the flames. But the chair crumbled like wax, and Christopher came away from it unharmed. Then the king had him lashed to a pillar and ordered four hundred bowmen to shoot arrows at him, but the arrows hung in midair and not a single one of them could touch him. But when the king, thinking that he had been mortally wounded, came to mock him, suddenly one of the arrows came through the air, turned back, and struck the tyrant in the eye, blinding him. Christopher said to him: "Tyrant, I will be dead by tomorrow. Then make a paste with my blood and rub it on your eyes, and you will recover your sight!"

By the king's order the saint was led away to the place of execution, where after praying he was beheaded. The king took a little of his blood and rubbed it on his eyes, saying: "In the name of God and Saint Christopher," and his sight was restored immediately. Then he was baptized and issued a decree that whoever blasphemed against God or Saint Christopher was to be beheaded at once.

Ambrose in his Preface says of this martyr: "O Lord, you granted such a wealth of virtue and such grace of teaching to Christopher that by his gleaming miracles he recalled forty-eight thousand men from the error of paganism to the cult of Christian dogma. Nicaea and Aquilina had been engaged in prostitution in a public brothel, but he won them over to the practice of chastity and schooled them to receive the crown of martyrdom. For this he was strapped into an iron chair in the middle of a blazing fire but feared no harm from the heat. For a whole day the storm of arrows shot by the soldiers could not pierce him; yet one arrow struck the executioner in the eye, and the blessed martyr's blood mixed with earth restored his sight and by removing the body's blindness also illumined his mind; for the saint besought your forgiveness and by his supplications obtained the cure of diseases and infirmities."

4. St. James the Dismembered (BHL 4101)

St. James, called the Dismembered because of the way he was martyred, was noble by birth and yet more noble by his faith. He was a native of the city of Elape in the land of the Persians, born of most Christian parents and wedded to a most Christian wife. To the king of the Persians he was well known, and stood first among his peers. It happened, however, that he was misled by the prince and his close friendship with him, and was induced to worship the idols. When his mother and his wife found this out, they wrote him a letter, saying: "By doing the will of a mortal man, you have deserted him with whom there is life; to please one who will be a mass of rottenness, you have deserted the eternal fragrance; you have traded truth for a lie; by acceding to a mortal's wish you have abandoned the judge of the living and the dead. Know therefore that from now on we are strangers to you and will no longer live in the same house with you."

When James read this letter, he wept bitterly and said: "If my mother and my wife have become strangers to me, how much more must I have estranged God?" He therefore inflicted harsh penances on himself in expiation of his fault. Then a messenger went to the prince and told him that James was a Christian, and the prince sent for him. "Tell me," he said to James, "are you a Nazarene?" "Yes," James answered, "I am a Nazarene." The prince: "Then you are a sorcerer!" James: "Far be it from me to be a sorcerer!" The prince threatened him with many kinds of torture, but James said: "Your threats do not bother me, because just as the wind blows over a stone, your anger goes quickly in one ear and out the other!" The prince: "Don't be a fool, or you may die a dreadful death!" James: "That is not death but should rather be called sleep, since in a short time resurrection is granted." The prince: "Don't let the Nazarenes deceive you by telling you that death is a sleep, because even great emperors fear it!" James: "We do not fear death, because we hope to pass from death to life!"

Upon the advice of his friends, the prince now sentenced James to death member by member, in order to strike fear into others. When some people wept out of compassion for him, he said: "Don't weep for me, but mourn for yourselves, because I go on to life, while eternal torment is your due!"

Now the torturers cut off the thumb of his right hand, and James cried out and said: "O Nazarene, my liberator, accept this branch of the tree of your mercy, for the husbandman trims the dry branches from the vine in order to let it grow stronger and be crowned with more fruit!" The headsman said: "If you wish to give in, I shall spare you and bring ointments for your wound." James: "Haven't you ever examined the trunk of a tree? The dry tendrils are cut away, and in due season, when the earth warms, each nub left by the pruning puts forth a new shoot. If therefore the vine is thought to need pruning in order to grow and bear fruit as the seasons revolve, how much greater the need of a man of faith who is grafted into Christ, the true vine!"

The torturer cut off the forefinger, and James said: "Accept, O Lord, the two branches that your right hand planted." The third finger was cut off; and James said: "I am now set free from the threefold temptation, and I will bless the Father, the Son, and the Holy Spirit. With the three youths rescued from the fiery furnace I will confess to you, O Lord, and amidst the choir of the martyrs I will sing psalms to your name, O Christ!" The fourth finger was severed, and James said: "Protector of the sons of Israel, you were foretold in the fourth blessing [Jacob's blessing on Judah in *Gen.* 49, 8–12]. Accept from your servant the confession of the fourth finger as blessed in Judah." The fifth was cut off, and he said: "My joy is complete."

Then the executioners said to him: "Now is the time to spare your soul, lest you perish. And don't be sad because you've lost one hand. Many men have only one hand, yet abound in wealth and honors!" Blessed James responded: "When shepherds shear their sheep, do they take off the fleece from the right side and leave the left side unsheared? And if the sheep, a dumb animal, wants to lose all its fleece, how much the more should I, a rational man, not think it beneath me to die for God?" Therefore those impious men proceeded to amputate the little finger of his left hand, and James said: "You, Lord, were great, but you chose to become little and least for us, and therefore I give back to you the body and the soul that you created and redeemed by your blood." The seventh finger was taken, and James said: "Seven times a day I have given praise to the Lord." The eighth was removed and he said: "On the eighth day Jesus was circumcised, and the Hebrew male child is circumcised on the eighth day in order to pass over to the ceremonies of the Law: so let the mind of your servant pass over from these uncircumcised men with their unclean foreskins, and let me come and look upon your face!" The ninth finger was cut off and he said: "At the ninth hour Christ yielded up his spirit on the Cross, and so I, Lord, confess to you in the pain of the ninth finger and give you thanks!" The tenth was taken, and he said: "Ten is the number of the commandments, and J is the initial letter of the name Jesus Christ."

Then some of the bystanders said: "O you who were so dear to us in the past, just profess their god before the consul so that you can go on living; and even though your hands are cut off, there are expert physicians who will be able to ease your pain!" To them James said: "Far be it from me to be guilty of so unspeakable a deception! No one who puts his hand to the plow and looks back is fit for the kingdom of God!" The angry torturers came and cut off the great toe of his right foot, and James said: "Christ's foot was pierced and blood poured out!" They took the second toe and he said: "Great above all days is this day to me, for today I shall be turned and go to almighty God." They cut off the third toe and threw it in front of him, and James smiled and said: "Go, third toe, to your fellow toes, and as the grain of wheat bears much fruit, so you at the last day will rest with your companions." The fourth went, and he said: "Why are you sad, my soul, and why do you disquiet me? I hope in God for I will still give praise to him, the salvation of my countenance and my God." The fifth was taken, and he said: "Now I shall begin to say to the Lord that he has made me a worthy companion to his servants."

Then they went to the left foot and took off the little toe, and James said: "Little toe, be comforted, because the big and the little will all rise again, and not a hair of the head will perish. How much less will you, the littlest, be separated from your fellows!" The second was taken, and James said: "Destroy the old house, a more splendid one is being prepared." After the third, he said: "The anvil is made more solid by the blows of the hammer." The fourth toe was amputated, and he said: "Comfort me, God of truth, for I trust in you, and in the shade of your wings I will hope until iniquity passes away." The fifth went, and he said: "Look upon me, O Lord, I offer sacrifice twenty times!"

Next, the executioners cut off James's right foot, and he said: "Now I shall offer a gift to the King of heaven, for love of whom I endure these pains." They cut off the left foot and he said: "It is you who work wonders, Lord! Hear me and save me!" They cut off his right hand, and he said: "May your mercies help me, O Lord!" After the left hand, he said: "You are the God who works wonders." Off with his right arm, and he said: "Praise the Lord, my soul, in my life I will praise the Lord, I will sing to my God as long as I shall be!" Now his left arm, and he said: "The sorrows of death surrounded me, and in the name of the Lord I will be avenged." Next it was the right leg, which they cut off at the thigh. Blessed James, stricken with unspeakable pain, cried out, saying: "Lord Jesus Christ, help me, because the groans of death have surrounded me!" And he said to the torturers: "The Lord will clothe me with new flesh, upon which the wounds you inflict will not be able to leave a stain." They were exhausted, having toiled from the first to the ninth hour of the day at dismembering blessed James, but now they returned to their task, taking off the calf of the left leg up to the thigh. Blessed James cried out: "O Lord and Ruler, hear me half alive, Lord of the living and the dead! Fingers, Lord, I have none to hold out to you, nor hands to extend to you; my feet are cut off and my knees demolished, so that I cannot kneel to you, and I am like a house that is about to fall because the columns that support it have been taken away. Heed me, Lord Jesus Christ, and lead my soul out of prison!"

When James had said this, one of the executioners cut off his head. Then Christians came secretly, seized his body, and buried it with honors. He suffered on the twenty-seventh day of November.

9. CATHERINE OF SIENA: HER LIFE AND LETTERS

Such is the importance of Catherine of Siena (1347-80) that she is paired with Francis of Assisi as patron saints of Italy. She was born in Siena, the youngest child of Jacopo Benincasa, a dyer, and his wife Lapa. As a child she was exceptional, experiencing her first vision at the age of six and dedicating herself to Christ a year later. As a young woman, she imposed increasingly harsh disciplines upon herself, particularly in fasting. She overcame the fierce opposition of her family, who wanted her to marry, and eventually entered the order of St. Dominic as a tertiary, a member of a group of devout women living under religious rule but in their own homes. Gradually, her reputation grew and she acquired a group of disciples around her with whom she remained close, while becoming increasingly involved in public affairs.

During her lifetime, violent warfare erupted between the forces of the pope and the nobles of the Italian city states. Catherine played the role of peacemaker with varying success, traveling between the opposing groups like a modern-day diplomat while attempting to bring them together. In 1377 she was able to persuade Pope Gregory XI (who had taken refuge in Avignon) to return to Rome, only for him to die the following year. He was replaced by Urban VI, who was less receptive to her advice, and the two years before her death saw the disastrous development of the Great Schism which divided Europe: Urban, supported by England, reigned in Italy, while Clement VII, supported by France, asserted his claims to the papacy from Avignon. Catherine died after a lengthy and painful illness with a deep sense of sorrow at the increasing corruption of the Church and abiding guilt for what to her was a personal failure in not accomplishing more.

Her 'Life' was written by her friend and confessor, Raymond of Capua (1330-99), a Dominican priest. As her biographer, Raymond situates himself between his subject and spiritual superior, Catherine, and his audience and spiritual inferiors; while admiration dominates the former, a need to convince, instruct, and assure the accuracy of his sources dominates the latter. However, Raymond knew Catherine intimately and is able to bring her to life despite his strong didactic tone. He recalls that whenever Catherine talked about God, her conversation often continued for so long that he sometimes nodded off. On one such occasion she rebuked him: "My dear man, do you really want to miss things useful to your soul, just for the sake of sleep? Am I supposed to be talking to you or the wall?" She emerges as a person of enormous willpower and feeling, affectionate and considerate toward friends and family, stern and impassioned toward those she saw as betraying the Church, always reserving the harshest judgment for herself.

These and other characteristics are displayed in a collection of 380 letters, of which six are included below. They show the range of her writing from descriptions of her visions and ecstasies, to her concern for friends and, for her mother, especially, to her ability to address the highest officials in Christendom in terms both tactful and demanding.

Sources: trans. George Lamb, *The Life of St. Catherine of Siena, by Raymond of Capua* (Rockford, IL: Tan Books and Publishers, Inc., 2003), pp. 36–45, 46–50, 150–63, 164–67. repr. with permission. Trans. Vida D. Scudder, *Saint Catherine of Siena as Seen in Her Letters* (London and New York: Dutton, 1906), pp. 102–03, 110–14, 117–23, 186–88, 233–35, 346–52.

Excerpts from *The Life of St. Catherine of Siena by Raymond of Capua*

Part I, Chapter 4
Bitter Struggles

... When this virgin dedicated to the Lord reached the marriageable age of about twelve she began to be kept at home – according to the local custom, for in Siena it is not usual for unmarried girls of that age to be allowed out of the house.

Besides this, her mother and father and brothers, not knowing her intentions, were already thinking of getting her married, and were trying to find a suitable match for her.

Her mother especially, with her daughter's goodness and wisdom in mind, had dreams of rejoicing in some distinguished son-in-law – though her daughter had in fact already obtained a greater son-in-law than she could possibly have imagined!

Lapa began to bother about her daughter's appearance, teaching her how to behave, making her wash her face and neck properly, keeping her hair combed and tidy – in short, doing all she could to make her attractive so that if anyone should come along to ask for her they should find her pretty. But Catherine had quite different ideas, however much, out of respect, she kept quiet about the vow she had made, and she refused to do any of these things: she was fully occupied trying to please, not men, but God.

Her mother anxiously watched the way she was behaving, and one day she summoned her married daughter Bonaventura and told her to get Catherine to follow her mother's advice and make herself beautiful like everyone else. Lapa knew that Catherine was very fond of Bonaventura and that she would listen to her more than to anyone else, as in fact she did; and as a result of Bonaventura's determined efforts the Lord permitted the young girl to agree to pay more attention to her dress, though at the same time keeping firmly to her vow not to take a husband.

Later, in confession, she used to acknowledge this fault with so many sobs and tears that one would have thought she had committed heaven knows what sin. Now that she has ascended into heaven I can reveal these things which redound so much to her glory, though in the first place they were meant to be kept secret, and I may mention the argument that arose between us during one of the many general confessions she made to me, when arriving at this point she turned on herself, sobbing and crying and harshly upbraiding herself.

Though experience has taught me that pious souls can find sins where there are no sins, and turn quite small ones into big ones, nevertheless, since Catherine was upbraiding herself as though she had committed some fault worthy of everlasting punishment I was constrained to ask her whether she had thought of breaking her vow of virginity. She answered that no such thought had ever come into her head. I next asked her whether, apart from this matter of her virginity, she had dressed up to please any particular man or men in general, and she said that nothing had so upset her as to see or be seen by men or to find herself in their company. Whenever the apprentices in her father's dye works, who lived with the family, came near her, she would rush off as though there were serpents after her – much to everyone's amazement. Nor would she ever stand at the window or the front door to see who was passing. So I asked her, "Why ever should you have deserved eternal punishment for trying to make yourself look pretty, if you didn't carry it to excess?" Catherine replied that the real trouble was that she had loved her sister more than she should have done, and in fact seemed to have loved her more than God; and that that was what made her cry and why she had to do such severe penance for it. And when I said that although there may have been some slight excess, nevertheless it had been very slight indeed and free from any vain intention in itself and so had contained nothing against the law of God, she raised her eyes and her voice to God and exclaimed, "Oh, Lord God, what kind of a spiritual father is this you have given me, who finds excuses for my sins!" Then, growing angry with herself, she turned to me and went on, "Father, is this vile miserable creature who has received so many graces from her creator without any labor or merit on her own part supposed to spend her time beautifying her putrid flesh to deceive some poor mortal? I don't believe," she went on, "that hell itself would have been a sufficient punishment for me if the divine pity had not had mercy on me." I could not but be silent.

... And now let us return to our story.

Bonaventura went on trying to cajole the holy girl into imitating her example and dressing up in her best clothes, but she could never get her to feel an inclination for any man or even to be voluntarily seen by men, even though her prayers and assiduity in meditating were gradually losing their fervor. But Almighty God, unable to bear the sight of his chosen bride being drawn even the slightest bit further away from him, himself removed the obstacle that was preventing her from uniting herself with him; for Bonaventura, having led her holy sister into the ways of vanity, shortly afterwards found herself about to give birth, and, young as she was, died in doing so.

And here, reader, note how hateful and displeasing to God are people who do anything to interfere with those who desire to serve him. Bonaventura was in herself a perfectly good woman from every point of view, but because she had tried to draw one who wished to serve him towards the world, God came down heavily upon her and punished her with death. She obtained mercy, however, for, as was subsequently revealed to the virgin, after finding herself in purgatory and undergoing severe punishment she ascended to heaven as a result of her sister's prayers; this the latter told me in confidence.

On her sister's death the holy virgin, now seeing clearly the vanity of the world, turned to her Eternal Bridegroom with greater fervor and desire, and acknowledging her culpability and upbraiding herself, prostrate with Mary Magdalene at the feet of her Lord, she gave herself to tears, imploring his to have mercy on her, praying and pondering on her sin, hoping to hear the words once addressed to Mary herself, "Thy sins are forgiven thee." She began to develop a particular devotion towards the Magdalene, doing everything she could to imitate her to obtain forgiveness. This devotion grew and grew until, as with the Lord's help I shall explain in detail later, the Bridegroom of all holy souls and his glorious Mother assigned the Magdalene to the holy virgin as her own mistress and mother.

Things had reached such a state, in fact, that the age-long Enemy, seeing the virgin now running with the utmost speed to the safe refuge of the tabernacle of all mercy (her Bridegroom), found to his dismay that the prey which he had hoped gradually to make his own was escaping out of his hands, and to prevent this from happening he determined to set a trap for her through her own people at home, hoping that opposition and persecution would in the end draw her to the things of this world.

He put it into their heads, in fact, to find Catherine a husband somehow or other and so get themselves a new member of the family. They were further encouraged to do this because of the loss of their other daughter Bonaventura and hoped that Catherine would make up for the bereavement they had suffered. And so especially after Bonaventura's death they did all they could to find the holy maiden a husband.

When the virgin began to realize this, and, under the Lord's inspiration, saw what the Devil was up to, she began to pray more than ever, devoting herself entirely to meditation and penance and eschewing all masculine society, thereby making it quite clear to her family that she had absolutely no desire for a mortal corruptible husband – because from her earliest years she had been betrothed in grace to the immortal king of all the ages.

The holy maiden kept on making this quite clear in every way she could, but her parents decided to force her and went to see one of the Order of Preaching Friars, a friend of the family, who is still alive. They implored him to try to persuade her to give way and this he promised to do; and in fact he went to see the virgin, and, finding her firm in her holy intention, felt bound in conscience to give her this sensible advice: "Since there seems to be absolutely no doubt that you wish to serve the Lord," he said, "and these people keep pestering you to do the opposite, show them you mean what you say – cut your hair off, and then perhaps they'll keep quiet!" Accepting this advice as though it came from heaven, Catherine seized a pair of scissors and joyfully cut her hair off to the roots, hating it as the cause of her grievous sin. Then she covered her head with a cap. From then on, in fact, unlike other girls, but in accordance with the teaching of the Apostle, she began to go about in a veiled cap.

When her mother Lapa noticed this she asked her why she was wearing this strange kind of headgear, but she could not get any precise answer out of her, for Catherine did not want to lie or prevaricate, and so she mumbled instead of replying openly; whereupon her mother went up to her, snatched the cap off her head, and found her head close-cropped. This gave her a big shock, for Catherine had had very beautiful hair. "Whatever have you done, daughter?" she wailed. Catherine simply put the cap back on her head and walked away, but Lapa's shrieks had brought her husband and sons running up, and when they discovered what had happened they were furious with the girl.

This was the beginning of Catherine's second battle, a fiercer one even than the first; but with the help of heaven it resulted in a victory so complete that the very things that had seemed as though they were bound to act against her worked miraculously to her advantage and united her more closely with the Lord.

In the house they started persecuting her openly, threatening and abusing her. "You wretched girl," they said, "you may have cut off your hair, but don't imagine that you have succeeded in your purpose. Your hair is bound to grow again, and we will force you to take a husband, even if it breaks your heart; you will have no rest until you do what we want you to."

It was decided that from now on Catherine was not to have a room of her own and was to be kept busy doing housework so that she would have no opportunity for praying and uniting herself with her bridegroom. So that she would realize she was in disgrace the maid was given a rest, and she was made to do all the dirty work in the kitchen in her place, and every day she was deluged with insults, taunts and jeers of a kind especially designed to hurt her feelings as a girl. Finally they managed to find her a young man, whom, according to what I have been told, they would have been very glad to have in the family, and then they attacked her even more fiercely to force her to give her consent to him.

The age-old adversary, whose guile and malignancy had started all this, imagined that he was triumphing over the girl, but in fact he was only making Catherine stronger, for she was quite unperturbed by all these upsets, and under the inspiration of the Holy Spirit she began to build up in her mind a secret cell which she vowed she would never leave for anything in the world. She had begun by having a room in a house, which she could go out of and come into at will; now, having made herself an inner cell which no one could take away from her, she had no need ever to come out of it again.

These were heavenly victories that could never be taken away from her, and they chained Satan down; for Truth itself has declared that the Kingdom of God is within us, and we know from the Prophet that all the glory of the eternal King's daughter is within. Within us, in fact, is the clear understanding, the free will, the tenacious memory; and into us is infused the unction of the Holy Spirit, which perfecting these powers overcomes and annihilates all obstacles outside; within us, if we are good strivers, lives that guest who said, "Have confidence, I have overcome the world."

Trusting in this guest, Catherine built for herself a cell not made with human hands, helped inwardly by Christ, and so was untroubled about losing a room with walls built by men. I remember – it has just come into my mind – that whenever I used to find myself pressed with too much business, or had to go on a journey, Catherine would say again and again, "Make yourself a cell in your own mind from which you need never come out." At that time I only understood what she meant superficially; but now, thinking back on her words, I am constrained to say with John the Evangelist, "These things his disciples did not know at the first: but when Jesus was glorified, then they remembered ..." It is remarkable how often it happens that I and the others who lived with her understand what she said and did better today than when she was amongst us.

Let us return to the story.

The Holy Spirit put into the virgin's mind another idea that enabled her to triumph over all the jeers and insults; this she revealed to me once when we were alone together, and I asked her how she had managed to retain her self-possession in the midst of all this ill-treatment. She told me that she had imagined her father as our Lord and Savior Jesus Christ, her mother as his most glorious mother, and her brothers and the other members of the family as the holy Apostles and disciples. With this in her mind, she had been able to serve them quite conscientiously and contentedly – much to their amazement. And also, while she was serving them, she could think about her bridegroom and imagine she was serving him too, and so when she was working in the kitchen she was all the time in the Holy of Holies and when she was waiting at table her soul could feed on the presence of the Savior. O height of the riches of the eternal counsel, in how many different and wonderful ways can you liberate those who trust in you from every kind of misery, guiding them through Scylla and Charybdis to the haven of eternal salvation!

So the matter remained: the holy virgin, with her eyes fixed unwaveringly on the reward promised her by the Holy Spirit, bore every offence with joyful patience, proceeding forward on the path marked out for her so that the joy of her soul might be complete. Unable now to have a room of her own and forced to be with the rest of the family all the time, with holy cunning she adopted her brother Stefano's room, as he had no wife or children, and during the day when he was out she could be alone there, and at night when he was asleep she could pray as much as she liked. Thus, ever seeking the face of the bridegroom, she stood knocking untiringly at the door of the divine tabernacle, praying continuously to the Lord that he would protect her virginity and singing with St. Cecilia the words of David, "Let my heart be undefiled in thy justifications."

Thus wondrously fortified by silence and hope, the fiercer the persecutions became, the more she was sustained by graces and consolations, until her brothers, seeing her constancy, said to each other, "She has defeated us." But her father, a better person than the others, silently pondered his daughter's behavior, and became more and more convinced every day that she was not being guided by any spirit of youthful caprice but by the spirit of God.

What I have said in this chapter has been told me by Lapa, Catherine's mother, and Lisa, the wife of one of her brothers; and what I could not be told by the other people in the house I learned from the holy virgin herself.

Chapter 5
Catherine's Victory

While the events narrated in the previous chapter were proceeding, the handmaid of Christ was one day praying fervently in her younger brother's room. The door was open because she had been forbidden by her parents to shut herself up anywhere, and her father Giacomo came in looking for something, knowing his son was out. When he entered he looked round, and instead of seeing what he wanted he found his daughter there – though she seemed to be more God's than his, for she was kneeling in a corner praying, and above her head was a snow-white dove, which flew up as soon as he came in, and then, as it seemed to him, flew out through the window. Giacomo asked his daughter whose dove it was that had just flown away but Catherine said she had not seen any dove, or anything else. This amazed him, and he kept all these things in his heart, going over them in his mind again and again.

At this time, as has been said above, there was increasing in the mind of the holy virgin the desire which had first come to her as a child, and which she now wished to realize so as to safeguard her virginity, that is to say, to take the habit of the Order of Preaching Friars, whose founder and organizer and father had been the most blessed Dominic. Day and night she turned untiringly to the Lord, imploring him to grant this wish of hers, developing too, as has been said above, a great devotion towards St. Dominic, who had always had such a splendid and most fruitful zeal for the salvation of souls. The Lord in his goodness, seeing the wisdom and fortitude with which his little disciple fought her battles and the fervor with which she was trying to make herself pleasing to him, willed to grant her wish and, to give her a greater sense of security, comforted her with the following vision.

It was given, then, to the handmaid of Christ to see in a dream many holy fathers, and the founders of various Orders, including the most blessed Dominic. She recognized him at once because he was holding in his hands a most beautiful dazzling white lily, which, like Moses' bush, burned brightly without ever being consumed. All the people present advised her in turn to enter one of their Orders but she kept her eyes fixed on St. Dominic and gradually moved towards him. Suddenly he came forward to meet her, holding in his hand the habit of the Sisters of Penance of St. Dominic of whom there have always been a great number in the city of Siena. When he came up to her he comforted her saying, "Sweetest daughter, take courage and fear no obstacle, for you will undoubtedly put on this habit, as is your wish." These words filled her with great joy, and with tears of happiness she gave thanks to God and to Dominic, the famous athlete of the Lord, for giving her such perfect consolation. Then she was awakened by her tears and came back to her senses.

The virgin felt so encouraged and fortified by this vision that she was emboldened that same day to call her parents and brothers together and speak to them as follows: "For a long time you have been talking amongst yourselves and planning to marry me off to some mortal, corruptible man, as you have told me; and though I cordially detest the idea, as you must have been able to see from a number of signs I have given you, nevertheless, I have kept quiet until now from the feeling of reverence that God commands us to show our parents. But now the time for keeping quiet is over, and I must tell you plainly what is in my heart and what my real intentions are. They did not

163

come to me today; on the contrary, I have had them ever since I was a child, and they have only grown stronger with the passage of time. You must know then that when I was quite a little girl I made a vow of virginity to our Lord Jesus Christ, the Savior of the world, and his most glorious mother; and I did not do this childishly, but after long reflection and intentionally, and I promised him that I would never marry anyone but him through all eternity. Now that with the grace of God I have reached years of discretion and have more understanding you must know that there are some things so firmly established within me that it would be easier to soften a stone than to remove them from my heart. The more you go on about this the more you will be wasting your time; so I advise you to throw all thoughts of an engagement for me to the winds, because I have no intention whatsoever of obliging you in that respect: I must obey God rather than men. Further: if you want to keep me in this house as a servant I am quite prepared to stay and will willingly do my best to serve you; but if you prefer to cast me out you can rest assured that I shall not deviate from my intention by a hair's breadth. I have a rich and powerful husband who will never let me die of hunger, and I am certain that he will never let me go without any of the things I need."

When the family heard this they burst into tears, and what with the sobs and the sighs no one was in a fit condition to say a word for some time. They had now fully realized the seriousness of the virgin's holy intention and did not dare oppose it, and they gazed dumbstruck at this girl who had hitherto always been so silent and shy but who had now revealed her thoughts so clearly and bravely and in such well-chosen words; and when they saw that she was prepared to leave home rather than break the vow she had made, which meant that there was no hope of her ever getting married, they were so moved that they found tears easier than words.

After a while they began to recover, and Catherine's father, who loved her tenderly, and who also feared God more than the others, remembered the dove he had seen and a number of other things he had noticed with amazement and said, "God forbid, darling daughter, that we should oppose the divine will from which it is clear your holy intention proceeds. We have realized this for some time as a matter of fact, but now we know for certain that you are not moved by youthful caprice but by an impulse of divine love. So keep your vow. Do exactly as you wish, and as the Holy Spirit teaches you. From now on we shall leave you in peace to your holy works, and put no more obstacles in the way of your holy exercises. Pray for us all a great deal, that we may be worthy of the promises of your husband who in his grace singled you out from your earliest years." Then turning to his wife and sons he said, "From now on let no one upset this my dearest daughter or dare to interfere with her; let her serve her Husband freely and pray to him for us unceasingly. We could never find a relative in any way comparable to this one, and we have no reason to lament if instead of a mortal man we are to have God and an immortal man in our family."

The matter ended in general lamentation, especially from Lapa, who loved her daughter very much in a worldly way, but the holy virgin, exulting in the Lord, gave thanks to her triumphant bridegroom for leading her to victory. Then she humbly thanked her parents and prepared to make the utmost of the privileges that had been granted her.

Part 2, Chapter 5
How Catherine Lived

One day, while the virgin was praying in her little room, the Lord and Savior of the human race appeared to her and announced what was to happen in these words: "Know, sweetest daughter," he said, "that in the time to come your earthly pilgrimage will be distinguished by such marvelous, new gifts from me that the hearts of ignorant carnal men will be amazed and incredulous. Many even of those who love you will have doubts, and believe that what you do is all a deception, whereas in fact it will be a result of a superabundance of love on my part. I shall infuse such a fullness of graces into your soul that they will overflow, and even your body will feel their effects and begin to live in an unprecedented way. Furthermore, your heart will burn so strongly for the salvation of your fellow-men that you will forget your sex and change your present way of life; you will not avoid the company of men and women as you do now, but for the salvation of their souls will take upon yourself every kind of labor. Many people will be scandalized by the things you do, and oppose you, so that the thoughts of their hearts may be revealed. But you must not be anxious or afraid, for I shall be always with you, and I shall free your soul from the evil tongues and the lips that utter lies. Carry out undauntedly whatever the Spirit prompts you to do, for through you I shall snatch many souls from the jaws of hell and by my grace transport them to the kingdom of heaven."

To these words, which, as she confessed to me herself, the Lord repeated several times, especially, "You must not be anxious or afraid," the holy virgin replied, "You are my Lord, and I am the least of your servants. May your will be done always, but remember me according to your great mercy, and do not forsake me."

The vision vanished, and the maiden of Christ remained lost in thought, wondering what this future change would mean.

From that moment the grace of Jesus Christ began to increase daily in Catherine's heart and the Spirit of the Lord to overflow within her; so that even she was astounded, and almost fainted from the wonder of it, singing with the Prophet, "For thee my flesh and my heart have fainted away: thou art the God of my heart, and the God that is my portion for ever." And, "I remembered God, and was delighted, and was exercised; and my spirit swooned away."

The virgin of Christ languished with love of her Lord, and the only relief she could find was in weeping of soul and body. Every day there were groans and tears. But not even incessant tears could bring alleviation of her pain. Then the Lord, as it seemed good to him, inspired her to have frequent recourse to the altar of God, to receive our Lord Jesus Christ, the joy of her body and soul, in the sacrament from the hands of the priest as often as she could, so that during her earthly pilgrimage she might at least taste him sacramentally, even if she could not as yet sate herself fully on him, as she longed to, in heaven.

But this led to still greater love, and hence still greater languishing; but by the power of faith it helped to assuage the furnace of charity which the breath of the Holy Spirit fanned in her heart more brightly every day. She developed the habit of communicating almost daily, and was only prevented from doing so, as frequently happened, by illness or through her concern for the good of souls.

Her longing to receive the Lord was so strong that when she could not satisfy it, her body suffered hardship and faintness, for as it shared in the abundance of her spirit so it was obliged to share in its afflictions. But of this, with the Lord's help, we shall speak at greater length elsewhere.

Now let us return to her admirable manner of life.

Thus, then, as she herself confessed to me in secret, and as I have also seen in the writings of the confessor who preceded me, after the vision described above there began to descend into her soul, especially when she received Holy Communion, such an abundance of graces and heavenly consolations that, overflowing and pouring out into her body, they affected the radical humor itself; changing the nature of her stomach in such a way that not only did she have no need of food but she could not in fact take any without it causing her pain. If she forced herself to eat, her body suffered extremely, her digestion would not function, and the food had to come out with an effort by the way it had gone in. It is difficult to estimate the amount of suffering that this holy virgin experienced through swallowing food.

At the beginning, such a way of life seemed incredible to everyone, even to the people in her own home and those most intimate with her; and what was in fact an extraordinary gift from God they called a temptation and a trick of the devil.

This mistake was also made by her confessor who has already been mentioned several times by name, for, out of zeal for goodness, certainly, but without a great deal of insight, he decided that the virgin had been led astray by the enemy, disguised as an angel of light; and so he forced her to eat every day, and told her not to believe in her visions because they came from the devil. Though Catherine told him that she knew from experience that she felt stronger and healthier when she refrained from eating, and tired and ill when she did eat, he remained unconvinced and went on insisting that she must eat. Being a true daughter of obedience she did her best to obey, but this so exhausted her that she seemed almost on the brink of death.

At this stage she went to see this confessor and said: "Father, if I went in for an excessive fast that was likely to bring me to death's door, it is true, isn't it, that you would forbid me to do it, so that I would avoid dying and being guilty of self-murder?"

"Certainly," he answered, "of course!"

So she said, "Isn't it worse to die from over-eating than from fasting?" and when he answered yes, she went on; "Well then, if, as you have seen again and again, and can see now, I am not at all well when I eat, why not forbid me to eat in the same way as you forbid me to fast?" To this reasoning he had not a word to reply; and as he could see quite clearly that Catherine showed all the signs of being on the point of death, he said, "Do as the Holy Spirit prompts you to do, for I can see that God is doing great things in you."

And this seems a good opportunity, reader, to beg you to consider how much Catherine suffered – beyond all description from the people in her home, who simply would not understand that the Lord was granting her extraordinary gifts. The holy virgin herself revealed this to me in confession when I first began to enjoy the honor of knowing her, and she repeated the same thing again later when we had occasion to discuss the matter.

These people judged her words and actions, not by the standard set by the Lord himself in shedding his graces so lavishly into his bride's soul, but by the usual standard, and often their own private one. Standing in the valley, they pretended to be able to measure the high tops of the mountains; ignorant of first principles, they nevertheless drew final conclusions, and blinded by the brilliance of so much light, they rashly criticized the colors. And so they foolishly complained about the rays that came from this star; tried to teach her, failing to realize that it was she who was teaching them; and, being themselves in the dark, took it upon themselves to argue with the light. They found fault with her amongst themselves, and behind a facade of righteousness did their best to disparage her to others. They even complained to her confessor, and got him against his will to agree to reprimand the virgin.

How much spiritual unhappiness Catherine had to endure from this behavior of theirs cannot easily be described, though I could easily go into it all if I had the time.

Obedient as she was, and rooted in contempt of self, she was no expert in the art of finding excuses for herself, nor did she dare set herself up against anything her confessor said or did. The result was that, knowing quite clearly that the will of the Highest was in conflict with all their opinions, and yet from fear of the Lord not wanting to fail in obedience or give scandal to anyone, she found herself in a state of uncertainty. On all sides were causes of grief, and her only consolation was prayer. To the Lord she shed tears of sorrow and hope, praying to him with humble persistence to reveal his will to her opponents, and especially her confessor, whom she was most fearful of offending....

... After the virgin had had the first vision she was so full of the Holy Spirit that she went without food or drink for the whole of Lent until the feast of Our Lord's Ascension; and yet despite this she was always bursting with life and happiness. No wonder, for as the Blessed Apostle says, "the fruit of the Spirit is charity, joy and peace." And the First Truth announced that "Not by bread alone doth man live but by every word that proceedeth from the mouth of God." It is also written that "the just man liveth by faith."

In the end, as the Lord had predicted, and as she herself had told her confessor, she was able to eat on Ascension Day, when she had wheaten bread and oil and vegetables. For it was not possible for any rich food to enter her stomach, either by natural or by supernatural means. When that day was over, however, she resumed her habitual fasting. Then she gradually reached a state of total abstinence almost unheard of in our times. But if her body took nothing, her spirit fed most sumptuously in its stead. While these things were happening, in fact, the holy virgin was devoutly receiving Holy Communion very frequently indeed, and on each occasion she was given so much grace that, with her bodily senses and all their inclinations thoroughly mortified, her soul and body were both equally nourished by the power of the Spirit. From this anyone with any faith must conclude that her life was wholly miraculous.

I myself have often seen that poor body, sustained by no more than a few glasses of cold water, reduced to such a state of exhaustion that we were all worried, imagining that she was about to die at any moment. Instead, as soon as any opportunity arose to honor the divine name, or do good to some soul, there would be a sudden wonderful change, and without the help of any medicine Catherine would regain all her life and strength and be strong and cheerful. She would get up, walk about, and go about her work as easily as the people who were with her and who were in good health: she did not know the meaning of fatigue.

I ask you: where did all this come from, if not from the Spirit who delights in such works? What could not be done by nature, he did by miracle. Is it not perfectly clear that it was he who gave strength to her soul and body?

Further: when the virgin first began to live without eating, her confessor, Fra Tommaso, asked her if she ever felt any desire for food and she replied, "I feel so satisfied by the Lord when I receive his most adorable Sacrament that I could not possibly feel any desire for any other kind of food." Then, when he wanted to know whether she felt any pangs of hunger when she did not receive the Sacrament, she replied, "When I am unable to receive the Sacrament, I am quite satisfied if I can be near it and see it; in fact I get so much pleasure out of merely seeing a priest who has touched the Sacrament that I lose all desire for food even then."

Such, then, was the virgin of the Lord; satisfied, though fasting, empty without but full within, dry to look at but inwardly watered by rivers of living water and at all times full of life and happiness.

... to silence the faultfinders and prevent people from being scandalized by her fasting, [Catherine] decided to sit down with the family once a day at table and find out whether she could make herself eat like everyone else. The food she forced herself to take did not include meat or wine or fish or eggs or cheese or even bread; nevertheless, this eating, or rather attempt at eating, produced such pains in her body that anyone who had seen her would have felt sorry for her, no matter how hard-hearted he was.

As we have shown above, her stomach could not digest anything, the heat did not consume the vital humors, with the result that what she had taken in had to come out by the same way as it had gone in, otherwise it caused her acute pains and swellings over most of her body. The holy virgin did not swallow any of the vegetables or other things that she masticated, for she spat out all the large bits; but because it was impossible for some little bits of food or juice not to go down into her stomach, and because she liked to drink fresh water to refresh her throat and jaws, she was obliged to throw up everything she had swallowed every day. To do this she often had to introduce a small branch of fennel or some other shrub into her stomach, despite the great pain it caused her, as this was generally the only way in which she could get rid of what she had swallowed. She did this throughout the rest of her life because of the grumblers, particularly those who were scandalized by her fasting.

Seeing the pain she endured in getting rid of the food she had eaten in this way, I once out of compassion tried to persuade her to leave the critics to their criticizing and not go on putting up with such a martyrdom simply on their account. With a contented smile she said: "Father, don't you think it is better for me to have my sins punished in this world rather than to have to face a punishment without end? Their criticisms are highly useful to me, because they help me to pay my creator back in a finite way, whereas I owe him something infinite. Should I try to escape from divine justice? Of course not! I am receiving a great grace, because justice is being done to me in this life." What could I answer? I preferred to say nothing, for if I had spoken I should not have been able to find anything suitable or worth saying.

With such considerations in mind, she called this painful behavior "doing justice," saying to her companions, "Let us go and do justice to this miserable sinner." Thus she drew some particular kind of profit from everything that happened to her, whether it was the devil's wiles or being persecuted by humans; and every day, too, she taught us to do the same.

One day, discussing the gifts of God with me, she said, "If everyone knew how to use the grace God gave them they would benefit from everything that happens to them." And she added, "This is what I would like you to do whenever something new happens to you, whether you like it or not: think to yourself and say, I intend to get some benefit from this. If you really did this you would be rich in no time."

Unhappy man that I am, I failed to treasure up these and all her other precious words! Don't you, reader, be as lazy as I was, but remember the words, "Blessed is the man who learns from the misfortunes of others." And I pray the author of all piety to enlighten you, and to goad me into imitating this virgin as hard as I can all my life.

Part 2, Chapter 6
Ecstacies and Revelations

At this time, when the Lord had granted his bride a particular way of living as regards the body, he likewise comforted her soul with great and extraordinary revelations, and the supernatural vigor of her body certainly resulted from this abundance of spiritual graces. And now that we have described in the utmost detail Catherine's bodily life, it is requisite to go on to recount the vigor of her spirit.

Know then, reader, that from the time when this virgin drank the water of life from the Lord's side, she abounded in such fullness of graces that she was almost always in a state of contemplation, and her spirit was so absorbed in the Creator that she spent most of her time in a region beyond sense. This, as I have shown in Part One, I experienced personally time and time again, and so did others, who saw and touched, as I did, her arms and hands, which remained so numb while she was in a state of contemplation that it would have been easier to break them than to get them to move. Her eyes remained tightly shut, her ears could not hear the loudest noise, and none of her bodily senses performed its accustomed functions. You will not find this astonishing if you follow carefully all that follows.

The Lord began to appear to his bride not only privately, as he had done at first, but in public too, in fact before everyone's eyes and quite familiarly, both when she was walking about and when she was standing still, and he set such a fire blazing within her heart that she herself told her confessor that she could not find words to express the divine experiences she had.

Once, when she was praying to the Lord with the utmost fervor, saying to him as the Prophet had done, "Create a clean heart within me, O God, and renew a right spirit within my bowels," and asking him again and again to take her own heart and will from her, he comforted her with this vision. It appeared to her that her Heavenly Bridegroom came to her as usual, opened her left side, took out her heart, and then went away. This vision was so effective and agreed so well with what she felt inside herself that in confession she told her confessor that she no longer had a heart in her breast. He shook his head a little at this way of putting it, and in a joking way reproved her; but she repeated it and insisted that she meant what she said. "Truly, Father," she said, "in so far as I feel anything at all, it seems to me that my heart has been taken away altogether. The Lord did indeed appear to me, opened my left side, took my heart out and went away." Her confessor then pointed out that it is impossible to live without a heart, but the virgin replied that nothing is impossible to God, and that she was convinced that she no longer had a heart. And for some time she went on repeating this, that she was living without a heart.

One day she was in the church of the Preaching Friars, which the Sisters of Penance of St. Dominic in Siena used to attend. The others had gone out, but she went on praying. Finally she came out of her ecstasy and got up to go home. All at once a light from heaven encircled her, and in the light appeared the Lord, holding in his holy hands a human heart, bright red and shining. At the appearance of the author of light she had fallen to the ground, trembling all over, but he came up to her, opened her left side once again and put the heart he was holding in his hands inside her, saying, "Dearest daughter, as I took your heart away from you the other day, now, you see, I am giving you mine, so that you can go on living with it for ever." With these words he closed the opening he had made in her side, and as a sign of the miracle a scar remained on that part of her flesh, as I and others were told by her companions who saw it. When I determined to get to the truth, she herself was obliged to confess to me that this was so, and she added that never afterwards had she been able to say, "Lord, I give you my heart."

After the reception of this heart, then, in such a gracious and marvelous way, from the abundance of its graces poured forth Catherine's great works and her most marvelous revelations. In point of fact she never approached the sacred altar without being shown many things beyond the range of the senses, especially when she received Holy Communion. She often saw a baby hidden in the hands of the priest; sometimes it was a slightly older boy; or again, she might see a burning fiery furnace, into which the priest seemed to enter at the moment when he consumed the sacred species. When she herself received the most adorable Sacrament, she would often smell such a strong sweet smell that she almost fainted. Seeing or receiving the Sacrament of the Altar always generated fresh and indescribable bliss in her soul, so that her heart would very often throb with joy within her breast, making such a loud noise that it could be heard even by her companions. At last, having noticed this so often, they told her confessor Fra Tommaso about it. He made a close inquiry into the matter, and on finding it was true, left the fact in writing as an imperishable record. This noise bore no resemblance to the gurgling that goes on naturally in the human stomach; there was nothing natural about the noise at all.

There is nothing surprising in the fact that a heart given in a supernatural way should act in a supernatural way too, for, as the Prophet says, "My heart and my flesh have rejoiced in the living God," that is to say, "They have jumped out, into the living God."

The Prophet says, "the living God", to signify that this special beating or heart action, being caused by the true life, does not bring death to the person to whom it happens, as it would in the ordinary course of nature, but Life.

After the miraculous exchange of hearts the virgin felt a different person, and she said to her confessor Fra Tommaso, "Can't you see, Father, that I am not the person I was, but am changed into someone else?" And she went on, "If only you could understand how I feel, Father! I don't believe that anyone who really knew how I feel inside could be obstinate enough not to be softened or be proud enough not to humble himself, for all that I reveal is nothing compared to what I feel." She described what she was experiencing, saying, "My mind is so full of joy and happiness that I am amazed my soul stays in my body." And she also said, "There is so much heat in my soul that this material fire seems cool by comparison, rather than to be giving out heat; it seems to have gone out, rather than to be still burning." And again, "This heat has generated in my mind a renewal of purity and humility, so that I seem to have gone back to the age of four or five. And at the same time so much love of my fellow-men has blazed up in me that I could face death for them cheerfully and with great joy in my heart." All this she told her confessor alone, in secret; but from others she hid as much as she could.

Words and happenings like this give some idea of the abundance the Lord had infused into the holy virgin's soul at this time, in a way far beyond the ordinary. But if I tried to describe everything in detail it would mean writing several books; so I have decided to collect together only a few things that nevertheless provide extraordinary evidence of Catherine's sanctity.

Letter from Catherine to Raymond of Capua

During the political upheavals in Siena, a young aristocrat from Perugia, Niccolò Tuldo, was arrested and condemned to death by the Sienese government. Here Catherine describes his execution and her own role in helping him become resigned to his death. The letter was written after 1374, the date when Raymond replaced Father Tommaso as her Confessor.

In the Name of Jesus Christ crucified and of sweet Mary:

Most beloved and dearest father [Raymond] and dear my son in Christ Jesus: I Catherine, servant and slave of the servants of Jesus Christ, write to you, commending myself to you in the precious blood of the Son of God; with desire to see you inflamed and drowned in that his sweetest blood, which is blended with the fire of his most ardent charity. This my soul desires, to see you therein, you and Nanni and Jacopo my son. I see no other remedy by which we may reach those chief virtues which are necessary to us. Sweetest father, your soul, which has made itself food for me – (and no moment of time passes that I do not receive this food at the table of the sweet Lamb slain with such ardent love) – your soul, I say, would not attain the little virtue, true humility, were it not drowned in the blood. This virtue shall be born from hate, and hate from love. Thus the soul is born with very perfect purity, as iron issues purified from the furnace.

I will, then, that you lock you in the open side of the Son of God, which is an open treasure-house, full of fragrance, even so that sin itself there becomes fragrant. There rests the sweet bride on the bed of fire and blood. There is seen and shown the secret of the heart of the Son of God. Oh, flowing source, which gives to drink and excites every loving desire, and gives gladness, and enlightens every mind and fills every memory which fixes itself thereon so that naught else can be held or meant or loved, save this sweet and good Jesus! Blood and fire, immeasurable love! Since my soul shall be blessed in seeing you thus drowned, I will that you do as he who draws up water with a bucket, and pours it over something else; thus do you pour the water of holy desire on the head of your brothers, who are our members, bound to us in the body of the sweet bride. And beware, lest through illusion of the devils – who I know have given you trouble, and will give you – or through the saying of some fellow creature, you should ever draw back: but persevere always in the hour when things look most cold, until we may see blood shed with sweet and enamored desires.

Up, up, sweetest my father! and let us sleep no more! For I hear such news that I wish no more bed of repose or worldly state. I have just received a head in my hands, which was to me of such sweetness as heart cannot think, nor tongue say, nor eye see, nor the ears hear. The will of God went on through the other mysteries wrought before; of which I do not tell, for it would be too long. I went to visit him [Niccolò Tuldo] whom you know: whence he received such comfort and consolation that he confessed, and prepared himself very well. And he made me promise by the love of God that when the time of the sentence should come, I would be with him. So I promised, and did. Then in the morning, before the bell rang, I went to him: and he received great consolation. I led him to hear Mass, and he received the Holy Communion, which he had never before received. His will was accorded and submitted to the will of God; and only one fear was left, that of not being strong at the moment. But the measureless and glowing goodness of God deceived him, creating in him such affection and love in the desire of God that he did not know how to abide without him, and said: "Stay with me, and do not abandon me. So it shall not be otherwise than well with me. And I die content." And he held his head upon my breast. I heard then the rejoicing, and breathed the fragrance of his blood; and it was not without the fragrance of mine, which I desire to shed for the sweet Bridegroom Jesus. And, desire waxing in my soul, feeling his fear, I said: "Comfort thee, sweet my brother; since we shall soon arrive at the wedding feast. Thou shalt go there bathed in the sweet blood of the Son of God, with the sweet name of Jesus, which I will never to leave thy memory. And I await thee at the place of justice." Now think, father and son, his heart then lost all fear, and his face changed from sorrow to gladness; and he rejoiced, he exulted, and said: "Whence comes such grace to me, that the sweetness of my soul will await me at the holy place of justice?" See, that he had come to so much light that he called the place of justice holy! And he said: "I shall go wholly joyous, and strong, and it will seem to me a thousand years before I arrive, thinking that you are awaiting me there." And he said words so sweet, as to break one's heart, of the goodness of God.

I waited for him then at the place of justice; and waited there with constant prayer, in the presence of Mary and of Catherine, Virgin and martyr. But before I attained, I prostrated me, and stretched my neck upon the block; but my desire did not come there, for I had too full consciousness of myself.

Then up! I prayed, I constrained her, I cried "Mary!" for I wished this grace, that at the moment of death she should give him a light and a peace in his heart, and then I should see him reach his goal. Then my soul became so full that although a multitude of people were there, I could see no human creature, for the sweet promise made to me.

Then he came, like a gentle lamb; and seeing me, he began to smile, and wanted me to make the sign of the cross. When he had received the sign, I said, "Down! To the bridal, sweetest my brother! For soon you shall be in the enduring life." He prostrated himself with great gentleness, and I stretched out his neck; and bowed me down, and recalled to him the blood of the Lamb. His lips said naught save Jesus! and, Catherine! And so saying, I received his head in my hands, closing my eyes in the divine goodness, and saying, "I will!"

Then was seen God-and-Man, as might the clearness of the sun be seen. And he stood wounded, and received the blood; in that blood a fire of holy desire, given and hidden in the soul by grace. He received it in the fire of his divine charity. When he had received his blood and his desire, he also received his soul, which he put into the open treasurehouse of his side, full of mercy; the primal truth showing that by grace and mercy alone he received it, and not for any other work. Oh, how sweet and unspeakable it was to see the goodness of God! with what sweetness and love he awaited that soul departed from the body! He turned the eye of mercy toward her, when she came to enter within his side, bathed in blood which availed through the blood of the Son of God. Thus received by God through power – powerful is he to do! the Son also, wisdom the word incarnate, gave him and made him share the crucified love with which he received painful and shameful death through the obedience which he showed to the Father, for the good of the human race. And the hands of the Holy Spirit locked him within.

But he made a gesture sweet enough to draw a thousand hearts. And I do not wonder, for already he tasted the divine sweetness. He turned as does the bride when she has reached the threshold of her bridegroom, who turns back her head and her look, bowing to those who have accompanied her, and with the gesture she gives signs of thanks.

When he was at rest, my soul rested in peace and in quiet, in so great fragrance of blood that I could not bear to remove the blood which had fallen on me from him.

Ah me, miserable! I will say no more. I stayed on the earth with the greatest envy. And it seems to me that the first new stone is already in place. Therefore do not wonder if I impose upon you nothing save to see yourselves drowned in the blood and flame poured from the side of the Son of God. Now then, no more negligence, sweetest my sons, since the blood is beginning to flow, and to receive the life. Sweet Jesus, Jesus Love.

To Sir John Hawkwood

Sir John Hawkwood (c. 1320-94) was an English mercenary who for thirty years played various roles in the Italian wars, fighting primarily for Florence but at times on the side of the pope. For his services to the former he was made an honorary citizen of Florence and given a civic funeral when he died. Catherine writes to him here clearly hoping to divert him into a holier cause (a crusade to the Holy Land).

In the Name of Jesus Christ crucified and of sweet Mary:

To you, most beloved and dear brothers in Christ Jesus: I Catherine, servant and slave of the servants of Jesus Christ, write in his precious blood: with desire to see you a true son and knight of Christ, in such wise that you may desire to give your life a thousand times, if need were, in service of sweet and good Jesus. This is a gift which would pay off all our sins, which we have committed against our Savior. Dearest and sweetest brother in Christ Jesus, it would be a great thing now if you would withdraw a little into yourself, and consider, and reflect how great are the pains and anguish which you have endured by being in the service and pay of the devil. Now my soul desires that you should change your way of life, and take the pay and the cross of Christ crucified, you and all your followers and companions; so that you may be Christ's company, to march against the infidel dogs who possess our holy place, where rested the sweet primal truth and bore death and pains for us. I beg you, then, gently in Christ Jesus, that since God and also our Holy Father have ordered a crusade against the infidels, and you take such pleasure in war and fighting, you should not make war against Christians any more – for this is a wrong to God; but go against the infidels! For it is a great cruelty that we who are Christians, and members bound in the body of holy Church, should persecute one another. We are not to do so; but to rise with perfect zeal, and to uplift ourselves above every evil thought.

I marvel much that you, having, as I heard, promised to be willing to go to die for Christ in this holy crusade, are wanting to make war in these parts. This is not that holy disposition which God demands from you if you are to go to so holy and venerable a place. It seems to me that you ought now, at this present time, to dispose you to virtue, until the time shall come for us and the others who shall be ready to give their lives for Christ: and thus you shall show that you are a manly and true knight.

There is coming to you this father and son of mine, Brother Raymond, who brings you this letter. Trust in what he tells you; because he is a true, faithful servant of God, and will advise you and say to you nothing except what will be to the honor of God and the safety and glory of your soul. I say no more. I beg you, dearest brother, to keep in memory the shortness of your time. Remain in the holy and sweet grace of God. Sweet Jesus, Jesus love.

Letter to Pope Gregory XI (1375)

Catherine writes to Pope Gregory in Avignon, addressing him affectionately as "Babbo" (a diminutive of 'father') but at the same time passionately condemning his overly conciliatory approach to corrupt church officials and to the rebellious Italian nobles of Pisa and Lucca.

In the name of Jesus Christ crucified and of sweet Mary:

To you, most reverend and beloved father in Christ Jesus, your unworthy, poor, miserable daughter Catherine, servant and slave of the servants of Jesus Christ, writes in his precious blood; with desire to see you a fruitful tree, full of sweet and mellow fruits, and planted in fruitful earth – for if it were out of the earth the tree would dry up and bear no fruit – that is, in the earth of true knowledge of yourself. For the soul that knows itself humbles itself, because it sees nothing to be proud of; and ripens the sweet fruit of very ardent charity, recognizing in itself the unmeasured goodness of God; and aware that it is not, it attributes all its being to him who is. Whence, then, it seems that the soul is constrained to love what God loves and to hate what he hates.

Oh, sweet and true knowledge, which carries with it the knife of hate, and stretches out the hand of holy desire, to draw forth and kill with this hate the worm of self-love – a worm that spoils and gnaws the root of our tree so that it cannot bear any fruit of life, but dries up, and its verdure lasts not! For if a man loves himself, perverse pride, head and source of every ill, lives in him, whatever his rank may be, prelate or subject. If he is lover of himself alone – that is, if he loves himself for his own sake and not for God – he cannot do other than ill, and all virtue is dead in him. Such a one is like a woman who brings forth her sons dead. And so it really is; for he has not had the life of charity in himself, and has cared only for praise and self-glory, and not for the name of God. I say, then: if he is a prelate, he does ill, because to avoid falling into disfavor with his fellow-creatures – that is, through self-love – in which he is bound by self-indulgence – holy justice dies in him. For he sees his subjects commit faults and sins, and pretends not to see them and fails to correct them; or if he does correct them, he does it with such coldness and lukewarmness that he does not accomplish anything, but plasters vice over; and he is always afraid of giving displeasure or of getting into a quarrel. All this is because he loves himself. Sometimes men like this want to get along with purely peaceful means. I say that this is the very worst cruelty which can be shown. If a wound when necessary is not cauterized or cut out with steel, but simply covered with ointment, not only does it fail to heal, but it infects everything, and many a time death follows from it.

Oh me, oh me, sweetest "Babbo" mine! This is the reason that all the subjects are corrupted by impurity and iniquity. Oh me, weeping I say it! How dangerous is that worm we spoke of! For not only does it give death to the shepherd, but all the rest fall into sickness and death through it. Why does that shepherd go on using so much ointment? Because he does not suffer in consequence! For no displeasure visits one and no ill will, from spreading ointment over the sick; since one does nothing contrary to their will; they wanted ointment, and so ointment is given them. Oh, human wretchedness! Blind is the sick man who does not know his own need, and blind the shepherd-physician, who has regard to nothing but pleasing, and his own advantage – since, not to forfeit it, he refrains from using the knife of justice or the fire of ardent charity! But such men do as Christ says: for if one blind man guide the other, both fall into the ditch. Sick man and physician fall into hell. Such a man is a right hireling shepherd, for, far from dragging his sheep from the hands of the wolf, he devours them himself. The cause of all this is, that he loves himself apart from God: so he does not follow sweet Jesus, the true shepherd, who has given his life for his sheep. Truly, then, this perverse love is perilous for one's self and for others, and truly to be shunned, since it works too much harm to every generation of people. I hope by the goodness of God, venerable father mine, that you will quench this in yourself, and will not love yourself for yourself, nor your neighbor for yourself, nor God; but will love him because he is highest and eternal goodness, and worthy of being loved; and yourself and your neighbor you will love to the honor and glory of the sweet name of Jesus. I will, then, that you be so true and good a shepherd that if you had a hundred thousand lives you would be ready to give them all for the honor of God and the salvation of his creatures. O "Babbo" mine, sweet Christ on earth, follow that sweet Gregory [the Great]! For all will be possible to you as to him; for he was not of other flesh than you; and that God is now who was then: we lack nothing save virtue, and hunger for the salvation of souls. But there is a remedy for this, father: that we flee the love spoken of above, for ourselves and every creature apart from God. Let no more note be given to friends or parents or one's temporal needs, but only to virtue and the exaltation of things spiritual. For temporal things are failing you from no other cause than from your neglect of the spiritual.

Now, then, do we wish to have that glorious hunger which these holy and true shepherds of the past have felt, and to quench in ourselves that fire of self-love? Let us do as they, who with fire quenched fire; for so great was the fire of inestimable and ardent charity that burned in their hearts and souls, that they were hungry and famished for the savor of souls. Oh, sweet and glorious fire, which is of such power that it quenches fire, and every inordinate delight and pleasure and all love of self; and this love is like a drop of water, which is swiftly consumed in the furnace! Should one ask me how men attained that sweet fire and hunger — inasmuch as we are surely in ourselves unfruitful trees — I say that those men grafted themselves into the fruitful tree of the most holy and sweet Cross, where they found the Lamb, slain with such fire of love for our salvation as seems insatiable. Still he cries that he is athirst, as if saying: "I have greater ardor and desire and thirst for your salvation than I show you with my finished Passion." O sweet and good Jesus! Let pontiffs shame them, and shepherds, and every other creature, for our ignorance and pride and self-indulgence, in the presence of so great largess and goodness and ineffable love on the part of our Creator! He has revealed himself to us in our humanity, a tree full of sweet and mellow fruits, in order that we, wild trees, might graft ourselves in him. Now in this way wrought that enamored Gregory, and those other good shepherds: knowing that they had no virtue in themselves, and gazing upon the word, our tree, they grafted themselves in him, bound and chained by the bands of love. For in that which the eye sees does it delight, when the thing is fair and good. They saw, then, and seeing they so bound them that they saw not themselves, but saw and tasted everything in God. And there was neither wind nor hail nor demons nor creatures that could keep them from bearing cultivated fruits: since they were grafted in the substance of our tree, Jesus. They brought forth their fruits, then, from the substance of sweet charity, in which they were united. And there is no other way.

This is what I wish to see in you. And if up to this time, we have not stood very firm, I wish and pray in truth that the moment of time which remains to be dealt with manfully, following Christ, whose vicar you are, like a strong man. And fear not, father, for anything that may result from those tempestuous winds that are now beating against you, those decaying members which have rebelled against you. Fear not; for divine aid is near. Have a care for spiritual things alone, for good shepherds, good rulers, in your cities — since on account of bad shepherds and rulers you have encountered rebellion. Give us, then, a remedy; and comfort you in Christ Jesus, and fear not. Press on, and fulfill with true zeal and holy what you have begun with a holy resolve, concerning your return, and the holy and sweet crusade. And delay no longer, for many difficulties have occurred through delay, and the devil has risen up to prevent these things being done, because he perceives his own loss. Up, then, father, and no more negligence! Raise the gonfalon [banner] of the most holy cross, for with the fragrance of the cross you shall win peace. I beg you to summon those who have rebelled against you to a holy peace, so that all warfare may be turned against the infidels. I hope by the infinite goodness of God that he will swiftly send his aid. Comfort you, comfort you, and come, come, to console the poor, the servants of God, your sons! We await you with eager and loving desire. Pardon me, father, that I have said so many words to you. You know that through the abundance of the heart the mouth speaks. I am certain that if you shall be the kind of tree I wish to see you, nothing will hinder you.

I beg you to send to Lucca and to Pisa with fatherly proposals, as God shall instruct you, supporting them so far as can be, and summoning them to remain firm and persevering. I have been at Pisa and at Lucca, up to now, influencing them as much as I can not to make a league with the decaying members that are rebelling against you: but they are in great perplexity, because they have no comfort from you, and are constantly urged to make it and threatened from the contrary side. However, up to the present time, they have not wholly consented. I beg you also to write emphatically to Messer Piero: and do it zealously, and do not delay. I say no more.

I have heard here that you have appointed the cardinals. I believe that it would honor God and profit us more if you would take heed always to appoint virtuous men. If the contrary is done, it will be a great insult to God, and disaster to Holy Church. Let us not wonder later if God sends us his disciplines and scourges; for the thing is just. I beg you to do what you have to do manfully and in the fear of God.

I have heard that you are to promote the master of our order to another benefice. Therefore I beg you, by the love of Christ crucified, that if this is so you will take pains to give us a good and virtuous vicar. The Order has need of it, for it has run altogether too wild. You can talk of this with Messer Niccola da Osimo and the Archbishop of Tronto; and I will write them about it.

Remain in the sweet and holy grace of God. I ask you humbly for your blessing. Pardon my presumption, that I presume to write to you. Sweet Jesus, Jesus love.

To Monna Lapa

In 1376 Catherine traveled to Avignon to persuade the pope to return to Rome. Having succeeded in her purpose, she herself set out for home but was delayed on her journey by the illness of her companions. Here she writes to console her mother (with a touch of rebuke), for complaining at her continued absence.

In the name of Jesus Christ crucified and of sweet Mary:

Dearest mother in Christ sweet Jesus: your poor, unworthy daughter

Catherine comforts you in the precious blood of the Son of God. With desire
have I desired to see you a true mother, not only of my body but of my soul;
for I have reflected that if you are more the lover of my soul than of my body,
all disordinate tenderness will die in you, and it will not be such a burden
to you to long for my bodily presence; but it will rather be a consolation to
you, and you will wish, for the honor of God, to endure every burden for
me, provided that the honor of God be wrought. Working for the honor
of God, I am not without the increase of grace and power in my soul. Yes,
indeed, it is true that if you, sweetest mother, love my soul better than my
body, you will be consoled and not disconsolate. I want you to learn from
that sweet mother, Mary, who, for the honor of God and for our salvation,
gave us her Son, dead upon the wood of the most holy cross. And when
Mary was left alone, after Christ had ascended into heaven, she stayed with
the holy disciples; and although Mary and the disciples had great consolation
together, and to separate was sorrow, nevertheless, for the glory and praise of
her Son, for the good of the whole universal world, she consented and chose
that they should go away. And she chose the burden of their departure rather
than the consolation of their remaining, solely through the love that she had
for the honor of God and for our salvation. Now, I want you to learn from
her, dearest mother. You know that it behooves me to follow the will of God;
and I know that you wish me to follow it. His will was that I should go away;
which going did not happen without mystery, nor without fruit of great
value. It was his will that I should come, and not the will of man; and whoever might say the opposite, it is not the truth. And thus it will behoove me
to go on, following his footsteps in what way and at what time shall please
his inestimable goodness. You, like a good, sweet mother, must be content,
and not disconsolate, enduring every burden for the honor of God, and for
your and my salvation. Remember that you did this for the sake of temporal
goods, when your sons left you to gain temporal wealth; now, to gain eternal
life, it seems to you such an affliction that you say that you will go and run
away if I do not reply to you soon. All this happens to you because you love
better that part which I derived from you — that is, your flesh, with which
you clothed me — than what I have derived from God. Lift up, lift up your
heart and mind a little to that sweet and holiest cross where all affliction
ceases; be willing to bear a little finite pain, to escape the infinite pain which
we merit for our sins. Now, comfort you, for the love of Christ crucified,
and do not think that you are abandoned either by God or by me. Yet shall
you be comforted, and receive full consolation; and the pain has not been so
great that the joy shall not be greater. We shall come soon, by the mercy of
God; and we should not have delayed our coming now, were it not for the
obstacle we have had in the serious illness of Neri. Also Master Giovanni and

Fra Bartolommeo have been ill.... I say no more. Commend us.... Remain in the holy and sweet grace of God. Sweet Jesus, Jesus love.

To Gregory XI (c. 1378)

In this letter written after Gregory's return to Rome, Catherine addresses his continuing failure (in her view) to address the problems of the Church. He died shortly afterwards, in March 1378, and was succeeded by Urban VI.

In the name of Jesus Christ crucified and of sweet Mary:

Most holy and sweet father, your poor unworthy daughter, Catherine in Christ sweet Jesus, commends herself to you in his precious blood: with desire to see you a manly man, free from any fear or fleshly love toward yourself, or toward any creature related to you in the flesh; since I perceive in the sweet presence of God that nothing so hinders your holy, good desire and so serves to hinder the honor of God and the exaltation and reform of holy Church, as this. Therefore, my soul desires with immeasurable love that God by his infinite mercy may take from you all passion and lukewarmness of heart, and re-form you another man, by forming in you anew a burning and ardent desire; for in no other way could you fulfill the will of God and the desire of his servants. Alas, alas, sweetest "Babbo" mine, pardon my presumption in what I have said to you and am saying; I am constrained by the sweet primal truth to say it. His will, father, is this, and thus demands of you. It demands that you execute justice on the abundance of many iniquities committed by those who are fed and pastured in the garden of holy Church; declaring that brutes should not be fed with the food of men. Since he has given you authority and you have assumed it, you should use your virtue and power: and if you are not willing to use it, it would be better for you to resign what you have assumed; more honor to God and health to your soul would it be.

Another demand that his will makes is this: he wills that you make peace with all Tuscany, with which you are at strife, securing from all your wicked sons, who have rebelled against you, whatever is possible to secure without war – but punishing them as a father ought to punish a son who has wronged him. Moreover, the sweet goodness of God demands from you that you give full authority to those who ask you to make ready for the holy crusade – that thing which appears impossible to you, and possible to the sweet goodness of God, who has ordained it, and wills that so it be. Beware, as you hold your life dear, that you commit no negligence in this, nor treat as jests the works of the Holy Spirit, which are demanded from you because you can do them. If you want justice, you can execute it. You can have peace, withdrawing from the perverse pomps and delights of the world, preserving only the honor of God and the due of Holy Church. Authority also you have to give peace to those who ask you for it. Then, since you are not poor but rich – you who bear in your hand the keys of heaven, to whom you open it is open, and to whom you shut it is shut – if you do not do this, you would be rebuked by God. I, if I were in your place, should fear lest divine judgment come upon me. Therefore I beg you most gently on behalf of Christ crucified to be obedient to the will of God, for I know that you want and desire no other thing than to do his will, that this sharp rebuke fall not upon you: "Be cursed, for you have not used the time and the strength entrusted to you." I believe, father, by the goodness of God, and also taking hope from your holiness, that you will so act that this will not fall upon you.

I say no more. Pardon me, pardon me; for the great love which I bear to your salvation, and my great grief when I see the contrary, makes me speak so. Willingly would I have said it to your own person, fully to unburden my conscience. When it shall please your Holiness that I come to you, I will come willingly. So do that I may not appeal to Christ crucified from you; for to no other can I appeal, for there is no greater on earth. Remain in the holy and sweet grace of God. I ask you humbly for your benediction. Sweet Jesus, Jesus love.

To Raymond of Capua

Catherine was dying in Rome in 1380 when she wrote this letter to her Confessor. She had longed for martyrdom, but instead she experienced a 'natural' death as a terrifying assault by demons, a period of guilt, fear, and pain interspersed with visions and marked by continued concern for the state of the Church and for her 'family' of disciples.

In the name of Jesus Christ crucified and of sweet Mary:

Dearest and sweetest father in Christ sweet Jesus: I Catherine, servant and slave of the servants of Jesus Christ, write to you in his precious blood; with the desire to see you a pillar newly established in the garden of holy Church, like a faithful bridegroom of truth, as you ought to be; and then shall I account my soul as blessed. Therefore I do not wish you to look back for any adversity or persecution, but I wish you to glory in adversity. For by endurance and in no other wise we show our love and constancy, and give glory to God's Name. Now is the time, dearest father, wholly to lose one's self, not to think of one's self an atom: as the glorious workmen did who were ready with such love and desire to give their life, and watered this garden with blood, with humble continual prayer, and with endurance unto death. Beware lest I see you timid; let not your shadow make you afraid; but be a manly fighter, and never desert that yoke of obedience which the highest pontiff has placed on you. Moreover, in the Order do what you see to be to the honor of God; for the great goodness of God demands this of us, and he has appointed us for nothing else.

Behold what necessity we see in holy Church; for we see her left utterly alone! Thus the truth showed, as I write you in another letter. And as the bride has been left solitary, so is her bridegroom. Oh, sweetest father, I will not be silent to you of the great mysteries of God, but I will tell them the most briefly that I can, so far as the frail tongue can express them by telling. And further, I say to you what I want you to do. But receive what I say to you without pain, for I do not know what the divine goodness will do with me, whether it will have me remain here, or will call me to itself.

Father, father and sweetest son, wonderful mysteries has God wrought, from the day of the Circumcision till now; such that no tongue could suffice to tell them. But let us pass over all that time, and come to Sexagesima Sunday, when occurred, as I am writing you briefly, those mysteries which you shall hear: never have I seemed to bear anything like them. For the pain in my heart was so great, that the tunic which clothed me burst, as much as I could clasp of it; and I circled around in the chapel like a person in spasms. He who had held me had surely taken away my life. Then, Monday coming, in the evening I was constrained to write to Christ on earth and to three cardinals. So I had myself helped, and went into the study. And when I had written to Christ on earth, I had no way of writing more, the pains had so greatly increased in my body. And, waiting a little, the terror of demons began, in such wise that they stunned me entirely; raging against me as if I, worm that I am, had been the means of taking from their hands what they had possessed a long time in holy Church. So great was the terror, with the bodily pain, that I wanted to fly from the study and go to the chapel – as if the study had been the cause of my pains. So I rose up, and not being able to walk, I leaned on my son Barduccio. But suddenly I was thrown down; and lying there, it seemed to me as if my soul were parted from my body; not in such wise as when it really was parted, for then my soul tasted the good of the immortals, receiving that highest good together with them; but this now seemed like a special case, for I did not seem to be in the body, but I saw my body as if it had been someone else. And my soul, seeing the grief of him who was with me, wished to know if I had any power over the body, to say to him: "Son, do not fear"; and I saw that I could not move the tongue or any member of it, any more than a body quite dead. Then I let the body stay just as it was; and the intellect was fixed on the abyss of the Trinity. Memory was full of recollection of the need of holy Church and of all the

Christian people; and I cried before his face, and demanded divine help with assurance, offering to him my desires, and constraining him by the blood of the Lamb and the pains that had been borne. And so eager was the demand that it seemed to me sure that he would not deny that petition. Then I asked for all you others, praying him that he would fulfill in you his will and my desires. Then I asked that he would save me from eternal condemnation. And while I stayed thus for a very long time, so that the family [of her disciples] was mourning me as dead, at this point all the terror of the demons was gone away. Then the presence of the humble Lamb came before my soul, saying: "Fear not: for I will fulfill your desires, and those of my other servants. I will that you see that I am a good master, who plays the potter, unmaking and remaking vessels as his pleasure is. These my vessels I know how to unmake and remake; and therefore I take the vessel of your body, and remake it in the garden of holy Church, in different wise than in past time." And as this Truth held me close, with ways and words most charming, which I pass over, the body began to breathe a little, and to show that the soul was returned to its vessel. Then I was full of wonder. And such pain remained in my heart that I have it there still. All pleasure and all refreshment and all food was then taken away from me. Being carried afterward into a place above, the room appeared full of devils: and they began to wage another battle, the most terrible that I ever had, trying to make me believe and see that I was not she who was in the body, but an impure spirit. I, having invoked the divine help with a sweet tenderness, refusing no labor, yet said: "God, listen for my help! Lord, haste thee to help me! You have permitted that I be alone in this battle, without the refreshment of the father of my soul, of whom I am deprived for my ingratitude."

Two nights and two days passed in these tempests. It is true that mind and desire received no break, but remained ever fixed on their object; but the body seemed almost to have failed. Afterward, on the day of the Purification of Mary, I wished to hear Mass. Then all the mysteries were renewed; and God showed the great need that existed, as later appeared; for Rome has all been on the point of revolution, backbiting disgracefully, and with much irreverence. Only that God has poured oil on their hearts, and I think the thing will have a good end. Then God imposed this obedience on me, that during the whole of this holy season of Lent I should offer in sacrifice the desires of all the family, and have Mass celebrated before him with this one intention alone – that is, for holy Church – and that I should myself hear a Mass every morning at dawn – a thing which you know is impossible to me; but in obedience to him all things have been possible. And this desire has become so much a part of my flesh, that memory retains nothing else, intellect can see nothing else, and will can desire nothing else. Not so much that the soul turns aside from things here below for this reason – but, conversing with the true citizens, it neither can nor will rejoice in their joy, but in their hunger, which they still feel, and which they felt while pilgrims and wayfarers in this life.

In this way, and many others which I cannot tell, my life is consumed and shed for this sweet bride [holy Church]. I by this road, and the glorious martyrs with blood. I pray the divine goodness soon to let me see the redemption of his people. When it is the hour of terce, I rise from Mass, and you would see a dead woman go to St. Peter's; and I enter anew to labor in the ship of holy Church. There I stay thus till near the hour of vespers: and from this place I would depart neither day nor night until I see this people at least a little steadily established in peace with their father. This body of mine remains without any food, without even a drop of water: in such sweet physical tortures as I never at any time endured; insomuch that my life hangs by a thread. Now I do not know what the Divine Goodness will do with me: as far as my feelings go, I do not say that I perceive his will in this matter; but as to my physical sensations, it seems to me that this time I am to confirm them with a new martyrdom in the sweetness of my soul – that is, for holy Church; then, perhaps, he will make me rise again with him. He will put so an end to my miseries and to my crucified desires. Or he may employ his usual ways to strengthen my body. I have prayed and pray his mercy that his will be fulfilled in me, and that he leave not you or the others orphans. But may he ever guide you in the way of the doctrine of truth, with true and very perfect light. I am sure that he will do it.

Now I pray and constrain you, father, and son given by that sweet Mother, Mary, that you feel that if God is turning the eye of his mercy upon me, he wills to renew your life; and as dead to all fleshly impulse do you cast yourself into that ship of holy Church. And be always discreet in your conversations. You will be able to have the actual cell little; but I wish you to have the cell of the heart always, and always carry it with you. For as you know, while we are locked therein enemies can do us no wrong. Then every act you shall do will be guided and ordered of God. Also, I beg you that you ripen your heart with holy and true prudence; and that your life be an example to worldly men by your never conforming to the world's customs. May that generosity toward the poor and that voluntary poverty which you have always practiced, be renewed and refreshed in you with true and perfect humility. Do not slacken in these, for any dignity or exaltation that God may give you, but descend more deep into that valley of humility, rejoicing in the table of the cross. There receive the food of souls: embracing the Mother, humble, faithful, and continual prayer, and holy vigil: celebrating every day, unless for some special reason. Flee idle and light talking, and be and show yourself mature in your speech and in every way. Cast from you all tenderness for yourself and all servile fear, for the sweet Church has no need of such folk, but of persons cruel to themselves and compassionate to her. These are the things which I beg you to study to observe. Also I beg you that you and Brother Bartolomeo and Brother Tommaso and the Master should gather together in your hands the book, and any writing of mine that you might find, and do with them what you see will be most to the honor of God: you and Messer Tommaso too – things in which I found some recreation. I beg you also, that so far as shall be possible to you, you be a shepherd and ruler to this family, as a father, keeping them in the joy of charity and in perfect union; that they be not scattered as sheep without a shepherd. And I think to do more for them and for you after my death than in my life. I shall pray the eternal truth that he pour forth upon you others all plenitude of grace and gifts which he may have given to my soul, so that you may be lights placed in a candlestick. I beg you to pray to the eternal bridegroom that he make me manfully fulfill his obedience, and pardon me the multitude of my iniquities. And I beg you that you pardon me every disobedience, irreverence, and ingratitude which I showed to you or committed against you, and all pain and bitterness which I may have caused you: and the slight zeal which I have had for our salvation. And I ask you for your blessing.

Pray earnestly for me, and have others pray, for the love of Christ crucified. Pardon me, that I have written you words of bitterness. I do not write them, however, to cause you bitterness, but because I am in doubt, and do not know what the goodness of God will do with me. I wish to have done my duty. And do not feel regret because we are separated one from the other in the body; although you would have been the very greatest consolation to me, greater are my consolation and gladness to see the fruit that you are bearing in holy Church. And now I beg you to labor yet more zealously, for she never had so great a need: and do you never depart for any persecution without permission from our lord the Pope. Comfort you in Christ sweet Jesus, without any bitterness. I say no more to you. Remain in the holy and sweet grace of God. Sweet Jesus, Jesus love.

INDEX OF TOPICS

Topics are listed by document number and, in some cases, by books or chapters and sections within that document. Thus, 2.1.4 is a reference to document number 2 (*Christianity in the Desert: St. Antony the Great*), Book 1, section 4; 3.4 is a reference to document number 3, section 4. If a topic appears several times in a document, no chapter or section number is given.

SOURCES

DUTTON, Paul Edward (Translator). "The Translation and Miracles of the Blessed Martyrs, Marcellinus and Peter," from *Charlemagne's Courtier*. Peterborough, ON: Broadview, 1998. Copyright © 1998 Paul Edward Dutton. Reprinted by permission of Broadview Press.

FAHY, Benen (Translator). "The Official Life of St. Francis: The Stigmata," from *Major and Minor Life of St. Francis with excerpts from other works by St. Bonaventure* in *St. Francis of Assisi: Writings and Early Biographies; English Omnibus of the Sources for the Life of St. Francis, 4th Edition Revised*. Edited by Marion A. Habig. Quincy, IL: Franciscan Press, 1991. Reprinted with permission.

HOGARTH, James (Translator). "The Pilgrim's Guide to St. James of Compostella," from *The Pilgrim's Guide: A 12th-Century Guide for the Pilgrim to St. James of Compostella*. London: Confraternity of St. James, 1992. Reprinted by permission of the Confraternity of St. James.

MCNAMARA, Jo Ann (Translator). "Venantius Fortunatus's Life of St. Radegund," from *Sainted Women of the Dark Ages*, Chapter 4: Radegund, Queen of the Franks and Abbess of Poitiers. Durham and London: Duke University Press, 1992. Copyright © 1992 Duke University Press. Reprinted by permission of Duke University Press.

MUSURILLO, H.R. (Translator). "The Passion of SS. Perpetua and Felicitas," from *Acts of the Christian Martyrs*. Oxford: Clarendon Press, 1972. Reprinted by permission of Oxford University Press.

PLACID, Hermann (Translator). "The Conversion of St. Francis of Assisi and the Founding of his Order," from *St. Francis of Assisi: First and Second Life of St. Francis by Thomas of Celano*. Chicago: Franciscan Herald Press, 1963. Abridged. Reprinted with permission.

RYAN, William Granger (Translator). "Four Lives from *The Golden Legend*," from *Jacobus de Voragine: The Golden Legend. Readings on the Saints Volume 1 and 2*. Princeton, NJ: Princeton University Press, 1993. Copyright © 1993 Princeton University Press, © 1995 Paperback Edition. Reprinted by permission of Princeton University Press.

ZIMMERMAN, Odo John (Translator). "The Life and Miracles of St. Benedict," from *St. Gregory the Great: Dialogues*. New York: Fathers of the Church, Inc., 1959. Reprinted with permission.

Cover Image: Osservanza Master (Italian [Siena], active second quarter of 15th century), Saint Anthony Abbot Tempted by a Heap of Gold, ca. 1435, Tempera on panel; Overall 18¾ x 13⁹⁄₁₆ in. (47.8 x 34.5 cm); painted surface 18⁷⁄₁₆ x 13¼ in. (46.8 x 33.5 cm).

The Metropolitan Museum of Art, Robert Lehman Collection, 1975. (1975.1.27) Image © The Metropolitan Museum of Art.